Homiletical Theology

The Promise of Homiletical Theology

Volume 1

Homiletical Theology

Preaching as Doing Theology

The Promise of Homiletical Theology

Volume 1

Edited by
DAVID SCHNASA JACOBSEN

Foreword by David Buttrick

CASCADE *Books* • Eugene, Oregon

HOMILETICAL THEOLOGY
Preaching as Doing Theology

The Promise of Homiletical Theology 1

Cascade Books
An Imprint of Wipf and Stock Publishers
199 W. 8th Ave., Suite 3
Eugene, OR 97401

www.wipfandstock.com

ISBN 13: 978-1-62564-565-4

Cataloguing-in-Publication Data

Homiletical theology : preaching as doing theology / edited by David Schnasa Jacobsen.

xiv + 186 p. ; 23 cm. Includes bibliographical references.

The Promise of Homiletical Theology

ISBN 13: 978-1-62564-565-4

1. Preaching. 2. Postmodernism—Religious aspects—Christianity. 3. Preaching—History—20th century. I. Jacobsen, David Schnasa.

BV4211.3 H656 2015

Manufactured in the U.S.A. 02/04/2015

Contents

Foreword | vii
—David Buttrick

Acknowledgments | xi

Contributors | xiii

Background to Homiletical Theology

Introduction | 3
—David Schnasa Jacobsen

Homiletical Theology: Constructive Visions

1 What is Homiletical Theology?: An Invitation to Constructive Theological Dialogue in North American Homiletics | 23
—David Schnasa Jacobsen

2 The Unfinished Task of Homiletical Theology: A Practical-Constructive Vision | 39
—David Schnasa Jacobsen

3 Preaching as Soft Heresy: Liturgy and the Communicative Dimension of Homiletical Theology | 56
—John S. McClure

4 In Our Own Native Tongue: Toward a Pentecostalization of Homiletical Theology | 72
—Luke A. Powery

Homiletical Theology as Practical Wisdom

5 The Company of Sages:
Homiletical Theology as a Sapiential Hermeneutic | 87
—Alyce M. McKenzie

6 Dietrich Bonhoeffer: On Becoming a Homiletic Theologian | 103
—Michael Pasquarello III

Homiletical Theology and Method

7 Preaching as Spark for Discovery in Theology | 129
—Ronald J. Allen

8 The Way and the Way of Homiletic Theology | 153
—Teresa Stricklen Eisenlohr

Bibliography | 177

Foreword

—*David Buttrick*

Many years ago I wrote a little book called *Preaching Jesus Christ* (Fortress, 1987). The book was put together from different lectureships; one dealing with how Christian faith must speak in different changing cultures, the other on the nature of Christology these days. The book was subtitled *An Exercise in Homiletic Theology*, as indeed it was. Whenever you talk about trying to speak a first-century gospel to a congregation in a twenty-first-century world, you are practicing "homiletic theology," whether you intend to or not.

There are two kinds of cultural change preachers must struggle with. There are multicentury epochal periods—there have been three since our Gospels were written: a classical Greco-Roman world, the Catholic Medieval world, and the modern world, which began with the Renaissance and the Protestant Reformation. The Reformation turned out to be a game of follow the leaders: Martin Luther, Ulrich Zwingli, John Calvin, Thomas Müntzer, Jacobus Arminius, and the Wesley brothers. Ultimately the game ended up in denominations! No wonder Paul Tillich labeled our modern world "the Protestant Era."

Within each of the epochal periods, there have been short eras, usually lasting about a decade at a time. These short eras have also affected the ways in which we brood and preach. In modern times, think how the "Protestant Era" reacted to cultural change in the last half century—the romantic '50s, the silent '70s, the quizzical '80s. Then in the '90s there was a sudden realization that after 400 years, an epoch, Tillich's "Protestant Era" was drawing to an end. Now preachers are finding themselves in the twenty-first century, an emerging new epoch they have yet to understand.

In every epoch there has been a great work of literature that in many ways defined the age. In the Greco-Roman world it was clearly the *Iliad*, written by Homer; in the medieval world, Dante's *The Divine Comedy* dominated the age. The Renaissance/Reformation was surely defined by Shakespeare's dramatic works. Some readers suppose that the twenty-first century has already been captured by David Foster Wallace's *Infinite Jest.* Probably the same sort of delineation could be worked out by the fine arts. How do preachers grasp their cultural epochs and eras? They must learn how to read cultural presentments: everything from novels, drama, art forms, and styles, all the way to TV sitcoms and the like.

Actually, the problem of faith and culture arises every Sunday with every sermon that begins with Scripture. Check the stages: (1) There is the matter of translation from an ancient language to twenty-first-century speakers' English. When you switch languages, original meaning is bound to be modified. Perhaps preachers equipped with knowledge of Hebrew and Greek can "roll their own," but average preachers will at least look at different translations—the KJV, the NIV, the NRSV, the recent CE (Common English), and others. (2) As a second step, the preacher must not only be familiar with the biblical world, the preacher must be familiar with his or her own world. Grasping our own cultural moment is not easy. (3) The preacher must know his or her congregation as a subcultural group within the wider epoch. Please notice that stage by stage the sermon is forcing preachers to do theology, not in the style of Karl Barth, but more likely as Paul Tillich might.

Finally there is the problem of a gospel involving Jesus Christ. The historical Jesus is not entirely known, but there have been historians who have dug around and tried to rediscover the figure of Jesus. The research started in the mid-1700s with Hermann Remairus, who argued Jesus was a largely failed political figure. Then in the mid-1800s, David Friedrich Strauss wrote a widely circulated study of Jesus in which he dismissed miracles, resurrection accounts, and birth narratives, tossing them out as difficult-to-believe "myth." Strauss ended up picturing Jesus as a kind of universal teacher. But then came Albert Schweitzer, who wrote *The Quest for the Historical Jesus* in the last year of the nineteenth century. He argued that Jesus was not a universal teacher at all, but that he was an apocalyptic figure who believed that God would soon end our present age and usher in a new world. Thus any teachings Jesus offered were merely an interim ethic, which to some degree could be ignored.

So what do we know now? We know of Jesus, a young Jew, who was first influenced by John the Baptist. After John's death, Jesus began his own preaching and organizing. He assembled twelve disciples, and with them, he aimed to renew the faith of Israel. He announced the coming of God's new world, a "kingdom of God." In Greek the word is *basileia,* and it means nothing more than a social order, but with *theou* added, it becomes "God's social order," what the KJV translated as "Kingdom of God." Jesus was trying to prepare human beings to become citizens of God's new social order. He was arrested and brutally crucified by the Roman military under Pontius Pilate, after Jesus, who was outraged by the selling of sacrifices in the temple, caused a public uproar. During Passover, Jerusalem was packed with pilgrims and Rome could not risk public disturbances.

Facts are few. So how can we handle a gospel that celebrates Jesus of Nazareth when all we have are four Gospels plus some earlier writings of the Apostle Paul? Paul's letters can be dated roughly from 48 to 60, when apparently he was executed by Rome. Thus we have five semi-Christologies. Paul calls Jesus "the Anointed" who suffered an appalling death, but in all was faithful, so God "adopted" him as a Son. In Mark (68–72 CE?), Jesus is an apocalyptic figure much like Schweitzer proposed. Mark has no birth narrative and no real resurrection account. Jesus is an eschatological prophet, but in the Gospel he is served up along with a collection of healing miracles, and nearly two dozen conflict stories (Jesus versus Jewish leaders) followed by a harsh, highly detailed crucifixion narrative. Matthew (85 CE?) was perhaps written for a Jesus synagogue being persecuted by traditional synagogues. In Matthew, of course, Jesus is Messiah. Next, there's Luke (90–95 CE?). Luke writes as a Roman citizen to Roman citizens, telling a more evangelical story of Jesus, the world-class Savior. As we all know now, Luke also produced the book of Acts, picturing a sort of ideal early Christianity (which was not always true). Though he writes for a Roman audience, he is somewhat subversive, for he actually wants the whole world to become Christian. The fourth Gospel, the Gospel of John (100 CE?) was written and rewritten, not once, but perhaps at least five times, until somehow the little community that produced the Gospel stumbled into oblivion. John sees Jesus as God's Word become flesh dwelling among us. Jesus says, "I and the Father are one." So the Gospel of John borders on Docetism. It is an odd book that begins in something like a wisdom style and tumbles toward Gnosticism. So we have four Gospels and a small batch of Paul's letters: five different Christologies. Preachers must struggle with the five different Christologies, picking and patching, but trying to be faithful to the tradition and yet be understood and believed by a contemporary cultural world. Homiletic theology happens every time a preacher preaches.

David Jacobsen is a friend, previously a smart graduate student, who with a crew of other grad students had to spend time dealing with the peculiar Professor Buttrick. After defending a splendid dissertation, Dr. David Jacobsen left Vanderbilt for a position at Waterloo Lutheran Seminary on the campus of Wilfrid Laurier University in Canada. Now David is a professor of homiletics at the Boston University School of Theology, where he has established a program dedicated to the study of homiletic theology. In the pages that follow, David will explain his own grasp of homiletic theology; then, by invitation, he has brought in a number of major homiletic scholars to join the discussion.

David G. Buttrick
Drucilla Moore Buffington Professor
of Homiletics and Liturgics, Emeritus
Vanderbilt University

Acknowledgments

It had not occurred to me until just now how odd it is to write the acknowledgments for a work with multiple contributors. No book is the product of a single hand; this one even less so. "Acknowledgments" just seems too small a word! Still, I am grateful first and foremost to the members of the 2013 Consultation on Homiletical Theology: Ron Allen, Teresa Stricklen Eisenlohr, John McClure, Alyce McKenzie, Michael Pasquarello III, Luke Powery—and the Academy of Homiletics that hosted us. We all gathered to share our thoughts on homiletical theology at our annual meeting in Louisville in December, 2013. The consultation conversation was fantastic. I hope readers catch a sense of it in these pages. The six colleagues in homiletics who helped write this first volume in this series of homiletical theology will always have a special place in my heart.

I want also to thank my dean at the Boston University School of Theology, Mary Elizabeth Moore. After spending fifteen years working at a small denominational seminary in Canada, in 2011 I found myself at a research university in Boston and face-to-face with a theological leader whose first interest was in my research trajectory. She encouraged me to develop the work of the consultation through the Homiletical Theology Project (www.bu.edu/homiletical-theology-project) and was instrumental in making it all happen. I am grateful, Mary Elizabeth, for all you've done. You are the most generative and generous scholar I know.

Some of the early stages of this research were also underwritten by the Center for Practical Theology at Boston University. I am grateful to the center's correctors, Drs. Bryan Stone, Claire Wolfteich, Phillis Sheppard, Courtney Goto, and the aforementioned Mary Elizabeth Moore, for their early support as well. I count myself fortunate to have such good colleagues in a vibrant research community.

Now that I am at Boston University, I also have the high privilege of working with graduate students serving as TAs and RAs. My web assistant,

Andrew Tripp, a brilliant practical theology PhD candidate at Boston University, has helped with the Homiletical Theology Project generally and also done much of the formatting work in helping to prepare this particular book for publication. He is an emerging scholar who has shown great care, wisdom, and perseverance throughout the process. I thank you, Andrew, for your steadfastness, and look forward to seeing your scholarly labors come to fruition.

Finally, I want to thank my teacher, David Buttrick, for providing the foreword to this book. My interest in homiletical theology goes back in so many ways to my time as a graduate student with him at Vanderbilt. In fact, I studied with David Buttrick twice: once for my MDiv, and again for my PhD. If I could, I would even do it again as an expression of my gratitude. But for now, this book will have to suffice. Thank you, David.

I write these words excited about the new things happening in my field, especially the exciting and diverse ways that it manifests its turn to theology. Preaching is not just application; nor is it mere technique. Preaching *is* doing theology. May the many ways we approach this vision in these pages help to renew preaching from its theological center.

David Schnasa Jacobsen
Pentecost, 2014
Boston, MA

Contributors

Ronald J. Allen, Professor of Preaching and Gospels and Letters at Christian Theological Seminary

John S. McClure, Charles G. Finney Professor of Preaching and Worship at Vanderbilt Divinity School

Alyce M. McKenzie, George W. and Nell Ayers Le Van Professor of Preaching and Worship at Perkins School of Theology, Southern Methodist University

Michael Pasquarello III, Granger E. and Anna A. Fisher Professor of Preaching at Asbury Theological Seminary

Luke A. Powery, Dean of the Chapel and Associate Professor of the Practice of Homiletics at Duke University

David Schnasa Jacobsen, Professor of the Practice of Homiletics and Director of the Homiletical Theology Project at the Boston University School of Theology

Teresa Stricklen Eisenlohr, PhD, Associate for Worship, Office of Theology and Worship, Presbyterian Church (U.S.A.)

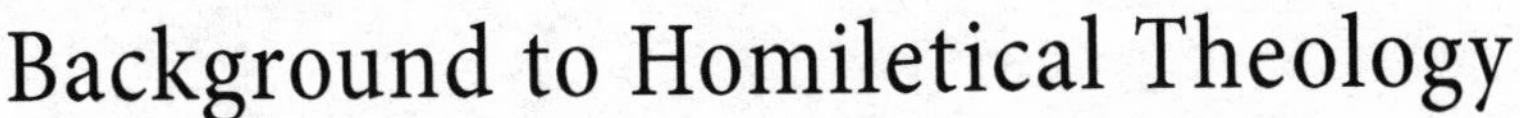

Background to Homiletical Theology

Introduction

—*David Schnasa Jacobsen*

This book makes the case that homiletical theology offers a unique vista for doing theology today. It argues that preaching is not about consuming theology, but a place where theology is "done," or produced. In doing so, it aims to concretize a commitment to seeing preaching as a thoroughgoing theological act, relating deeply to its practice, theories, and contexts.

At first hearing, the term *homiletical theology* may sound like just another trendy variation on theology proper. We could add it to a long list of qualifiers for theology: biblical, historical, or philosophical, among many others. Yet even if we were to focus on, say, systematic theology as somehow representative of theology as a whole, the proliferation of theologies is clear. In our day, even systematic theology has devolved into a series of theological loci now covered piecemeal or brought together in a kind of bricolage of what is today called constructive theology. As for practical theology, under the pressure of disciplinary specialization that emerged in the Enlightenment, university practical theology itself has given way to pastoral theology, liturgical theology, spiritual theology . . . and now, it might seem with this book, to yet one more variation: *homiletical* theology.

Yet this is not the intention in these pages. This volume is an attempt not to regionalize theology yet again, nor to add to the list of qualifiers that make theology so confusing. Rather, this volume on homiletical theology expresses a desire to make connections, to start conversations across theology and among theological disciplines. It promotes homiletical theology as a different way of *doing* theology.

DOING THEOLOGY HOMILETICALLY

Some in the field of homiletics might be surprised at such a notion. In fact, not everyone in homiletics even agrees that there is such a thing as homiletical theology. Yet there are in the field, since the high point of the so-called "new homiletic" in the seventies and eighties, some developments that lead us in such a direction.[1] In an important piece in the journal *Homiletic,* Paul Scott Wilson argued over a decade ago that homiletics was already making "a theological turn."[2] Indeed, one can find books from over the last twenty years arguing that the work of the homiletician should be informed by kerygmatic theology, liberation theology, postliberal narrative theology, contextual theology, pastoral theology, revisionist theology, and many more. What this book offers, however, is a theological reframing of homiletics itself. Homiletics is not merely where theologies are applied or completed; it is rather a place for doing theology in light of its own practices, theories, and contexts. In these pages homiletics is not a venue for applying theologies, but a place for *doing theology* that sees the activity of preaching as a locus of theological conversation between preachers and hearers. What homiletical theology does is put these theological turns in the field in a new light.

HOMILETICAL THEOLOGY AS THEOLOGY IN A CONVERSATIONAL, RHETORICAL MODE

The homiletical term in the pairing may be instructive for promoting just what homiletical theology can be. The English word *homiletics* is derived from a Greek verb that appears in the New Testament. In Luke 24:14 two dejected post-crucifixion disciples are getting out of Jerusalem on the way to Emmaus while they "converse" with one another about "all that had happened." The word *converse* here comes from the Greek word *homileō.*

1. The so-called new homiletic refers to an important shift in homiletic theory and its turn to the hearer by appeal to an eventful experience of the gospel in preaching. The term was first coined in connection to developments in post-Bultmannian approaches to hermeneutics through the work of Randolph, *The Renewal of Preaching.* The term *new homiletic* was later applied to the work of five particular homileticians with varying interests in inductive, narrative, story, and phenomenological approaches to preaching: Charles Rice, Fred Craddock, Henry Mitchell, Eugene Lowry, and David Buttrick (Eslinger, *A New Hearing).* Since its heyday in the 1980s, the new homiletic has come under critique for theological and ethical reasons from several quarters—and in one case for not even really being "new" at all given the long history of such experientially oriented preaching in African-American church traditions (Andrews, "Response" in Allen, ed., *The Renewed Homiletic,* 96–99).

2. Wilson, "Is Homiletics Making a Theological Turn?," 15.

The use of this word, transliterated from Luke 24:14 in the verb form *hōmiloun*, to name the outwardly troubled conversation of two dejected disciples might not augur well for *homiletical* theology. It certainly tamps down any hubris about the theological contribution homiletics can make when it is first attributed to the conversation of two hapless disciples using the ephemeral, evanescent medium that is the spoken word. Unlike its liturgical cousin, homiletical theology cannot lay claim to being *theologia prima*.[3] It is too human, too *broken* for that. Homiletical theology is theology on the way—sometimes even on the way out of town. It is provisional.

Homiletical theology emerges, I suspect, in the fits and starts of knowing you need to say something, yet not really knowing just what to say. The Apostle Paul, himself quite possibly a provisional, contingent homiletical theologian,[4] at least had the sense to place all theological claims under the eschatological reservation in 1 Corinthians 13:12: "for now we see through a glass darkly" (KJV). Homiletical theology is theology in a rhetorical, even conversational mode.[5] It speaks of God because it must. But it also speaks of God in full awareness that it can never do true justice to its subject matter.

3. The field of liturgical theology is, by contrast, quite well developed. A large part of the dialogue in liturgical theology is built on the notion of *lex orandi, lex credendi*—the law of prayer is the law of belief. For this reason, liturgical theologians like David Fagerberg argue that the liturgy itself is the font of theology and that it is *theologia prima*, from which any reflective theology (theology in the sense of a field) is only secondary. Liturgical theologians are to be congratulated for placing theology at the center of their field. As Fagerberg puts it, theology is the "work of the liturgical assembly." *Theologia Prima*, ii. Like other practical-theological disciplines, liturgics has often ignored theological judgments for the sake of those offered by other fields: sometimes historical, sometimes anthropological, sometimes even aesthetic. On the other hand, the argument that the liturgy offers some raw, primal *theologia prima* that is free from theological criticism would build a fence around its object of study. For two important works on liturgical theology see Fagerberg, *Theologia Prima*, and Lathrop, *Holy Things*.

4. The "contingent" side of this description of Paul goes back to Beker's work in *Paul the Apostle*. The homiletical side represents a surmise on my part, especially in terms of the marks that many of Paul's letters bear that they may have been intended for reading in the assembly. Paul, at any rate, thinks carefully and theologically about the practice of preaching (Rom 10, 1; Cor 1–4) and the nature of the gospel (Gal) in his letters.

5. Many in the field of homiletics would be reluctant to elide the two terms I am using here: rhetorical *and* conversational. I am aware that some embrace conversation as a way of avoiding the kind of coercion that they fear always attends persuasion. I have had many conversations about this with my colleagues, but find myself unpersuaded! I am not using *rhetoric* or *persuasion* in such a pejorative sense. What is more, I am not convinced that even conversation escapes the trap of words that influence. In either event, I view both as intentional activities—which is the key for me. A preacher engages rhetorically and conversationally with some sort of end in view. The terms here are merely designed to describe the mode of homiletical theological reflection: it is done with hearers and conversation partners in mind.

And yet, it trudges dejectedly into the pulpit, shuffles its note cards, and clears its throat only to discover that in the huge silent gap between the reading of the Scripture lesson and the sermon's beginning, a yearning expectation has opened up. Theologically, this gap is probably the high point of a Sunday service. For a moment, a number of people actually sit there silent, expecting that there might still be a word from the Lord today—at least before our feeble homiletical efforts have had the chance to dissuade those hearers of their resilient hope! It is, for me as a homiletical theologian, the most gracious gap I know.

But this also entails one other limitation of homiletical theology. Because homiletical theology is theology in a conversational or rhetorical mode it can never make pretensions to universality. Preachers preach with some sort of construal of an audience in mind. In his book *The Realm of Rhetoric*, Chaim Perelman argues there is a fundamental difference between mathematical or philosophical discourse, which is designed to convince a universal audience, and rhetoric, which is designed to persuade or increase adherence to a value among particular interlocutors.[6] Representatives of the former might just be able to envision something of a universal audience for their work. In a rhetorical, persuasive context, however, a degree of specificity, or context, enters in. The former makes its case with a view toward certitude; the latter aims for belief or opinion among a certain group. As a result, homiletical theology must naturally conceive its task relative to hearers and the medium in which it takes place. For this reason, homiletical theology is also unique among theologies. It is not because preaching is primary or in some way foundational for all theology. The two Lukan disciples *hōmiloun*, beginning to converse, who are making their way out of town, will testify to that! No, it is rather because homiletical theology is just so fragile, so contingent. It starts not with great themes or pretensions or grand ideas, but with Sundays and hearers, at least in most cases. It starts quite simply with the practices, theories, and contexts of preaching. It begins with a rhetorically invested theological conversation.

HOMILETICAL THEOLOGY: TURNING BARTH ON HIS HEAD

To his credit, Karl Barth tried hard to reinvigorate the relationship of theology to preaching. In his book based on his time teaching preaching in Bonn, *Homiletics*, Barth asserts that all theology is sermon preparation.[7] In some

6. Perelman, *The Realm of Rhetoric*, xiv, 17.

7. Barth, *Homiletics*, 17.

ways, Barth was being kind to us hapless preachers on the way to Sunday. After all, preachers have usually been relegated to the theological task of "application"—as if what homiletics did was all about packaging content already delivered from headquarters. What Barth did, however, was to place preaching in a very powerful relationship to theology. To paraphrase Ebeling, theology's job was essentially to make preaching as hard as it had to be.[8]

At the same time, making theology preparation for the sermon in the Barthian sense also had the effect of putting preaching on a kind of posttheological pedestal. Some say that being "put on a pedestal" does not always result in a relationship of mutuality and respect, but can still have the effect of placing a person outside of the realm where real thinking is done and real decisions are made. It can therefore be that such a Barthian salute to preaching may have ended up being something less than intended.

This made all the more interesting homiletician David Buttrick's response to Barth. Buttrick wrote a surprising foreword to Barth's *Homiletics* when it was translated two decades ago. Toward the end of his foreword Buttrick wondered out loud in his conversation with Barth: perhaps the issue is not so much whether all theology is sermon preparation, but whether all sermon preparation is theology.[9]

To my mind Buttrick's statement concretized what was really missing in the relationship between theology and preaching. Homileticians fall, like many practical theologians, into the trap of assuming that their preaching task is reducible to method.[10] There is, of course, good reason for that. A practical-theological field should be about *practice*. And practice is worthy of reflection and methodological refinement. While method can get out of hand and reduce even ends to mere means, it seems something of a necessary evil. Even Augustine, who stands with his *On Christian Doctrine* at the beginning of the homiletical tradition, cannot help himself.[11] Augustine actually thinks that eloquence cannot be taught—after all, who can think of the rules of speaking, *while speaking*! Nonetheless, by the end of his four-part work he is at it: giving practical advice on style and admiring a few of the Bible's own rhetorical and homiletical tropes. But while he does this, Augustine is quick to frame his methodological offerings within a theological perspective. Preaching, for Augustine, is about theologically norming what it is that preachers do when preparing to preach. Thus, when working

8. Ebeling, *Word and Faith*, 424.

9. Buttrick, "Foreword," 10.

10. Edward Farley has pointed out that practical theological disciplines and ministerial practitioners have long run the risk of being captive to the methodological rigor of a sister discipline outside of theology. See *Practicing Gospel*, 13.

11. Augustine, *On Christian Doctrine*.

with texts that seem to push immorality (like stories of biblical patriarchs with multiple wives) or make a claim about God that is somewhere beneath the divine, Augustine does not advocate a methodological norm, but a theological one: namely, whatever in the literal meaning of a biblical text does not tend toward love of God or neighbor should be interpreted figuratively.

Yet a steadfast theological vision does not mean method is *absent* from Augustine either. If Augustine's prologue to *On Christian Doctrine* is to be taken at face value, apparently some of Augustine's opponents thought it silly that he should actually try to teach people to interpret the Bible for preaching—an ostensible purpose of his writing *On Christian Doctrine* in the first place. Biblical interpretation was *Spirit* work, Augustine's opponents claimed, not something that could be taught at all—least of all, using that filthy, pagan *rhetoric* which Augustine had so mastered in his earlier years. But Augustine had a different point of view. Method was fine, so long as it was in its place. In the meantime, no cultural product, no method, no technique was beyond the pale for enhancing the practice of preaching. Just as the Hebrews plundered the Egyptians before leaving to go worship God, so preachers could feel free to put rhetoric and other such tools to the use of Christian preaching so long as they were put to nonidolatrous uses.

To my mind, homiletical theology operates from just such a principle—and one that makes sense of Buttrick's clever inversion of Barth. It is not the kind of theology that can exist apart from its rootage in a practice, to put it simply, as sermon preparation. It is theology done in earshot of hearers, with hearers in mind, and reflects this theologically through the practices, theories, and contexts that matter to it most deeply.[12] Buttrick's inversion of Barth invites homiletical theology, at the same time, to refuse to split off matters of theology and method, or ends and means. In this respect it stands within its own tradition since Augustine wrote *On Christian Doctrine* in which matters of theology, practice, theory, and even context exist side by side. When a homiletical theologian works with a troublesome biblical text, the problem takes theological life in relation to these hearers, this context. When a homiletical theologian organizes and arranges her discourse, she is doing more than making methodological choices. She is doing theology in a rhetorical or conversational mode—that is, with hearers in mind.

Imagine the unique theological problems that a homiletical theologian faces! What kinds of tropes dare we use for a God whom preachers would proclaim as Wholly Other? Will analogy ever carry such freight? Or must we grope toward God with our speech, only to recognize the gap

12. For an excellent example of reading homiletical theory and method with a view toward grasping its explicit and implicit theological norms, see chapter 1 of Bond's *Contemporary African American Preaching*.

between our little human words and the divine by appealing to "how much the more," as in the rhetorical trope of the lesser to the greater, or invoking some tensive paradox, or trailing off intentionally into solecisms when correct grammar just cannot contain the infinite? How do we engage in any of these rhetorical practices as contexts and hearers change? To speak of the cross, do we appeal to first-century images of ransoming slaves, to the satisfaction metaphors of Anselm's feudal world; or is the homiletical theologian charged to work the edges of speech to discern new or more local ways of conversing about Jesus' death? These are the kinds of practical, theoretical, and contextual decisions that preachers make, not as tacticians, but as *homiletical theologians*. I wonder if homiletical theology can be like *that*: a unique venue for doing theology in light of things that matter for sermon preparation, its practices, theories, and contexts. If so, it would be a different way of doing theology conversationally, in a rhetorical mode.

LEVELS OF HOMILETICAL THEOLOGY: PEDAGOGICAL, PROFESSIONAL, AND SCHOLARLY

Homiletician Charles Bartow makes a distinction between the various levels at which homiletical theology is practiced. In his article on "Homiletical (Theological) Criticism" in the *New Interpreter's Handbook on Preaching*, Bartow argues for three levels of what we are calling homiletical theology: the pedagogical, the professional, and the scholarly.[13]

On one level, homiletical theology is what homileticians train their students to do. In the homiletics classroom we do more than lay out methods or hand out skills. Homileticians as teachers help students to see homiletics and their own work as preachers theologically. This pedagogical level refers firstly to the way students become theologians in the classroom: a mix of method and theology that, through sermon feedback and reflection, aims toward assisting students to become residential theologians.

On another level, homiletical theology is something that all preachers do professionally. On this professional level homiletical theology is the self-reflective capacity of practitioners. Homiletical theology here is the ability of practicing preachers to think through what sermons have done in light of what the next sermon might do. Professionally, every preacher is this kind of homiletical theologian as a matter of calling to the practice.

13. Bartow, "Homiletical (Theological) Criticism," 154. What follows below is a summary of Bartow's discussion.

On the third level, which is the focus of most of this book's contributors, we consider homiletical theology in what Bartow calls a scholarly activity, that is, as critical research. Here homiletics lifts its eyes from the trees of Sunday-to-Sunday sermons in the hope of seeing them in relation to the forest of the homiletical tradition and wider scholarly inquiry. As a scholarly practice, homiletical theology tries to understand itself more deeply in relation to the practices, theories, and contexts of preaching so that preaching can see itself whole: what homiletical theology means in connection to the full range of its theological task.

WHAT HOMILETICAL THEOLOGY ENCOMPASSES: FIVE INTERSECTIONS

For this reason, homiletical theology at this scholarly level needs to begin to grasp the range of its activity. When homiletical theologians work, they often do so within certain theological genres, appealing to specific theological loci, and with specific kinds of theological concerns—all in intimate relation to the practices, theories, and contexts of preaching. I call these meeting places of preaching and theology *intersections*.[14] These are the places, the loci, where the theological task of the homiletician as academic or preacher as practitioner come into greatest relief: theologies of the gospel, theologies of preaching, theologies of word and sacrament, theology in preaching, and preaching *as* theology. While these intersections do at points overlap, they represent at least five distinct intersections where homiletical theologians can and do operate.

Theologies of the Gospel (Reflecting on Gospel as Lens for Preaching)

The concern here is focused on a theology of the basic message of Christian faith. Theologies of the gospel ask just this: what is the gospel that we preach? In much contemporary literature in homiletical theology (see chapter 1), this is typically the starting point for doing homiletical theology in the first place. Generally one's theology of the gospel influences and shapes how one interprets a scriptural text for preaching or how one makes sense of a situation or topic. It also impacts how homileticians tend to raise issues

14. You can find detailed bibliographies of all these "intersections" at my Homiletical Theology Project's website at http://www.bu.edu/homiletical-theology-project/theological-intersections.

that lead them to other intersections: especially a theology of preaching or a theology of word and sacrament (see further intersections below). In short, the gospel is something homileticians reflect on because without its center preaching is more likely to be an amalgam of textual theologies or cultural wisdoms. Being able to offer a homiletical theology of the gospel provides a center to preaching and the doing of theology as a whole. This interest, of course, does overlap with the intersecting genre theologies of preaching. Occasionally theologies of preaching include an explicit theology of the gospel. However, it is also true that many such works focus specifically on the gospel as an object of sustained theological reflection, especially in light of the relationship of gospel and culture or context. Here the homiletical theologian shares this genre of theological writing not only with theologians generally, but also with scholars in missiology and evangelism. In a theology of the gospel, the homiletical theologian aims to name what the gospel is in context and show how it might be useful for the practice of preaching in some respect.

Theologies of Preaching (Theological Reflection on the Act of Preaching)

That being said, the intersection with theologies of preaching represents the most common genre or working area of homileticians as a whole. Theologies of preaching, or theologies of the word, comprise a well-known genre in theological writing generally and among homileticians in particular. Theologies of preaching are concerned with reflecting on the activity of preaching theologically. Thus, their concerns range from discussing what is the word of God (Scripture, the sermon, Christology, revelation, or some combination of these), how the Spirit works with the word in the sermon (pneumatology), the descriptions of hearers theologically whether individually or corporately (theological anthropology, ecclesiology), and so on. This topic as a special locus came into greatest focus after the Reformation and again much later with the rise of neoorthodoxy. Having said this, there are important Roman Catholic and Orthodox theologies of preaching as well as liberationist, contextual, and revisionist theologies of preaching. This is also one area in the literature of preaching where systematic and dogmatic theologians have made their mark alongside homiletical and practical theologians in particular. Theologies of preaching are concerned with understanding the act of preaching from a theological frame. While this theological intersection is not the exclusive concern of homileticians, it is often what many people mean when they talk about homiletical theology in a more general way.

Theologies of Word and Sacrament (Reflecting on Means of Grace in the Context of Worship)

In this intersection and genre of theological writing, homileticians reflect on practices and theories of preaching in relation to the context of worship and therefore also in light of the theological locus of the "means of grace." Protestant and Roman Catholic theologians in particular have struggled to understand just how to describe preaching and the sacraments as means of divine grace. Is preaching merely preparatory for the great sacrament of the Eucharist? Are communion and baptism merely external confirmations or even ordinances which pale by comparison to the grace given in the word? These are some of the questions with which theologies of word and sacrament have struggled historically. This genre of theological writing, an important intersection for homiletical theology, does not belong solely to homiletical theologians either. There are many systematic, dogmatic, and constructive theologians who share an interest in this theological locus. It should not be surprising that liturgical theologians occupy this space as well. Among Protestants, this topic for homiletical theology, while popular among the Reformers themselves, received greater Protestant focus after Vatican II. Many Protestant theologians and liturgists, together with homiletical theologians, have gravitated increasingly toward this intersection. Therefore it is quite common that homiletical theologians occupy themselves in part with theologies of word and sacrament.

Theology in Preaching (Content of Theology in Sermons)

This particular genre of writing is probably the one theological intersection with which people most quickly assume homiletical theologians are chiefly concerned. This intersection of preaching and theology is focused on the theological *content* of the sermon. With respect to troublesome biblical texts, for example, it might explore how preachers wrestle theologically with what the Scriptures say and the theological problematics such texts embody. With respect to the theological tradition, such an intersection for homiletical theology would be concerned with the content of, say, a doctrinal or teaching sermon. With respect to difficult or recurring situations of life that must be addressed from the pulpit, it might ask how one theologizes in a sermon the Sunday after 9/11 or the catastrophic tsunami in Indonesia. While this literature overlaps a bit with other areas above, especially a theology of the gospel, its chief concern is to consider how best to do theological reflection in the sermon itself. It is an important part of the task of doing homiletical theology.

Preaching as Theology (Theological Method and/or Practical Wisdom)

This intersection is probably the least explored, but may be the most promising one of all for homiletical theologians. Its concern is to see preaching itself as an extension of theology, or theological method in particular. Some homiletical theologians pursue this in terms of the practical theological wisdom that forms both the preacher and the preachers' work.[15] Others may pose questions as to how homiletical theology itself deals with practical- or constructive-theological concerns. Still other homiletical theologians pursue this in line with theology's own modern concern with method.[16] What are the sources and norms for doing theology? For the homiletical theologian, these sources and norms are related to the activity of preaching itself as an instantiation of theological method. Although this region of homiletical theology is not as well-developed as others it is a rising area of concern and in fact has formed the mode of reflection in this volume. Just how is preaching "doing theology"? This is also an important question for homiletical theologians.

HOW HOMILETICAL THEOLOGY DIFFERS FROM THESE INTERSECTIONS

It would be a mistake to identify homiletical theology with any one of these five intersections. It would also be problematic to circumscribe the work of the homiletical theologian with them—if for no other reason than because preaching occasionally finds itself at the constructive-theological cutting edge of the church. The fact that homiletical theology does its work in light of the practice of preaching and its theories and contexts would seem to indicate that homiletical theology does in fact have a range of concerns and thus a wealth of opportunity for doing theological reflection. What it does do more specifically is to sharpen theological reflection along the very edge

15. Pasquarello, *Sacred Rhetoric*.

16. Stricklen Eisenlohr, "Analgesic Jesus and the Power of God for Salvation."

of the church's life. Week in, week out, preachers theologize. With every illustration, image, metaphor, or even stumbling syntax preachers invoke the divine presence and do so in ever-new and broadening contexts. The upshot is that homiletical theology is much more than the sphere of application; it is also a realm for the ongoing *constructive* theological task. Despite its own stammering, inadequacy, and yet persistent concern for practices, theories, and contexts, homiletical theology sometimes by grace actually names God into the world again. While much preaching can be hackneyed, too reliant on old tropes or tired images, or, on the other hand, too willing to sacrifice the depth of the tradition for the sake of using trendy ideas or superficial metaphors, what cannot be gainsaid is that Sunday-to-Sunday preaching across myriad contexts, denominations, and situations occasions a potentially ever-widening ambit of homiletical theology. In speaking of God, homiletical theology is more than simply the realm of application; it is the doing of theology itself with ever-new accents, perspectives, and articulations of good news.

In many ways, the idea of homiletical theology is not really a new one. Within the history of preaching, the sermon itself is one of the chief genres of theological reflection. The Cappadoccian fathers themselves were known for the role their theological sermons played even in the great Trinitarian theological struggles of their day. During the Reformation, sermons and pamphlets of sermons played a key role in the theological transition of a world somewhere between the medieval and the modern. In our own day we have witnessed preachers like Martin Luther King Jr., whose sermons stirred the conscience of a nation, along the way refiguring its own civil religion theologically! Sermons do not have to be the locus of the sentimental image, the trite thought, or the dogmatically reductive idea. They are sometimes places where theology takes up its unfinished task anew to name God into the world again. That, we propose, is the ultimate task of homiletical theology that views sermon preparation as theology—and why doing theology homiletically can be important today.

MOVING FORWARD: HOMILETICAL THEOLOGY ON THE WAY

This volume is an extended reflection on what homiletical theology is and what it can become. Immediately after this Introduction, chapter 1 sets up a context for that work going forward: a review of where it has been historically so that we can trace the outlines of where it might be heading. By the end of chapter 1, we discover that homiletical theology in contemporary research has taken three primary forms: a kind of kerygmatic theology that views the work of preaching as a completion of theology, a type of practical theology that aims either to refine homiletical practice or form its practitioners theologically in practical wisdom, and a kind of constructive theology that represents, in a sense, a beginning or a resumption of theology's "unfinished task" today. Readers should be careful not to construe these forms in a mutually exclusive way. In the process we will see important overlaps and ways that these divergent approaches help to inform important areas of work in homiletical theology.

Chapters 2 through 8 bear out the different forms that homiletical theology takes. These individual chapters represent the work of the seven members of the Consultation on Homiletical Theology—a group of scholars gathered together to articulate in a more thoroughgoing way just what homiletical theology is. This august group of homileticians will lead us through various perspectives on homiletical theology as they are emerging in recent literature in the field. The contributors to these chapters are for the most part homileticians who have adopted the use of the term homiletical theology in their writing: Ron Allen, John McClure, Alyce McKenzie, Michael Pasquarello, Luke Powery, and Teresa Stricklen Eisenlohr. Their contributions will serve to identify what homiletical theology can be and set possible directions for going forward. We will, from our different vantage points, envision a future for a homiletical theology that sees itself as a theology that works through the practices, theories, and contexts of preaching—in other words, that sees all sermon preparation as theology. The arrangement of the contributors in the chapters that follow is determined by the scope of each contributor's work. Chapters 2 through 4 are written by homileticians who put the primary accent on homiletical theology in its more constructive mode. Chapters 5 through 6 represent a more thoroughgoing practical-theological vision rooted in homiletical theology as practical wisdom. The final two contributors in chapters 6 and 7 take a step back to consider how homiletical theology might understand itself relative to questions about theological method.

The constructive portion begins with my chapter. In chapter 2 I argue that homiletical theology is a fusion of both practical- and constructive-theological concerns. I draw on the work of kerygmatic and practical homiletical theologians to show how homiletical theology's rhetorical tasks are taken up to refine preaching's practice and ground its more fundamental sense as a kind of wisdom. At the same time, the constructive task of the homiletical theologian is also named and described with reference to the diversity of scriptural texts and situations and their own "unfinished" theological task. For me, there is no way to *avoid* the constructive task of the homiletical theologian. I offer thoughts both about its limits and promise given the work of the homiletical theologian.

In chapter 3, "Preaching as Soft Heresy," John McClure ventures his own constructive vision for homiletical theology in the conversational mode. Using the dialogical nature of the context of worship as a starting point, McClure develops a way of thinking through the theological implications and dimensions of liturgical intersubjective communication for the worship context and the practice of preaching itself. What McClure envisions is a kind of shared theological reflection whereby the preacher ventures, by means of preaching's referential task, a "soft heresy," making a new choice on the way to truth. Preaching relies on worship to help achieve an intersubjective alignment sufficient for inventing such a "passing theory," or approximated act of reference. This communicational, conversational model for homiletical theology has implications for the work of homiletical theology, but has the final impact of opening the door to other rooms beyond preaching's liturgical spaces: to contexts beyond the church. At this point McClure broaches, I sense, the possibility of a conversational-*apologetic* task for homiletical theology in an age of pluralism.

In chapter 4, "In Our Own Native Tongue: Toward a Pentecostalization of Homiletical Theology," Luke Powery likewise explores the constructive nature of homiletical theology—in his case in a pneumatological vein. He calls Pentecost a constructive homiletical lens and uses it to pry open homiletical theology's constructive task. Along the way, Powery touches not just on preaching, but also hearing—better, *understanding*—as the Spirit's gracious work in ways both embodied and diverse. The result is a homiletical theology oriented to an "epistemic humility and a hermeneutics of trust" marked by prayer, an embrace of culture and context by means of embodiment, and an ecumenical openness based on the inherent provisionality of homiletical theology. Powery, in his own pentecostalized form of constructive homiletical theology, names both its gifts and limitations.

With Alyce McKenzie's contribution in chapter 5, "The Company of Sages: Homiletical Theology as a Sapiential Hermeneutic," we move toward emphasizing homiletical theology as a practical-theological enterprise, in this case, in the mode of wisdom. McKenzie is also aware of the constructive task, as she argues this is also the purview of a sapiential hermeneutic oriented toward a kind of inductive understanding. Yet its primary mode is practical-theological in this sense: the sapiential hermeneutic that she proposes for homiletical theology is no less than the exercise of practical wisdom. Such a view yields for her a homiletical theology that values complexity, ambiguity, humility, and respect for diversity on the part of the homiletical theologian, as well as a capacity for listening and attentiveness.

In a telling portion of her essay, she connects her own vision to those of others in this volume.

In chapter 6, "Dietrich Bonhoeffer: On Becoming a Homiletic Theologian," Michael Pasquarello likewise views homiletical theology in a practical-theological vein: that is, as a kind of practical wisdom or reasoning. In a very arresting way, Pasquarello helps readers understand this through an important theologian from history: Dietrich Bonhoeffer. Consistent with many of Pasquarello's other writings on homiletical theology, the chapter here explores deeply Bonhoeffer's own theology and historical context as a way of showing how his homiletical theology was "on the way." What is revealed is a focus on the gospel that, while immersed in classic Lutheran concerns like the word of God and the means of grace, also opened itself to emergent pneumatological and ecclesiological concerns—markers of Bonhoeffer's own theological journey. The result is a homiletical theology that is squarely focused on the gospel but also profoundly aware of the world—and that only by being formed through prayer, study, and shared ecclesial experience. In this way Bonhoeffer extends "the movement of the Spirit and the power of the gospel into the depths of human language and experience."

With chapter 7 we shift into the third and final part of our contributions and its focus on homiletical theology and theological method. Here, Ron Allen, in his chapter, "Theological Discovery in the Spiral of Homiletical Theology," begins to capture the transitions where preaching discovers a need to review theological frames and presuppositions. Allen is quick to remind us that homiletical theology itself is still on its way to definition. Indeed, even in his skepticism about the viability of the term itself, he helpfully prods homiletical theology to see itself within wider frames: the traditional and variegated families of theological reflection that already shape and form us, the importance of pluralism in homiletical theologies themselves, and the need for humility in pursuing any such enterprise that works through transitions prompting new homiletical-theological reflection. Through it all, Allen cautions that homiletical theologies see their methodological task in "recognizable continuity" with the tradition and in a way that is at home for preachers and congregations—congregations who themselves are optimally participants in theological reflection.

In chapter 8, Teresa Stricklen Eisenlohr, with her "The Way and the Way of Homiletic Theology," also touches on the relationship of homiletical theology to theological method. In doing so, she clears away the underbrush to come at a clear definition for homiletical theology. For her, homiletical theology is "the theological thinking required for preparing to preach the gospel in any given sermon at any given time and place." Much of her article is devoted to the *via negativa*, describing what homiletical theology is not:

neither preaching, nor homiletics, nor academic theology, nor even a theology of preaching. Her definition comes closest perhaps to Bartow's professional vision of homiletical theology, chiefly because she draws a sharp distinction from academic constructive theology in terms of audience and context (in contrast to Bartow, who allows for the possibility of a "scholarly" homiletical theology). At the same time, she describes theology as discerning the way of God, akin to what theologians would refer to as theological method, the work typically done in theological prolegomena. It is this definition that opens the way for her to see homiletical theology for what it is: not just a mastered body of doctrine, but a humble theological discernment done in relation to preaching's practices, theories, and contexts. She goes on to give an example of homiletical theology in action and sees its benefit in promoting a more provisional way of doing theology along with a deep pneumatological sense of its work. In the end, for Teresa Stricklen Eisenlohr, homiletical theology is linked with preaching itself and not with the purity of academic theology's typologies or methods.

CONCLUDING THOUGHTS ON THE WAY

By now you will no doubt have noticed that homiletical theology is far from a settled thing. It is at this point still in development, a focus of conversation, and not one whose end we can yet foresee. In fact, you will notice in the coming pages that we cannot even agree what to call it: *homiletical* theology or *homiletic* theology! What shall we think of this embryonic conversation about homiletical theology, a theology on the way?

Please note that, different as we are, we contributors to this volume are all still tending to the common conversation. At the end of each contributor's chapter, beginning with chapter 2, we have concluded our reflections with a section called "Implications for the Development of Homiletical Theology." In that section each of us makes an effort to bring his or her unique part of the conversation back in touch with others'. We hope it will help you on the way.

In conclusion, we should recall how homiletical theology had its linguistic conversational roots in two dejected disciples making their way out of Jerusalem for Emmaus. They were beginning to converse (*hōmiloun*) with one another about "all the things that had happened." It is a heavy load, when you think about it. At the same time, these two did not go alone. They were met along the way by a strange visitor who not only connected all the things that had happened to the Scriptures, but spoke with them in a way that made their hearts burn, and even connected their conversation to a mysterious breaking of bread along their journey. Homiletical theology is theology on the way. It may be located in concrete practices, theories, and contexts, but it is ultimately animated by Another who keeps the conversation going and sends those two dejected disciples scampering back to Jerusalem in the middle of the night with a new message and a new account of all that had happened: "'The Lord has risen indeed, and he has appeared to Simon!' Then they told what had happened on the road, and how he had been made known to them in the breaking of the bread" (Luke 24:34–35). They are perhaps good enough models for homiletical theologians—with their mysterious conversation with each other, leading to a meal with the stranger Jesus, they uncovered by grace a way forward: a way to name God into the world again.

Homiletical Theology:
Constructive Visions

—1—

What is Homiletical Theology?

An Invitation to Constructive Theological Dialogue in North American Homiletics

—David Schnasa Jacobsen

INTRODUCTION

The question about what constitutes homiletical or homiletic theology has been an open, unresolved one within the field. When surveying many of the significant monographs, articles, and papers over the last twenty-five years, one finds the phrase comes up with some frequency. Yet it is a term that homileticians often bandy about without ever actually defining. In recent years, "homiletical theology" has been reemerging among the work of younger scholars in theses and dissertations.[1] The term has also gained currency among historians interested in the theological analysis of sermons

1. Most but not all of the recent theses and dissertations below use the term *homiletical theology* in their titles or abstracts as an analytical tool to understand a theological perspective or a theology of preaching of a figure or movement of interest in the history of preaching: Eichhorn, "Ecclesial Preaching"; Holloway, "The Homiletical Theology of Jonathan Edwards, Gilbert Tennent, and Samuel Davies"; Tsai, "Preaching as 'Testimony, Publication, Prophesying'"; Yang, "Martin Luther King Jr.'s Homiletic Theology of Preaching on Violence and Reconciliation"; Clayborn, "A Homiletic of Spirituality"; Nappi, "First, Empty Your Cup." From the standpoint of defining homiletical theology, it may well embody what Paul Wilson pointed to in the late 1990s, in his "Is Homiletics Making a Theological Turn?," 15: that the turn to the hearer of the new homiletic is itself morphing into a return to theology—perhaps here of late, a *homiletical* theology.

in particular.[2] The purpose of this chapter is both to describe what homiletical theology is and to envision what it can be. Along the way, it seeks to trace the history of the use of the term *homiletical theology* in contemporary North American homiletics, especially in the work of David Buttrick, Susan Hedahl, Charles Bartow, Paul Scott Wilson, Robert Hughes and Robert Kysar, Teresa Stricklen Eisenlohr, Michael Pasquarello, Luke Powery, John McClure, and David Schnasa Jacobsen. In the end I offer a definition of the term to ground a more developed and self-reflective conversation about actually doing homiletical theology going forward.

HISTORY

Homiletical Theology as Clergy Practice and Application

The term has some history in relation to understandings of theology from the time after the Reformation. According to Edward Farley, the dominant notion of theology in this period was in the form of knowledge rather than discipline. As knowledge, it represented a unified *habitus* or wisdom that "disposes the life of the individual as the result of revelation and redemption."[3] Nonetheless, in anticipation of later developments, there began to be different *levels* of this unified sense of theology as knowledge or wisdom as a result of its connection to theological institutions rather than a more general reflective way of being in the world under God.[4] Thus, in the period of Protestant Orthodoxy, the term *homiletical theology* could appear as a designation within the arc of exegetical theology from theologians like Vitringa, whose five classes of theology included "exegetical, dogmatic, elenctical, moral, and historical."[5] Within Lutheran Orthodoxy Quenstedt uses the term in his *Theologia didacto polemica*, where he considers it to be one branch of acroamatic theology, a theology for clerics and academics, as distinguished from catechetical theology. Quenstedt writes, "Homiletical theology, which they also call ecclesiastical theology, informs those who will become ministers of the church about the method of public speaking and the practice of preachers."[6] From this view, where the scope of homiletics is significantly limited over against other theological branches, it is no great leap to the typical modern view of practical theological fields as areas

2. Collins, *A Faithful Witness*.
3. Farley, *Theologia* 51.
4. Ibid., 54.
5. Muller, *Post-Reformation Reformed Dogmatics*, 204.
6. Lund, *Documents from the History of Lutheranism*, 222.

of "application." Farley chronicles this uniquely modern form of practical theology in response to the Enlightenment and the development of the literature of theological encyclopedia.[7]

Homiletical Theology: Turning Barth on His Head?

In light of this, Karl Barth's famous dictum is initially a way of working against the application-oriented tendencies of modern theology: "theology should be nothing other than sermon preparation."[8] For Barth, theology is at the service of preaching. This is no small step forward. Yet in his foreword to Karl Barth's *Homiletics*, David Buttrick turns Barth on his head. Buttrick writes that Barth is worth studying for exactly the opposite reason than we would expect: "Barth's thoughtful [work] with homiletic definitions and issues and is still worthy of attention because, to reverse Barth's own claim, sermon preparation after all is nothing other than theology."[9] To my mind, the ways in which the term *homiletical theology* has emerged in the field of homiletics reflects the differences around precisely this inversion. In other words, to ask what homiletical theology is to ask fundamentally about its relationship to theology as a whole. The struggle around the inversion of Barth opens up space for a more distinctive way of thinking about homiletical theology and its connections to the practices, theories, and relationships that make up the preparation for preaching. We turn, therefore, to different formulations of homiletical theology in the contemporary literature of the field. In the following examples, I see three visions of what homiletical theology can be proceeding from different ways of connecting homiletical theology to a predominant theological orientation: dogmatic theology, practical theology, or constructive theology. Dogmatic theology shares the Barthian vision of homiletics as the completion of theology; the practical- and constructive-theological views relate the theological task to preaching itself—thus the latter argue that preaching *adds* something to theology. Accordingly, homiletical theology has something to contribute to theology generally, either as an instantiation of theology, a critical-theological move, or a constructive homiletical moment.[10]

7. Farley, "Theology and Practice Outside the Clerical Paradigm," 28.

8. Barth, *Homiletics*, 17.

9. Buttrick, "Foreword," 10.

10. Although Nora Tubbs Tisdale does not mention the term, her proposal for a more constructive vision of contextual theology in preaching comes close in her *Preaching as Local Theology and Folk Art*, 30.

HOMILETICAL THEOLOGY AS DOGMATIC THEOLOGY

Paul Scott Wilson and a Kerygmatic Homiletical Theology of Proclaiming the Gospel

Paul Wilson devotes a substantial section of chapters 11 and 12 in *The Practice of Preaching* to the topic of homiletical theology. However, these portions of his writing on homiletical theology are probably best understood in light of the final chapter of his book, "Proclaiming the Gospel." Because his kerygmatic theology of the gospel lies at the center of homiletical theology, Wilson's approach comes under the dogmatic umbrella.[11]

In chapter 11, Wilson is keenly aware that homiletical theology is a rhetorical enterprise. Just as in Aristotle, dialectical and rhetorical moments are needed at various points in the study of ethics, politics, and poetics, depending on whether theoretical or practical issues are in view. Homiletical theology does its work in light of "propositions, metaphors, images, stories, symbols, and emotions."[12] This is a context for homiletical theology that differentiates it from its systematic cousin.

Chapter 12 also has a long section devoted to homiletical theology. However, here the rhetorical task is linked even more explicitly to the issue of proclaiming the gospel. Wilson argues that an understanding of the gospel and its proclamation commends certain homiletic practices that support it: namely, finding a theological focus in the text, concentrating on core doctrines, discussing one doctrine per sermon, developing uniform theological movement, and inverting to amplify the gospel in the sermon when the text has too little of it.[13]

Chapter 13, the concluding chapter of the book, goes on to discuss what such an understanding of homiletical theology actually serves. Ultimately, for Wilson, the focus on God is the key. Yet the proclamation of the gospel is still core to Wilson's project. In this way he sees his work as actually completing the largely missing theological task of the new homiletic. Homiletical theology, Wilson argues, is essentially the end of theology: "The

11. Barth uses the term *dogmatic theology* in reaction to the older vision of systematic theology. As human theologians cannot obtain any sense of mastery over the divine subject of self-revelation in theology, Barth opts for the term *dogmatic* as a means of contrasting himself with the overreach of claiming systematic knowledge of God. To do so requires returning to the way God discloses Godself in the Word of God, Jesus Christ, in dialectical paradox.

12. Wilson, *The Practice of Preaching*, 214. See 219n17 for the connection to Aristotle.

13. Ibid., 234–45.

sermon, in a sense, is the completion of theology, made complete through Christ speaking it and constituting the church through it."[14]

Luke Powery and a Homiletical Theology of the Spirit

Through two books, Luke Powery has been pursuing a homiletical theology of the Spirit. On the one hand, Powery places his homiletical-theological reflections within the powerful dialectics of the kerygmatic tradition: trouble/grace, lament/celebration, and most recently, death/hope. However, Powery is also careful to do two other things that press beyond the boundaries of this kerygmatic tradition. First, he is beginning to subtly distinguish his way of speaking dialectically from a unified movement from lament to celebration or death to hope.[15] Second, Powery's vision for doing homiletical theology does not build solely on the sermon, but includes African-American musical traditions and contexts, especially worship.[16] It is this that allows Powery to expand his vision of homiletical theology to include the spirituals.[17]

In Powery's first book, homiletical theology treats both sides of this dynamic, the continuity and the discontinuity with its kerygmatic tradition.

14. Ibid., 214. Wilson's view also contains one more constructive moment that goes beyond the more strictly kerygmatic view. Wilson at one point argues from the tradition of systematic theology that it is important to identify one's own "theological method or approach. . . . The excellent preacher keeps pushing at a congregation's limits and boundaries calling people afresh to new claims of the gospel message; this can be done only within a relationship of mutual respect and trust." *Practice of Preaching*, 232–33. What Wilson leaves unanswered is whether such a task might also belong to the homiletical theologian and is not just an extension of the systematic task.

15. See Powery, *Spirit Speech* 95–97, especially 165n22, where a variation from that movement is envisioned. The difference becomes more pointed in Powery's latest work, *Dem Dry Bones*, 93–94. The shift is in questioning the necessity of unitary homiletical-theological movement.

16. At the beginning of *Spirit Speech* Powery lays his homiletical-theological position out clearly: "Preaching is a theological act of worship rooted in the triune God." xiv.

17. In personal correspondence with the author on January 29, 2013, Powery made this crucial point: "I am trying to distance myself from a rigid dialectic through my embrace of culture, particular African American. I would also add that my embrace of the Spirit, or should I say the Spirit's embrace of me, suggests a broader approach beyond the dialectic because the Spirit blows where she wills, even working in inverse (grace to trouble or celebration to lament) if and when necessary or moving in totally different ways. The Spirit frees us from being imprisoned to any paradigm or at least from [any] idolizing one. I have to say this because of a Pentecostal vision of preaching with its multilingual, multicultural nature." Powery points out that African American traditions antedate the development of kerygmatic theology in the early twentieth century. Ironically, this tension within the kerygmatic frame may just point to a crucial *constructive* and culture-open element in African American homiletical theology.

In talking about doxology as the third identity yielded by the dialectic of lament and celebration in *Spirit Speech*, Powery places himself in the center of the kerygmatic homiletical-theological tradition: "Thinking of doxology (lament and celebration) in relation to preaching can blaze the trail for a homiletic theology that burns with the fire of worship for God. Philosophical, rhetorical, or performance-oriented discussions about preaching may then take a backseat to the doxological, thus theological identity of preaching, leading all who engage in this act to celebrate, and even lament, before God in the Spirit."[18] The section is telling for its take on what comprises homiletic theology for Powery. It may be theory, but it is theory first at the service of his doxological vision. At the same time, Powery pushes beyond a kerygmatic view. As we have noted, the dialectic at the heart of the kerygmatic view does not mean an absolutely unchanging homiletical *ordo*. Moreover, Powery's project places culture at the center of his homiletical-theological work. Here he notes how lament and celebration in the African American tradition can be discerned in particular through cultural practices pointing to the Spirit's activity.[19]

In his most recent work, *Dem Dry Bones*, Powery expands on these homiletical-theological emphases. Here the focus is the theological claims of the musical tradition of the spirituals. The spirituals are not simply music but embody culturally the proclamation of death and hope in the face of oppression and with a view toward God's good eschatological purposes. This is why Powery begins with "the spirituals as historical and cultural musical sermons proclaimed in the midst of death as a key resource for exploring what it means to preach Christian hope today."[20] This is a response, says Powery, to a homiletical-theological problem: the rise of a prosperity gospel that ignores death as the proper ground for preaching hope. Powery writes that the problem is "the avoidance of dealing forthrightly with death as a part of life and not just primarily in funeral sermons. This is a theo-homiletical problem, especially in light of a contemporary context of death and violence in society on numerous levels, especially African American communities."[21] In the process, Powery rejects the "'candy' homiletical theology" of prosperity preaching.[22] Yet the antidote that the spirituals provide is more than what we might expect. The spirituals are the source, says Pow-

18. Powery, *Spirit Speech*, 97.

19. Ibid., 92–100.

20. Powery, *Dem Dry Bones*, 17.

21. Ibid.

22. Ibid., 5. The "candy" term Powery borrows from a poignant quote by Gardner Taylor.

ery, of a *musical* homiletical theology. In one substantial section, he reviews the musical homiletical theology of the spirituals: communal embodiment and the importance of death and hope in spiritual preaching in various forms.[23] Yet Powery goes further. Homiletical theology can then turn and reflect on its work in light of the spirituals: "Here I will discuss homiletical theology, theory, and practice *from* the spirituals, going beyond them for contemporary homiletical relevance."[24]

HOMILETICAL THEOLOGY AS PRACTICAL THEOLOGY

Homiletical theology is pursued not only in this kerygmatic, dogmatic vein. For other homileticians, homiletical theology is not simply the completion of theology. Instead it is more closely related to the practice of preaching itself. With this, we turn to two figures in homiletics who use a practical-theological frame for pursuing homiletical theology. While they do so in two different ways, and thus place very different values on the relation of practice and theory, they both begin, as practical theologians are wont to do, with the practice of preaching itself. Charles Bartow and Michael Pasquarello will be our chief exemplars for homiletical theology in the mode of practical theology.

Charles Bartow and Homiletical (Theological) Criticism

Charles Bartow pursues homiletical theology as an extension of his commitment to homiletical criticism. In his *New Interpreter's Handbook of Preaching* article "Homiletical (Theological) Criticism," Bartow says that homiletical criticism is nothing but the "theological practice of assessing preaching in relationship to theory or theory in relationship to it."[25] He argues for three types of such homiletical-theological criticism: pedagogical, professional, and scholarly. Pedagogical refers to the practice of theological criticism of student sermons and their delivery.[26] Professional refers to the practicing minister's week-to-week critique of his/her own homiletical efforts. Scholarly homiletical (theological) criticism refers to "critical research

23. Ibid., 57–69.

24. Ibid., 80.

25. Bartow, "Homiletical (Theological) Criticism," 154. What follows is a summary of Bartow's entry.

26. See Bartow, *The Preaching Moment*.

undertaken in order to discover implications for preaching theory from a rigorous study of exemplary practice."[27] It is this third sort that links Bartow's project in particular to practical theology. What makes it theological is chiefly its use of theological norms together with criteria, in Bartow's case, from performance theory and rhetoric that do the critical work. The theology Bartow articulates is one where the divine speech of *actio divina* is joined with human speech, *homo performans*, to effect God's human speech, an instantiation of the Trinity's ongoing act of self-disclosure, as the Scriptures attest through Jesus Christ in the power of the Holy Spirit.

What makes this project a practical-theological vision for homiletical theology is best understood through Bartow's work, *God's Human Speech: A Practical Theology of Proclamation*. Here Bartow relates his vision for homiletical criticism to the work of practical theology in general. Practical theology begins with a specific focus on the description of performative acts. An appeal to theory is done in light of that praxis. The fact that practical theology is also inductive and interdisciplinary means that it needs to *understand* precisely those performative acts as praxis. Here practical theology tries to explicate that significance and hold it up to theory and theology to see if it helps to deepen and strengthen that practice. Practical theology thus has descriptive, constructive, and critical moments.

Yet Bartow's work is not exhausted by his critical, practical, homiletical theology of proclamation. In the process of his practical-theological vision he also touches not only on a theology of the gospel, but on a theology of word and sacrament as well.[28] All this is to say that Bartow's vision of homiletical theology, while an important instantiation of practical theology in a performative and rhetorical mode, also shows a range of homiletical-theological reflection.

Michael Pasquarello and Homiletics as Theological Practice

With Michael Pasquarello's work the focus on homiletical theology shifts attention to ecclesial practices. Homiletical theology is not something one does as a matter of method. Instead, homiletical theology is a *habitus*, a wisdom imparted in the practice of preaching itself.

This idea takes interesting shape in Pasquarello's book, *John Wesley: A Preaching Life*.[29] Wesley, says Pasquarello, was no systematic theologian, but rather a homiletic theologian. The preached word was the medium in

27. Bartow, "Homiletical (Theological) Criticism," 154.

28. Ibid., 17–19.

29. Pasquarello, *John Wesley*.

which he reflected on and understood the gospel. Pasquarello invites readers to consider Wesley as a homiletic theologian tied deeply to the practices of the church as enmeshed in the life of the Trinity. The centerpiece for Pasquarello is a sense of wisdom that pervades the life of the preacher, a participation in the divine life that refuses to turn preaching into *techne.* Part of the move also presupposes a constant between Wesley and certain traditions that run from Aristotle to Aquinas: we are being formed in such wisdom and its virtues shape our practice and life in ways that go beyond mere *techne.* Pasquarello argues against splitting means and ends in preaching. In the process, Pasquarello also lifts up a Wesleyan mixing of law and gospel, as a kind of practical wisdom. Preaching theologians as such participate in its wisdom and life.

Yet the Wesley book actually points back to an earlier commitment to homiletic theology that Pasquarello makes in his book *Sacred Rhetoric: Preaching as a Theological and Pastoral Practice of the Church.* Pasquarello describes the project in its pages as "an essay in homiletic theology, a description of the enactment of Christian witness, the performance of God's word through the ministry of preaching . . . as shaped by theological wisdom, a form of primary theology that creates and sustains the church by nurturing and testing its faith."[30] It is this notion of *habitus*, a kind of practical wisdom, that dominates Pasquarello's scholarship on preaching and grounds the work of theology in the practice of the church.[31]

HOMILETICAL THEOLOGY AS CONSTRUCTIVE THEOLOGY

David Buttrick and Homiletic Theology

The language of homiletic theology emerges quite strongly in David Buttrick's work in particular. Buttrick himself describes the term in a series of writings: *Preaching Jesus Christ* (1988), *Speaking Jesus* (2002), and *Speaking Conflict* (2007). In the latter works, "homiletic theology," according to Buttrick, includes how to think through a biblical text, how to order one's thoughts homiletically, grasp the salient critical issues with theological

30. Pasquarello, *Sacred Rhetoric*, 1.

31. Some will recognize the term *habitus* from the work of Edward Farley, part of which is cited below in the treatment of Teresa Stricklen Eisenlohr's view of homiletical theology as method. With Pasquarello, however, the notion of *habitus* takes a decidedly postliberal hue, oriented chiefly to an ecclesial reality that stands in stark contrast to the surrounding culture, thus lacking the sense of the ecclesial relation to the worldly life of faith.

wisdom, and then "in a collision course with the cultural mind" ultimately think out rhetorical strategies in preaching theologically.[32] In this sense, it represents a vision consistent with his inversion of Barth. Yet even this does not actually reflect the true range of what homiletic theology can be.

In 1988 Buttrick published *Preaching Jesus Christ*, his first extended work to place homiletic theology, or perhaps better a homiletic *Christology*, at the center. With this book, something theologically expansive comes into view. Here we find a vision of how preaching can actually *do* theology. In the service of developing a homiletic Christology, Buttrick considers gospel, culture, metaphor as a means of relating gospel to lived experience, story, and image, all in connection to a mysterious God in relation to the complexities of human consciousness. Thus, in *Preaching Jesus Christ* Buttrick contrasts homiletic theology with attempts to either get an objective historical Jesus or put ourselves in the "mind" of an ancient community (e.g., apocalyptic thought). Instead, contemporary preachers as homiletic theologians interpret Jesus Christ, who comes as Word in the midst of broken yet being-saved communities.

For the purposes of developing a homiletic Christology this project entails working with theory: the problem of culture (preachers have to deal with gospel and cultural mind all the time), theories of metaphor (as means of relating gospel to lived experience—metaphors [and images and narratives] bridge the gap between traditional claims and modern life), phenomenology (God as mystery is not about gaps in nature or experience, but disclosed precisely in the complexity of human consciousness), and theology itself (here in the form of the "new age" that without apocalyptic baggage helps us to imagine "in time" how Christ saves and reflects the divine mystery in contemporary life).

At the end of the book Buttrick argues that preachers pursue a homiletic Christology through story and image. The implication here is that Buttrick views homiletic Christology as a theological activity understood through elements of human consciousness: its nature; structure; connection to culture, metaphor, narrative, image, and symbol; and its grounding in the relationship of the mystery of God in relation to humanity and God's ultimate purposes. In this way sermon preparation *is* theology.

In his book on preaching the Sermon on the Mount, *Speaking Jesus*, Buttrick also talks about homiletic theology, and here as a recurring structural feature of interpretation. In the book, homiletic theology occupies a middle position between biblical study and proclamation. In *Speaking Conflict* he uses the term somewhat similarly to the one above. Yet in this book,

32. Buttrick, *Speaking Jesus*, 2.

which focuses on conflict or controversy stories in the gospels, homiletic theology also includes understanding the tradition as well. It thus opens the door to a homiletic theology that encompasses the tradition more broadly.

Susan Hedahl and Homiletical Meaning Making

In her 1996 article "All the King's Men: Constructing Homiletical Meaning," Hedahl takes up something akin to this constructive-theological way of thinking about homiletical theology. Hedahl sees homiletical theology caught on the "horns of a dilemma," somewhere between meaning making and the older language of authority. Her proposal touches on three areas: "the role of the imagination in homiletical meaning making, the need for a rhetorical vision/version of homiletics, and an examination of the loving, vigorous challenges against traditional forms of the Word."[33] Hedahl calls for a homiletical theology more closely tied to meaning making, and in ways that move beyond its classic tensions with older models of authority. Along the way, Hedahl confesses herself open to culture and the theological-anthropological work of understanding hearers rhetorically.

Robert Hughes and Robert Kysar and Homiletic Theology

In 1997 Robert Hughes and Robert Kysar's book *Preaching Doctrine for the Twenty-First Century* also sought to carry forward a more constructive-theological vision for homiletics. Their concern is for a method of homiletic theology, that is, "how the preacher theologizes in sermon preparation and in the sermon itself."[34] The center point of their theological work is the gospel itself, which they interpret christocentrically (the good news is what God has done for us in Christ) and must be understood systematically, that is, tested across other doctrinal positions for clarity and coherence. The beginning point of such reflection for them is the experience of the gospel itself. We theologize as those under the gospel's claim, which roots homiletic theology in particular in the church. The task of homiletic theology is to reflect holistically on all the gospel's claims and to understand the whole of the relationship between the gospel and human experience. It is in fact this concern with the gospel that unites the work of the preacher and the homiletic theologian. Preaching begins with some sense of a theology of

33. Hedahl, "All the King's Men: Constructing Homiletical Meaning," 83.

34. Hughes and Kysar, *Preaching Doctrine for the Twenty-First Century*, 20. What follows is a summary of their work, 20–35.

the gospel, hence its importance for homiletic theology as a method. Its scope includes hermeneutics, wrestling theologically with texts of various theological persuasions, understanding congregational situations, theories of communication, and the content of the sermon itself. The nature of homiletic theology encompasses (1) overcoming the split between *kerygma* and *didache*, (2) bridging and reformulating experience and abstraction, (3) re-languageing and re-imaging tradition, (4) localizing theology, and (5) forming the people of God theologically. While its ambit described here is quite wide, items 2–4 certainly carry forward a more explicitly constructive position.

Teresa Stricklen Eisenlohr and Homiletic Theological Method

Teresa Stricklen Eisenlohr's 2003 article "Analgesic Jesus and the Power of God for Salvation: The Importance of Theological Method for Preaching" represents one of the most thoroughgoing attempts to make a case for viewing homiletic theology as a constructive enterprise.[35] Her view is to offer this vision of all sermon preparation as being theology in the specific form of theological method.

Her starting point for entering homiletic theology is, as we have often seen previously, the problem of the gospel. Whatever it is we think about preaching, it has to be more than simply Bible or rhetoric: preaching the gospel *is* a profoundly theological activity and therefore theological method is central to any homiletic theological project. The goal of this article is to spell out those elements of a homiletic theological method. Along the way, Stricklen Eisenlohr salutes McClure's attempt to profile various theologies in preaching.[36] These help us to identify important features: starting points for doing theology (e.g., Scripture, experience), and sources for theology, norms, and authorities. Theological method generally works with such realities; homiletic theology as an instantiation of theological method does so too, albeit with reference to sermon preparation, viz., real preaching moments. She writes, "Homiletic theology needs to begin, therefore, with thinking theologically through the complex issues involved in actual preaching events, theological thinking that is out of tradition and traditioned, but not traditional in the sense of conventional or it ceases to be news, which is not good for the ongoing revelation of God in redemptive ways for us here

35. Stricklen Eisenlohr, "Analgesic Jesus and the Power of God for Salvation."

36. This is ultimately concretized in Cooper and McClure, *Claiming Theology in the Pulpit*.

and now."[37] Such a move is not simply a capitulation to culture or experience, either. Again, she takes pains to identify homiletic theology as a critical praxis: "Preachers have the responsibility of testifying to the Holy One who relativizes all perceived human needs by placing them in submission to the real human need for God to be God—not human beings. Humans are to be conformed to God, not seek to have God conform to their wishes, and for preachers to just submit to the perceived needs of a culture nursed on narcissism is to render us ultimately ineffectual for the gospel since it puts us on equal footing with those who do infomercials hawking analgesic cream of Jesus."[38]

To this end, Eisenlohr turns to the theological method of Edward Farley. Theological method takes life to the degree to which it a *habitus* of the salvific knowledge of God, a "dimension of *ecclesia* and its worldly life of faith."[39] The mistake postliberal theology makes is to substitute the world of the Bible for the world of the gospel. Yet because the corruption of language can happen anywhere, it is important for a homiletic theological method to be critical, capable of reflecting on God's ultimate purposes in the gospel, even when our use of the Bible pulls us in another direction. The means by which homiletic theology does so should be familiar: it uses "images, metaphors, symbols, narratives, and thoughtful reflections."[40] Such a critical vision of homiletical theology requires the deployment of both a hermeneutic of suspicion and a hermeneutic of trust. To do this requires a four-step theological method:

> (1) Comparisons of faith's testimonies of ecclesial existence in a portraiture moment; (2) the emergence and coalescence of ecclesial universals and their intentionalities; (3) judgment regarding the truth of the various items in play in any given situation in order to discern the degree to which they are in accord with faith's ultimate intentionality—*basileia*—which functions as critical norm; and (4) return to the lifeworld with theologically deliberate being, word, and deed.[41]

37. Stricklen Eisenlohr, "Analgesic Jesus and the Power of God for Salvation," 244.

38. Ibid., 245.

39. Ibid., 247.

40. Ibid, 249. In this section, Stricklen Eisenlohr refers to the work of Edward Farley. See Farley, "Toward a Practical Theology of Popular Religion," in his *Practicing Gospel*, 51–53, as well as his treatment of religious language in *Divine Empathy*.

41. Stricklen Eisenlohr, "Analgesic Jesus and the Power of God for Salvation," 250–51.

Stricklen Eisenlohr returns to her gospel-oriented focus in describing homiletic theology as theological method: "If all we do as homileticians is teach preachers how to shape language without robustly attending to homiletic theological discernment, then the preaching of the church may work as an informercial for cream of Jesus, but not God's power for salvation."[42]

John McClure and "Preaching Theology"

The term *homiletical theology* does not appear with great frequency in the work of John McClure, whose own interest has been more focused on developing theological profiles of individual preachers.[43] In one article, however, McClure offers crucial thoughts for developing a more conversational *and* constructive vision for homiletical theology:

> Ultimately, semiotic approaches to practicing homiletical theology in parish contexts, as important as they are, leave something to be desired. Ethnographic study constitutes an essential analytic process and can contribute enormously to the process of socializing and resocializing congregational theologies. However, semiotic practical theology for preaching is able to work only at the level at which theology is *represented* (or signified) within congregations and does not begin to address the ways in which this theology is, in fact, *constituted* minute by minute in the inter-human and interactive life of the community. Ultimately, semiotic approaches do not take preaching and embed it within a living dialogical process in which theological meaning is being created and shaped by the ongoing conversations and verbal interactions that make up church (and cultural) life. Many theorists of language and communication have recognized this and have argued for post-semiotic philosophies of communication that are more dialogic in nature . . .[44]

For McClure, it is precisely this post-semiotic turn that opens up the true constructive nature of the homiletical theologian's work. Homiletical theology calls us forward to a post-semiotic communicative moment where theology in all its difference is actually constituted in interactions with others. This, of course, is guided by a preacher's own "theology of preaching"

42. Ibid., 252.

43. This type of focus on theology profiles in preaching is what McClure undertakes with theologian Cooper, *Claiming Theology in the Pulpit*.

44. McClure, "Preaching Theology," 257.

as a vocational focus to such work. But its nature opens it up to a kind of practical-constructive task.

David Schnasa Jacobsen and Homiletical Theology as Confessional-Correlational Theology

My own vision for homiletical theology for situational preaching can be described as a confessional-correlational theology in a rhetorical mode. The confessional part refers to a core sense of the gospel, not as a fixed entity, but as a starting point for homiletical-theological reflection. In *Kairos Preaching*, systematician Robert Kelly and I took on the problem of preaching the gospel in light of recurring, perplexing situations of parish ministry: funerals, weddings, public crises, injustice, etc. Following Ed Farley's work on a theology of gospel, we refused to reduce gospel to one single phrase. Instead, gospel is a mode of reflection in interaction with a situation and/or context. As a *confessional*-correlationist, I took the classic Reformation formulation of the gospel as a *starting point*: justification by grace through faith.[45] Yet rather than reduce gospel to one *theologoumenon*, I then brought that starting point into dialogue with the situation as a critical principle. This starting point of justification *shakes loose* a situation and starts a conversation that enables an overall sense of the gospel in *this* situation to emerge. The result is a series of "gospel commonplaces" that while beginning with justification quickly engage the situation with greater gospel specificity.

Because I am a confessional-*correlationist*, I am also convinced that situations and contexts are not merely recipients of gospel speaking, but also work back on gospel to broaden its vision and refocus it. For this reason, my approach combines two of contextual theologian Stephan Bevans's types for relating gospel and culture: the praxis orientation and the synthetic orientation. The praxis view argues that the relationship of gospel and culture is not static, but dynamic—hence my commitment to the confessional piece as *initiating a dialogue*. The synthetic view argues that a deep connection underlies the relationship of gospel and culture—both gospel and culture *need each other*—and the dialogue can actually change or enlarge the way gospel is understood in a given situation. For me, "The gospel as lens focuses on culture as a means of initiating a mutual dialogue and critique in order to move toward social change. Because culture relates back to the gospel lens,

45. Jacobsen and Kelly, *Kairos Preaching*, 14–20, 103. In this section I speak only for myself, not my coauthor.

however, [I] would be quick to point out that the culture, while passing into gospel view, occasions the focusing of the gospel lens."[46]

One more clarifying point will help to ground this confessional-correlational homiletical theology: its practice in a *rhetorical mode*. What this means for me is that homiletical theology is done with hearers in mind. This means that its end result takes a rhetorical shape. The theological task of a homiletical theologian uses well-thought-out arguments, but does so always in deep connection to image, metaphor, and story—with all their limitations and poetic power.[47]

CONCLUSIONS AND PROSPECTS

This review of the literature has revealed diversity at the heart of what homileticians have been calling "homiletical theology." This essay has identified three basic orientations for pursuing homiletical theology: a dogmatic mode represented by diverging kerygmatic approaches, a practical-theological mode with postliberal inclinations of various types, and a constructive mode shaped by critical-correlational or revisionist models. The turn to theology that Paul Scott Wilson identified in his article "Is Homiletics Making a Theological Turn?" in *Homiletic* in 1998 may actually be a turn to *theologies*, if this survey is a reliable indication.[48]

At the same time one marked difference does come to the fore. The three orientations to homiletical theology that I have identified do point to at least two fundamentally different views of the task of homiletical theology. Is homiletical theology the "completion" of theology, or is it more like a beginning? In other words, does the practice of preaching contribute anything more or new to theology generally? This is, to my mind, an important question and one worth continuing discussion. This summary also shows that homiletical theology remains on its way to being defined. Still, this much can be said: homiletical theology is a form of theological reflection that emerges in connection with the practices and theories of preaching and typically in relation to cultures, contexts, and situations. If so, homiletical theology is not merely application, but a way of doing theology.

46. Ibid., 33.

47. Ibid.

48. Wilson, "Is Homiletics Making a Theological Turn?," 15.

—2—

The Unfinished Task of Homiletical Theology

A Practical-Constructive Vision

—David Schnasa Jacobsen

We have been arguing that homiletical theology is more than simply a matter of applying theology to the pulpit. We have in fact made the claim that homiletical theology is a way of doing theology. I intend with this chapter to show not only the fruitfulness of such a notion for the discipline of homiletics, but also to make some proposals about the *character* of homiletical theology. My proposal is that homiletical theology takes the shape of both practical *and* constructive theology by virtue of reflecting on the gospel in connection to hearers. It is a form of theology that does its work with respect to preaching's practices, theories, and contexts, with a potentially widening ambit to include a range of theological intersections.

In order to do this, I want to consider first how theology and homiletics have related of late with a view toward placing a theology of the gospel more firmly at the center of homiletics. This will also occasion reflection on the genesis of a *homiletical* theology as a particular way of doing theology against the backdrop of the discipline's own attempts to see itself as no mere *techne*, but a theological discipline. I then want to sketch this relationship in connection with three elements of homiletical theology's unfinished tasks in late modernity: dealing with differences in the Scriptures and Christian doctrine, confronting the unfinished business and need for repair in the good gifts of Scripture and tradition, and the overarching problem of "speaking of God" and the gospel at all. These unfinished tasks, however, will also help to show how a focus on preaching's practices, theories, and contexts might yield a more uniquely theological way of pursuing our work. I then intend to make a case for thinking about homiletical theology as both a practical theo-rhetorical and constructive theo-conversational enterprise.

HOMILETICS AND THEOLOGY

The relationship of homiletics and theology has not always been assumed, least of all in the modern period. Under the pressure of the rationalism of the Enlightenment, homiletics was often tempted to view its task in purely technical terms. While this represents a situation that is something of an outlier in the history of the field, it is close enough to our own late-modern context to merit mention. There are several such hazards and roadblocks for developing and furthering homiletical theology. Theologian Edward Farley, in a series of important works on the place of theology in the university and the shape of the practical-theological disciplines, identified several ways in which homiletics has been tempted to abdicate its theological task.

First, there is the struggle that many or all practical-theological disciplines face in justifying themselves in the Enlightenment university. In careful studies of the place of theology in university education, Farley shows generally how the view of theology as a *habitus* and *scientia* eventually gave way to a view of theology as "discipline."[1] Like every discipline, theology needed a well-defined subject matter and methods of investigation that were defensible within the overall vision of the scientific enterprise of the Enlightenment university. Because over the course of its own development theology had been seen as encompassing three and sometimes four areas (Scripture, church history, systematic theology, and practical theology), all theological disciplines were subject to the same kinds of intellectual pressures. Within practical theology, the subdisciplines began to devolve to specific tasks of ministry, especially when, with Schleiermacher, the theological encyclopedia focused the efforts for theological education as a kind of clergy "professional education," commensurate with other university fields like law and medicine. As a result, individual clerical activities (preaching, pastoral care, Christian education) began to identify as separate fields with discrete subject matters and shared methods. In light of this reality, the practical disciplines themselves began to identify more with the critical methods that were key to their tasks: homiletics with rhetoric, pastoral care with

1. Farley, *Theologia* and *The Fragility of Knowledge*.

psychology, and Christian education with pedagogy.[2] Lost in the process was any enduring, overarching sense of "theology." The fields were left with discrete disciplines that understood their work largely in terms of methods from cognate disciplines in the humanities and social sciences.

A second struggle for practical-theological disciplines like homiletics had to do with an extension of the same issue that Schleiermacher introduced. If the proper focus of a field like homiletics is the education of clergy leadership, what does theology have to do with those who are not clergy? Farley, partly motivated by his own desire to reclaim theology not as discipline but as *habitus*, thought theology was also a kind of reflexive disposition of believers generally, a sense of openness in faith to things of God. He therefore rejected any "clericalization" of theology and suggested that practical theology in particular should have a more expansive view that included more than just clerical activities, but the shared life of the *ecclesia*, the church.[3]

A third issue emerged as a concrete form of the problem in homiletics in a landmark article published in *Theology Today* in the mid-1990s.[4] The problem of a lack of theological concern in homiletics here was extended to include how the bridge metaphor (preaching's purview "bridges" individual Bible passages to a rhetorically plausible sermon for contemporary hearers) actually *truncates* the theological task by assuming every biblical text's subject matter was in some sense a nugget of preachable truth. Through careful work with the range of biblical materials in light of contemporary criticism and explorations of the inadequacy of the theological assumption that every text or pericope bears "gospel" or "word of God," Farley challenged homiletics not to cede its theological task to "bridging" every portion of a subdivided Bible, but to see its work from start to finish as a theological one of naming gospel.

Here Farley posits a center to preaching that homiletical theology had already begun to pick up. The problem with the bridge paradigm rested chiefly on its failure to discern the true, theological nature of preaching. That is, preaching is not about bridging the world of the Bible to our world, but in relation to Bible and situations articulates ever-anew the world of gospel. This particular notion has already had a huge impact on scholars pursuing a self-conscious "homiletical theology," especially Paul Wilson, Robert Hughes and Robert Kysar, Teresa Stricklen Eisenlohr, and myself.

2. Farley, "Theology and Practice Outside the Clerical Paradigm."

3. Ibid., 35–40.

4. Farley, "Preaching the Bible and Preaching the Gospel."

The kinds of homiletical theology we pursue are very different, yet we seek to put a theology of the gospel at the center of the way we conceive the task.

Clearly, the sum total of Farley's critiques, both of practical-theological disciplines generally and homiletics in particular, helped the field to view itself as a more thoroughgoing theological task. Farley's trenchant analyses also point the way to a rethinking of the nature of such a task. Homiletics need not cede its theological work to its ancillary methods, nor even the Bible itself when viewed in the bridge paradigm. What is more, Farley wonders whether the theology that so emerges might also be seen in more profound connection to hearers who *share* in that theological task. Farley's work as a whole also calls for a reordering of the relationship. What is needed is not just a prioritizing of theology, but a way of *doing* theology in homiletics that sees its theological task in profound connection to gospel and hearers.

THE UNFINISHED TASK OF DOING HOMILETICAL THEOLOGY

Yet what Farley calls homiletics to do is actually to go back to the core of theology itself. Precisely this has stood at the heart of doing theology all along: Theology, in its broadest sense, has been about what generations of believers have done and continue to do in connecting the gospel to life. One popular introduction to theological reflection puts it this way:

> [W]e hold to a time-honored conviction that when Christians are baptized they enter into a ministry they all share, responding to a God-given call to disclose the Gospel (God's good news of Jesus Christ) through all they say and do. Their calling makes them witnesses of faith, and hence theologians as well. This is because the witness they make in the course of their daily lives sets forth their understanding of the meaning of the Christian faith, and—in keeping with another time-honored conviction—because Christian theology is at its root a matter of faith seeking understanding.[5]

This does not mean to level all distinctions in who "does" theology. The church and the world need specialists who do theology as a unique vocation. But this does mean, in a very important sense, that doing theology—even homiletical theology—is rooted in a shared theological task ever taken up anew. Theology is certainly not something to be regionalized, least of all

5. Stone and Duke, *How to Think Theologically*, 1–2.

to homileticians. Yet there is also no such thing as a finished theology, for every theology by definition takes up its task anew. Whatever homiletical theology should be, at the very least it takes up this *common* task: the task of naming gospel in this moment and in this context.

ACKNOWLEDGING DIFFERENCES IN SCRIPTURE AND TRADITION

Yet even this only begins to scratch the surface of homiletical theology's unfinished task. Ronald Allen has likewise consistently attempted to see the preaching task in all its dimensions in connection with his own sense of the gospel.[6] Allen argues that systematic theology has an important role to play here as a means of making sure that the gospel is intelligible and morally plausible. For him, the theological task of preaching begins at the very point where individual biblical texts disagree (in textual sermons) and doctrinal positions must be named in a way that has coherence from sermon to sermon (in topical sermons).[7] Systematic theology ensures a coherent way of preaching that acknowledges the otherness of texts and doctrines and thus the need of theology in preaching to differentiate and systematize across sermons. In the process, Allen offers a conversational approach along with his own revisionist (process) theological views as a way of showing how such homiletical work can be done by honoring texts and doctrines in their uniqueness while still holding to a coherent theological center in preaching.

In my view, Allen's work is important for understanding theology's unfinished task. The Bible, as Allen points out, is not a monolith, but is in fact a collection of diverse theologies and views. In this way, the theological task is no mere overlay to preaching, but goes to its heart in taking it up again. More than that, however, Allen's conversational approach moves profoundly in the direction of Farley's declericalized vision of theology:

> [S]ystematic theology helps the congregation name what we believe and make coherent sense of life from the perspective of God so that the community can live and witness with integrity. As the title of the book suggests, preaching is itself an act of

6. R. Allen notes in this text and in many others that "[t]he gospel is the dipolar news of God's unconditional love for each and all and God's will for justice for each and all." *Preaching Is Believing*, 17.

7. Ibid., 35–36. The notion also extends to texts and doctrines that we do not sufficiently treat in their otherness to hear on their own terms. Either way, his conversational vision for using systematic theology in preaching is designed to surface differences honestly to shape a conversation on what hearers might believe today.

> believing. The sermon bodies forth the deepest beliefs of the congregation . . . *and the preacher* . . . in the context of theological reflection.[8]

Here his irenic, congregational view reveals yet another way that what we propose as homiletical theology would likewise be taking up an unfinished task: that hearers themselves participate in theological reflection.

ACKNOWLEDGING THE NEED FOR REPAIR AND RESUMPTION OF THE THEOLOGICAL TASK

At the same time, the unfinished task of homiletical theology is also evident in other ways as we deal with the good gifts of the Scriptures and the tradition: that is, places where the tradition itself is still "unfinished" and perhaps in need of repair.[9] In some ways this is an extension of Allen's categories concerning intelligibility and moral plausibility. We stumble on some texts because they are in contemporary terms morally problematic or otherwise struggle to make sense after twenty or more centuries. There is, however, another way in which my distinction might be useful. In some cases, it may just be that our texts or traditions offer ways forward that themselves were never really resolved. German New Testament scholar Günter Wasserberg considers, for example, some New Testament texts, and in particular Luke-Acts, as a kind of "grief document."[10] Many New Testament commentators themselves acknowledge the massive crisis that the destruction of the temple produced in the final third of the first century. In many ways, New Testament writings from Mark onward are trying to work through this trauma and grief through their narrative theologies.[11] Sensitive interpreters of the New Testament struggle with some anti-Jewish elements that may have emerged in early New Testament narratives precisely because of these traumatic events. If so, the task of an unfinished theology is even more complicated than we might first imagine. Our resistance to anti-Judaism in our preaching texts may mean more than simply identifying such problematic elements in our theological conversations. They may be more like

8. Ibid., 2.

9. I treat this issue, described below, in much greater detail in "Preaching as the Unfinished Task of Theology."

10. Wasserberg, "Die Haltung der beiden grossen Kirchen in Deutschland nach 1945 zu Auschwitz," 53–57. Dr. Wasserberg treated this issue in our coauthored volume, *Preaching Luke-Acts*, 9–12.

11. Brown points out an analogous relationship to the theological development beyond atonement theories for preaching in *Cross Talk*.

theologizing through unresolved grief or trauma. At any rate, it recasts the unfinished task of homiletical theology. The issue is not just how we interpret Mark, or Matthew, or Luke, or any New Testament writer. The issue may also be whether we can "take up" their theological task again, beside them. It is in this extra sense in which I wish to talk about homiletical theology's unfinished task. As preachers we are continuing to take up the theological task of the tradition even while our responses are themselves provisional. The task of homiletical theology is not merely unfinished because of new times and new places, nor is it unfinished solely because of tensions between texts and doctrinal traditions; it is also unfinished because the good gifts of Scripture and tradition came to birth, at least in part, amidst grief and trauma.

We are, in other words, homiletical theologians also because the tradition continues to sustain us and yet also sometimes troubles us. We might think of a doctrinal parallel, for example, in the expanding critical reflection on a theology of the cross that runs from Luther to Moltmann to Deanna Thompson to James Cone. On occasion, preachers take up such unresolved issues as Gospel passion narratives because the remembrance and ritual of the calendar keep rolling around, as does the carnival of death and suffering that is human weakness, profound pain, and oppression. It is here where homiletical theology is ever ventured in the presence of others and communities, in face-to-face assemblies and before ever wider publics.

For reasons of this sometimes-unfinished theological task, I also wish to move more in the direction of seeing homiletical theology as a provisional and constructive enterprise rather than a systematic one. Ron Allen rightly identifies that systematic theology does not necessarily imply unyielding logical systems that are closed to transformation.[12] He also rightly emphasizes the need for coherence across texts and doctrines that are treated from the pulpit. At the same time, the shift away from a more systematic to a constructive-theological orientation is not simply to cede everything to a breezy postmodern relativism. The authors of an important text on constructive theology put it this way:

> We are not interested in merely describing what theology has been; we are trying to understand and construct it in the present, to imagine what life-giving faith can be in today's world. In doing so, as with any construction job, we are attempting to build a viable structure. In our case, that structure is an inhabitable, beautiful, and truthful *theology.*[13]

12. Allen, *Preaching Is Believing*, 3.

13. Jones, Lakeland, and Workgroup, *Constructive Theology*, 2.

The point is an important one for dealing with theology as an unfinished task in a *conversational* mode that moves beyond the clericalized vision that Farley critiques above.[14] If the tradition itself is sometimes the locus of its unfinished character, perhaps it is helpful—especially in a late-modern context like ours—to consider not an overarching systematic coherence as the goal of a homiletical theology, but what philosopher Charles Taylor calls a "best account."[15] A best account attempts to organize a way of viewing things that is plausible while acknowledging its limitations. The notion is not born solely of a late-modern, or even postmodern, concern about truth claims, but makes sense within the tradition's own modesty: "for now we see through a glass darkly, but then face to face" (1 Cor 13:12, KJV). Within this eschatological frame, we must all concede that our best accounts, in an age of theological construction, remain provisional and thus unfinished this side of heaven. It may be that such an approach is also more open to the kind of conversations across "best accounts" that may be necessary for Christian faith in a pluralistic context. It may also be a profound invitation to mystery in our linguistic practice as homiletical theologians.

A Starting Point for Homiletical Theology: Naming Gospel

The unfinished character of homiletical theology means that naming gospel, the starting point for doing such theology as I am proposing, is a moment of interactivity between Scripture/tradition and experience/culture. It is this moment of mediation that shapes homiletical theology most profoundly. Preachers occupy space between the two, knowing full well that they must articulate gospel not just to construed audiences in articles and monographs, but face-to-face as both a rhetorical and conversational act. The theo-rhetorical concern is chiefly one of clarity: how to speak gospel and not to say something else, that is, *not to say more than one needs to*. This mediation usually entails either a deepening of the shared practical wisdom that is theology or else bringing theory and theology to bear on practical moments so that preaching can be refined as a practice. But homiletical theology is not confined to this alone. Homiletical theology also occasionally bumps into moments when Scripture, tradition, or situations bring to the fore unfinished theologies which call forth a different kind of engagement:

14. I treat the importance of the conversational mode for homiletical theology in the Introduction to this volume.

15. In Taylor's work, the concern is making an ethical case in an age of scientific explanation. See Taylor, *Sources of the Self*, 58ff.

to say more when one needs to. In those occasions homiletical theology entails constructive, conversational moments where, in the interaction between gospel and experience/culture, something new is named—perhaps even just new in this time and place. In such occasions, a conversation is set loose and a constructive homiletical theology begins and a new way of being emerges through the word of gospel.[16] Such moments may not occur every day, since the gospel needs to be identifiable and consistent over time to be gospel. However, silence in the presence of our unfinished task will also prove untenable. The question is how we do so admitting both our limits as homiletical theologians and the mysteries to which we attend.

We should be clear that the naming of gospel is itself unfinished because the broken work of theology continues apace in the ever-new contexts in which the word is preached and its symbols are broken open, not just because preachers are hankering after innovation. Homiletical theologians know it when they face the question: What am I going to say this Sunday? Or how am I going to say *this* on Sunday? They are questions about the limits of what can be said in the face of mystery and the need to say more on occasions when situations emerge. Homiletical theologians know to ask such questions because they live with the practices, theories, and, most profoundly, contexts of preaching. They seek to be present at the times when the world of gospel, as Farley calls it, opens up a future in light of them in all its startling newness.

A TWOFOLD VISION: THE PROMISE OF A CONSTRUCTIVE AND PRACTICAL HOMILETICAL THEOLOGY

I have argued that the unfinished nature of homiletical theology conditions its work in profound ways. We turn now to twin visions for doing such theology: the former marked by the concerns of the homiletician as practical theologian, the latter shaped more by a need for constructive-theological engagement. The twin visions are deeply related and not mutually exclusive.[17] I treat them in turn because they represent distinguishable moments in the work of the homiletical theologian, as many in our guild amply illustrate through their research.

16. Here I am eliding notions hermeneutical *and* theological in the work of Ricoeur, *Interpretation Theory*, 87, and Farley, "Preaching the Bible and Preaching the Gospel."

17. For example, Poling, *Rethinking Faith*.

A Practical Theo-Rhetorical Vision of Homiletical Theology

Given its unfinished theological task, how can a practical, theo-rhetorical vision for homiletical theology help? Above all, such a view would help homiletical theologians "not to say more than they need to," that is, to speak the gospel with theo-rhetorical clarity. A practical, theo-rhetorical vision of homiletical theology will see part of its task in a traditional, practical-theological way: *refining practice*.

Although most may not identify the problem for preaching in the same way, several have championed a view of homiletical theology that sees it as a refinement of preaching practice. Paul Wilson, in his book *The Practice of Preaching*, dedicates much of his kerygmatic view of homiletical theology to developing criteria for preaching, both theological and methodological, that aim to ensure gospel is spoken and heard. The goal of his vision for homiletical theology is a sharpened view of how gospel properly conceived should be related to practices like finding a theological focus in the text, concentrating on core doctrines, discussing one doctrine per sermon, developing uniform theological movement, and inverting to amplify the gospel in the sermon when the text has too little of it.[18] At the same time, the means for doing so touch deeply on matters related to homiletical theory. As Wilson puts it, homiletical theology does its work in light of "propositions, metaphors, images, stories, symbols, and emotions."[19] The direction in this case is clear. Theology guides theory for the refinement of the practice of preaching.

A more explicit practical-theological vision for homiletical theology is found in the work of Charles Bartow. Bartow argues that homiletical theology (criticism) takes place on three levels: the pedagogical (for students learning preaching), professional (for critically reflective practitioners), and academic. Common to all three is Bartow's vision that homiletical theology is the "theological practice of assessing preaching in relationship to theory or theory in relationship to it."[20] The first two, the pedagogical and professional, epitomize the homiletical theology we are proposing here. For Bartow the vision is not so much rhetorical, but orients to performance theory. However, the question is largely analogous: how does theory serve to revise practice?

18. Ibid., 234–45.

19. Wilson, *The Practice of Preaching*, 214. See also 219n17 for the connection to Aristotle.

20. Bartow, "Homiletical (Theological) Criticism." What follows below is a summary of Bartow's article.

To this, the homiletical-theological work of Michael Pasquarello adds yet another important level: the importance attached to a practical-theological vision connected to preaching as a form of practical wisdom. In his book *Sacred Rhetoric: Preaching as a Theological and Pastoral Practice of the Church*, Pasquarello describes his project as "an essay in homiletic theology, a description of the enactment of Christian witness, the performance of God's word through the ministry of preaching . . . as shaped by theological wisdom, a form of primary theology that creates and sustains the church by nurturing and testing its faith."[21] It is this notion of *habitus*, a kind of practical wisdom, that dominates Pasquarello's scholarship on preaching and grounds the work of theology in the practice of the church.[22] He offers a vision of homiletical theology as practical theology viewed as *habitus* or wisdom. The recovery of such a vision for homiletical theology is important, as we have argued, not just for preachers but for the *ecclesia* as well. Homiletical theology in its practical-theological dimension must be cognizant of the practical wisdom that forms preachers and communities as theologians.

The upshot for me is a vision of homiletical theology that takes the close reading of sermons seriously again. Homiletical theology begins at least in the practice of preaching with a view toward understanding theory at the service of theology for the sake of refining preaching practice. This is a venue for doing homiletical theology that our guild has neglected. We have multiplied our perspectives and joined the work of homiletics to myriad theoretical partners—as we should. At the same time, we have rarely started with thick descriptions of preaching itself with a view toward refining its theological intention. This would entail a deepening of our practice and a more profound theological integration of our work in a practical-theological mode. Such a move need not be theo-rhetorical only. All that is needed is a desire to see how theory can connect preachers to hearers more deeply, so that sermons don't say more than they need to say theologically, but name gospel with clarity.

21. Pasquarello, *Sacred Rhetoric*, 1.

22. Some will recognize the term *habitus* from the work of Farley, part of which is cited above in the treatment of Stricklen Eisenlohr's view of homiletical theology as method. With Pasquarello, however, the notion of *habitus* takes a decidedly postliberal hue, oriented chiefly to an ecclesial reality that stands in stark contrast to the surrounding culture, thus lacking the sense of the ecclesial relation to the "worldly life of faith."

A Constructive Theo-Conversational Vision for Homiletical Theology

But in an age of the unfinished task of theology, homiletical theology cannot afford solely to dedicate itself to refining its own practice. It must be able to reflect not only on how sermons should not say more than they need to; it must also help preaching, and preachers, to say more *when* we need to—especially in those homiletical moments when theologies require reformulation or some semantic impertinence forces open new theological venues for God talk. Such moments are rare, but they do happen most often precisely because situations and contexts *change*. The constructive vision here is emphatically not that homiletical theology should be the site of a kind of hot desire for innovation for its own sake. It is the ongoing connection of preaching to the good gifts of its sources that gives it something identifiable to say. The point is definitely not to make homiletical theology a hothouse for the latest theological construction or theological novelty.

What is at stake, however, are those moments when in preaching something has shifted and the tradition's old namings, whether through texts or doctrines, clearly no longer hold, or cannot quite say all that is needed in the moment. Mary McClintock Fulkerson speaks movingly of theology as a response to a wound.[23] Paraphrasing Charles Winquist, she notes that creative thinking "originates at the site of a wound," or as she describes it, from "an inchoate sense that something must be addressed." This is not to argue that homiletical theology reasons from problems to solutions, but only that there is, as Fulkerson points out, a coconstituitive relationship in "belief-ful knowing" between our theological thinking and the situations in which we find ourselves. In those moments, rare as they may be, where homiletical theology needs to say something *more*, then it must be open to live out its constructive theo-conversational vision. In that way, it, too, can carry out its unfinished theological task.

The idea of homiletical theology as a constructive task is not new. There are intimations of it in Luke Powery's work where he begins to break down a unidirectional dialectical theology through a cultural-open embrace of the Spirit. His concern is for articulating gospel aright in light of a "candy theology" at work in culture. His resource is a cultural, musical-theological story or narrative that the spirituals provide in deep relation to Scripture and preaching.[24] Elements of this culture-open construction also show up

23. Fulkerson, *Places of Redemption*, 12ff. Here the idea also connects back to Pasquarello's interest in homiletical theology as practical wisdom in that she describes such theology as "a sensibility that initiates inquiry at the outset." 13.

24. Powery, *Dem Dry Bones*, 25–27.

in the work of David Buttrick with his "homiletic Christology" and Susan Hedahl's emphasis on "meaning making" in contrast with older models of authority.[25] Robert Hughes and Robert Kysar talk about the importance of homiletic theology's work of bridging and reformulating experience and abstraction, relanguageing and re-imaging tradition, and localizing theology—all important constructive-theological impulses.[26] To this, Teresa Stricklen Eisenlohr adds the importance of a critical relationship between gospel and culture and even gospel and Scripture. Since the corruption of language can happen anywhere, she argues, it is important for a homiletical-theological method to be critical, capable of reflecting on God's ultimate purposes in the gospel, even when our use of the Bible pulls us in another direction. All of these are helpful ways of thinking about the constructive task of the homiletical theologian. They name the struggle of preaching as a theological task and in ways that allow preachers to take up their own unfinished theological work.

A constructive homiletical-theological word is needed because there are times when preachers need to say more—even in the face of mystery. Luther distinguished between God preached and not preached, the hidden God and the revealed God. The Reformer was worried about the speculative turn in medieval theology. Luther was convinced that we cannot know everything about God, but even then we do offer assurance of what we do know: for him the gospel revelation of God in Christ. All such constructive moves require great modesty in theological claims, yet the option of saying nothing is likewise untenable. What is left for Luther is the proclamation of the gospel even in the face of that mystery, the paradox of the God preached and the God not preached.

What might this modest constructive homiletical-theological task look like? As a way of retrieving Luther in a late-modern context, I would propose that what preaching does in such moments is to say more when we need to *only in light of what we still can say in the gospel.* It is not a general invitation to solve all problems in Scripture or even the tradition. Yet what the homiletical theologian has in view is the gospel itself in relation to all these good gifts. In some moments, it may mean probing gently beyond texts and doctrinal traditions, or as Ronald Allen calls it, preaching the twenty-ninth chapter of Acts. This would prove especially helpful with those texts that themselves trail off into ellipses like Mark's ending. In other contexts, homiletical theology will turn constructive because the

25. See Buttrick, *Preaching Jesus Christ,* and Hedahl, "All the King's Men: Constructing Homiletical Meaning," 83.

26. Hughes and Kysar, *Preaching Doctrine for the Twenty-First Century*, 27–34.

problems lurk in Scripture and tradition themselves, such as the unresolved grief, loss, and trauma described above. I suspect in those moments the task of the homiletical theologian is proximate. It suffices to differentiate from a problematic text, but then we pick up the pieces from our texts and traditions, eyeing them for shards of the gospel in all their jaggedness to name God preached, even if we cannot say too much more. Such preaching as is shaped by homiletical theology will bear certain sermonic qualities: mystery, beauty, brokenness, and stammering provisionality—like strangely luminous shards of stained glass.

At the same time, these very qualities open up the possibility of a homiletical theology that is ever more eschatological in orientation. It is the qualities of mystery, beauty, brokenness, and provisionality that open to a rethinking of homiletical theology beyond purely ontological categories as well as apophatic denials and deferrals. It is in the interaction of particular hearers and problematic texts and traditions that a possibilizing of homiletical theology in an eschatological mode occurs.[27] Philosopher Richard Kearney may prove the greatest help with his notion of transfiguration in *The God Who May Be*. Kearney's project is to get beyond the God of "essence" and "being" (that is, onto-theology) and also beyond the purely negative, deconstructive view of God that is so eschatological it can only speak of divine absence. For Kearney, there exists a middle way: a kind of onto-eschatological view of God that embraces God's being but moves beyond it as a kind of "traversing" through the present. In this way, it is still possible to talk of God's presence, but as a moving, eschatological "transfiguration." The point for Kearney is that it allows him to speak of God not as timeless essence, but of potential in relation to human beings: not the God who is, but the God who *may be*. The idea, for Kearney, is to move to a view of God not caught up in the straitjacket of the timeless conception of Hellenistic thinking to one who embraces both action through promise *and* a relation to human beings whose capacity for struggling for justice is enabled by that promise and the necessary response to that promise.

Doing so, crucially, also holds the potential of opening up a way of doing that constructive work that leads to wider ecclesial conversation. Again, Mary McClintock Fulkerson envisions a similar kind of theological work in her book *Places of Redemption*. In her study of a congregation of racially diverse and differently abled persons, she uses a discerning reading of congregational life to identify a "logic of redemption" named in some common spaces of the pastors' preaching and carried forward in different

27. I owe this insight to my consultation colleague John McClure from correspondence on December 10, 2013.

congregational conversations.[28] Such a study allows for a vision of homiletical theology that is located in sermonic reception, or better sermonic participation. This vision of homiletical theology in a constructive form is thus also focused on the importance of preaching's theological task being seen as a conversational enterprise.

Such a development will push homiletics where it has not been. When it is done in connection with Scripture, it is not just a "sermon help"; it is sometimes doing theology *with* Scripture. When it deals in exceptional moments with an unfinished theology, it is not just a repackaging of the doctrinal tradition; it is an opportunity in the presence of hearers and in light of some eschatological, emerging sense of gospel to be engaged corporately in traditioning. Such a development is also not an ending, as in a terminus or application of something already arrived at somewhere else, but the first fruits of a truly homiletical theology.

IMPLICATIONS FOR THE DEVELOPMENT OF HOMILETICAL THEOLOGY

We have argued that homiletical theology has an unfinished task with respect to relating gospel in context to doctrine and Scripture. But what of homiletical theology itself? Is it not, itself, "unfinished" as well? Indeed, this does then impact the initial set of questions posed in this volume. Recall that we asked several key questions in chapter 1. What is homiletical theology? Are there different types? What is its subject matter? Here I would like to revisit some of the claims and initial explorations offered in the first chapter as a way of refining them for future conversation. I will do so in light of the very sense of "provisionality" that emerged in connection with our naming of homiletical theology as a practical and constructive form of theology. As it is, the very presence of so many contributors with so many different views clearly indicates that such a conversation is only just beginning—and can therefore be nothing but provisional at all! To the notion of

28. Fulkerson, *Places*, 117ff. The prospect of doing constructive theo-conversational work in homiletics has already begun to be named in our field. Conversational and collaborationist models already push us in this direction, although chiefly from the homiletic/representational "supply-side" of things: Tisdale, *Preaching as Local Theology and Folk Art*; Saunders and Campbell, *The Word on the Street*; McClure, *The Roundtable Pulpit*; Rose, *Sharing the Word*; and Allen, *The Homiletic of All Believers*. A chief challenge here will be to think even more deeply about hearers as theologians by means of sermonic reception and participation beyond pure homiletical representation. The intrusion of hearers is of course an important beginning as McClure (cf. also McClure's *Other-Wise Preaching*, 133–52), Rose, Campbell, and Allen point out, yet it is still just a beginning for such a homiletical-theological task.

provisionality, however, I would like to add another important feature of homiletical theology that emerged in Ron Allen's critical engagement with the notion (see chapter 7): that homiletical theology needs also to be "recognizable," that is, seen clearly in conversation with the givenness of tradition. Homiletical theology is, as was claimed in chapter 1, "on the way" because it operates theo-rhetorically and theo-conversationally, that is, in a way which is recognizable and provisional.

Homiletical theology deals chiefly with preaching's practices, theories, and contexts—true enough. In my own offering here all three have indeed come into play. In one respect chiefly it is ventured, however, in only the most provisional way. Homiletical theology is not only a matter of doing theology in a theo-rhetorical and theo-conversational mode, it does so precisely as a profoundly contextual act—that is, it is provisional and partial for both eschatological reasons and reasons of its location. The eschatological side of this is explored initially through an embrace of homiletical theology's own limits. As Paul writes in 1 Corinthians 13 (KJV): "For now we see through a glass darkly . . ." At a deeper level, however, it is also eschatological in the displaced way it engages in theology's unfinished task. In the face of struggles in the Bible and tradition, where the work of theology is unfinished, it is also eschatological in the sense of offering a provisional *newness*. In the face of new others and new historical moments, the gospel as homiletical theology's starting point is provisional as a situational and contextual possibilizing of the tradition. It is only in moments of ever-new injustices and human pain that the gospel finds eschatological voice in such a way as to enlarge vision and pry open the tradition. It is this second, eschatological sense that leads us to the issue of location. As contexts *change*, so also does the scope of the gospel. The gospel in meeting contexts focuses vision, but its lens has also enlarged in interaction with new cultural moments and epochs.[29] To say, therefore, that homiletical theology deals chiefly with preaching's practices, theories, and contexts is to say far too little. These very matters of practice, theory, and context are the grounds for its two-sided provisionality and locally enlarging contextuality.

Without recognizability, however, there is no real homiletical theology either. Surely Ron Allen is correct in identifying this key feature of homiletical theology. It begins with the givenness of Scripture and tradition, something shared between preachers and hearers. Those moments when homiletical theology articulates a dawning newness are only possible through a recognizable relationship with its gifted and yet sometimes

29. I make a similar point in my embrace of both praxis and synthetic approaches to a contextual theology of the gospel. See Jacobsen and Kelly, *Kairos Preaching*, xx.

troubled and unfinished biblical texts and traditions. It is recognizability, moreover, that makes possible our theo-rhetorical and theo-conversational moves. Without such recognizability neither persuasion nor dialogue can even happen. Homiletical theology may be "on the way," but it is nonetheless on the way *from somewhere.*

These insights, however, still leave open two important dimensions of homiletical theology: the levels at which it is done and the range of issues under its purview. We have contended that homiletical theology is indeed pursued at multiple levels. With Charles Bartow, we have distinguished between its pedagogical, professional, and scholarly versions. The pedagogical has been largely left out of this volume. It merits its own detailed study—especially if the purpose of teaching preaching is to induct students into becoming more than exegetes or technicians, but homiletical theologians in their own right. Clearly this important issue takes us far beyond the purview of this volume. Yet a volume such as this still needs to distinguish properly between homiletical theology's professional and scholarly practice. The line here, even in this volume, has not always been clearly drawn. It remains a desideratum for the development of a truly homiletical theology.

By contrast, the essay here has at least moved us down the road as to the purview of homiletical theology. In chapter 1 I argued that homiletical theology covers a range of interests: theologies of preaching, theologies of the gospel, theologies of word and sacrament, theology in preaching, and preaching itself as theological method. I am now willing to contend that the starting point of homiletical theology is a theology of the gospel itself. It seems to me that this particular locus really helps to drive the others and provide a center point for our work going forward.

—3—

Preaching as Soft Heresy

Liturgy and the Communicative Dimension of Homiletical Theology

—John S. McClure

In what follows, I approach homiletical theology in a way that resembles closely what David Jacobsen labels "constructive homiletical theology." I offer a way of thinking about how preaching actually *does* theological work. In this instance, I will outline a constructive homiletical theology of *communication,* identifying how it is that preaching, liturgically conceived, does theological work by transforming elements of human communication to make them adequate to the larger theological task of human-divine communication. By human-divine "communication" I wish to designate the entire process of entering into relationship, shared action, language negotiation, and meaning making with the God of Jesus Christ.

During years of teaching classes on Christian worship in divinity schools and local churches, I have periodically inquired into what the experience of worship means to each person present. Many answers contain within them some sort of communication metaphor: "Worship is time to be with God." "Worship is talking to God and hearing from God." "I come to worship each week to hear a word from the Lord." "We meet God in worship." These pragmatic notions of Christian worship as a kind of human-divine communication can also be found in literature on Christian worship in which worship is often spoken of as "dialogue with God,"[1] "revelation and response,"[2] "encounter,"[3] and so on.

Theologically, it is important with a term such as *communication* to avoid either a strict two-way "transmissive" verticality (individual/community to/from transcendent "Other"), or a kind of ritual immanentism (individual/community ritually attuning to a particular religious idea or feeling). Instead, it is important to include these elements within a broader sense of communication as taking place within a richly multivocal and multireceptive intersubjective space in which words to, with, and from God are spoken, heard, and acted upon. This space resembles the space of "conversation" identified by David Jacobsen in the Introduction to this volume, while focusing more directly on the ways in which this space engenders shared relation, action, language, and reference—as features more appropriate to a communicational perspective.

If we take this communicational root metaphor seriously, we might ask how it is that worship makes a particular kind of human-divine communication possible. And what role does preaching play in this process? Is there anything that we can learn from our historical liturgies about this communication process that can be carried forward as we rethink practices of worship in a post-Christendom, postdenominational, postliturgical era?[4]

If we limit our exploration to the so-called Liturgy of the Word in the Western church tradition, we might look within those liturgical texts and their enactment for clues.[5] The primary questions would be these: What does Christian worship do to transform what we know about human communication to make it adequate to human-divine communication? What aspects of human-divine communication does Christian worship address

1. See Furr and Price, *The Dialogue of Worship*; Chapell, *Christ-Centered Worship;* Crichton, *Understanding the Mass*; Plantinga and Rozeboom, *Discerning the Spirits*; and Hughes, *Worship as Meaning.*

2. See Quicke, *Preaching as Worship*; Edwards, *Worship Three Sixty-Five*; and Chan, *Liturgical Theology.*

3. See Christopherson, *A Place of Encounter*, and Rognlien, *Experiential Worship.*

4. By "postliturgical" I do not mean "postworship." Rather I refer to the movement away from both prayer book and worship directory traditions, as well as the abandonment of denominational expectations regarding the ordering of worship, whether written into polity or not. I also have in mind the migration of worship or elements of worship out of church sanctuaries into parachurch spaces (retreat centers, conference centers, small groups, etc.) and into the networks and flows of popular culture (fan cultures, festivals, coffee houses, bars, etc.).

5. One useful collection of these liturgies is Thompson's *Liturgies of the Western Church.*

and seek to transform? How can we keep these aspects alive as we develop new forms of worship and new understandings of preaching?

In my assessment, the Liturgy of the Word in the Western church tradition bears within it four *paradoxisms* that seem relevant to transforming human communication to make it adequate to this larger task.[6] *Paradoxism* is a term used by literary and cultural critic Roland Barthes to describe an "alliance of words" or an "unusual figure"[7] designed to "transgress" or overcome a seemingly unsolvable conundrum or "Antithesis."[8] These paradoxisms usually mix within themselves seemingly antithetical elements (humanity/divinity, inside/outside, good/evil, etc.) in such a way as to signal the possibility of a pathway "through the wall of an Antithesis."[9] As I interpret them below, each of these four paradoxisms within the Liturgy of the Word is bound up with overcoming one of four communicational "antitheses" or problematics within the practical theology of human-divine communication. And as we will see, each problematic, while distinct, impinges directly on the unique paradoxism we call the sermon.

1) PRIEST(S): WHO'S IN THE CONVERSATION?

The first communicationally significant paradoxism within the Liturgy of the Word is the worship leader, minister, or "priest." I use the word *priest* in the broadest and most generic way here to signify an ordinary person who becomes set apart in relation to divine power within a religious or ritual context. In some free church and nonsacramental traditions, such persons may be set apart through certain qualities of "sainthood" within congregations, through significant testimonial practices during worship (in some forms of revivalist or Anabaptist worship), or through other valued aspects of ritual leadership (in prayer, song, etc.). These "God-persons," some ordained, some not, are (of course inadequate) ciphers for overcoming what

6. In 1984, as a part of my dissertation, I conducted an extensive semiotic analysis of eighteen liturgies in the Western church tradition, searching for these "paradoxisms." Although my interpretation of these paradoxisms in relation to dialogue is quite different now, I believe that the semiotic analysis holds up under the weight of time. See McClure, "Preaching and the Pragmatics of Human/Divine Communication."

7. For Barthes, a *figure* is a technique of speech, like metaphor, alliteration, or synecdoche. The paradoxism is a figure of a unique mixture or confusion of qualities designed to surpass a boundary or limit condition.

8. Barthes, *S/Z*, 27.

9. According to Barthes, "Every joining of two antithetical terms, every mixture, every conciliation—in short, every passage through the wall of the Antithesis—thus constitutes a transgression." Ibid.

might be called the *Antithesis of human-divine relation*. The distance between humanity and God seems so far. Is a relationship possible? When we confront this first paradoxism, what is at stake for human-divine communication is authentic *relation*: becoming fully, and in the deepest sense, *with* God, in communication.[10]

To be more specific, the pragmatic issue for human-divine communication represented by the priestly liturgical figure is the problem of moving beyond role-taking and role-playing to an even deeper personal/communal relation with God characterized by integrity, immediacy, and transparency. During worship, leaders take roles for God (Father, healer, mother hen, savior, etc.), inviting worshipers to play corresponding roles (prodigals, wounded ones, dependents, sinners, etc.). These roles are designed to build a certain kind of relationship—to situate worshipers, as fully as possible, *with* the God witnessed to in Scripture and tradition. These roles exhaust themselves, however, especially in *confession* and *doxology*. In the Roman rite, the priest falls on the steps of the altar and pounds the chest wailing "*mea culpa*." In Reformed corporate confession of sin "Woe is me" falls from the assembly's lips as worshipers confront their distance from a real relation to God and self. In contemporary worship, during a musical crescendo, all eyes fasten on the music leader whose face is turned upward and hands outstretched to God. In doxology, worshipers cry out together "you alone are worthy" and struggle to push beyond role-play to direct personal and communal relationship.

Within the liturgy, the priestly paradoxism is a liturgical figure for the perfect, authentic relationship between humanity and divinity within the person of Christ. The human/divine person of Christ indicates the impossible possibility of a fundamentally "role-free" relationship between humanity and God. The metaphors used throughout the history of the church to describe this relationship within the person of Christ are all communicational in nature: "communication idiomatum," "mixtio," "confusio," "intercommunication," "communion of natures," and "communication" itself. Somehow, within the person of Christ there occurs a fundamental, consistent, and primary relation between God and humanity. Only "in Christ" can anyone expect to find a taste of this most interior and direct divine-human relation, but the priestly paradoxism becomes a liturgical figure for the *possibility* of

10. According to Lionel Trilling, authenticity can be contrasted with an older ideal, sincerity, which assumes a solid self that can be represented in public. Authenticity is a concept that emerged in late modernity in which this stable, solid self is problematized. The search for authenticity represents the search for, or awareness of, a fluid and hidden self, available in only in this *kairos* or opportune moment of communication. See Trilling, *Sincerity and Authenticity*, 9. See also Smith, *The New Measures*, 215, 305.

a journey toward and perhaps "through the wall" of the Antithesis of divine/human relation.

2) INTERCESSION: AM I COMPETENT TO COMMUNICATE?

In his lecture "The Affliction and Promise of Christian Proclamation," Karl Barth asks: "What are you doing, you human person, with God's word on your lips? How do you come to this role of mediator between heaven and earth?"[11] The second paradoxism in the Liturgy of the Word is the figure of the worshiper as "mediator between heaven and earth" in prayer, especially intercessory prayer. Intercessory prayer is a unique and unusual figure in the liturgy and it seeks to transgress what might be called the *Antithesis of human/divine mediation.* Beyond establishing relation, mediation implies activity: a way of *acting* within the divine/human relationship.[12]

When worshipers intercede, what is at stake for the pragmatics of human-divine communication is realizing an empathic "communicative competence" adequate to human-divine interaction. Communicative competence reaches beyond simple linguistic competence. It refers to the ability to use language appropriately in different situations. Such competence usually implies a high degree of empathy for others. In a well-known essay by M. V. Redmond, the perception of communicative competence and the perception of empathy are shown to be so closely aligned as to be virtually interchangeable.[13] In intercession, which Gregory Dix called the "priestly prayer of the whole church,"[14] the gathered worshiping community takes on itself the privilege of empathically "going between" (*inter* + *cedere*) God and humanity. Intercession (and prayer in its fullness) builds, over time, a new spiritually empathic competence—situating worshipers as mediators or "go-betweens" who take the things of God to the world, and the things of the world to God.

11. Barth, "Not und Verheißung," quoted in Denecke, *Gotteswort als Menschenwort*, 118. Taken from Deeg, "Disruption, Initiation, Staging," 6.

12. According to Grossberg, the "notion of expressive mediation calls for a vocabulary that will enable us to describe the agencies and sites of the production, mobilization, deployment, organization, management, and transformation of mediation as becoming." *Cultural Studies in the Future Tense*, 192.

13. Redmond "The Relationship Between Perceived Communication Competence and Perceived Empathy." See also Hymes, "Competence and Performance in Linguistic Theory."

14. Dix, *The Shape of the Liturgy*, 45.

The paradoxism of intercession is a liturgical figure for Christ as intercessor—the new high priest, entering the holy of holies and offering a completed, perfect sacrifice on behalf of the gathered church, appearing "before the face of God" (Heb 9:24). From the human side we say that the church engages in intercession in order to participate in the spiritual mediation of Christ at prayer and its power to transform communicative competence before God. From the divine side we say that Christ as high priestly intercessor identifies with this figure of local presence in order that we might share in Christ's unique empathic mediation between the human and the divine.[15]

3) SCRIPTURE: WHAT LANGUAGE SHALL WE SPEAK?

The third communicational paradoxism in the Liturgy of the Word is the Bible. Here we confront the *Antithesis of human/divine language*: human words/divine words. What code, what language, is large enough, strange enough, transformative enough, interruptive enough, transgressive enough, for us to eventually "speak"—with intercessory competence, and from within a transparent relationship with God? In this situation we raise the pulpit Bible, or perhaps kiss it. Or we take our well-worn personal Bible in hand and open its hallowed pages to follow along. Surely this is the code! Here alone we can trace the "messianic secret" as it finds its way into our own lives.

This sacred book of words is a paradoxism that becomes a unique liturgical figure for Christ as word or Logos, reconfigured within the Hebrew conception of *dabhar YHWH,* and present now in worship as Scripture (Bibles, church calendar, lectionary, quotations, lyrics, etc.). Here we confront in worship the creative, interruptive, dynamic word of God as a unique grammar and habitus. The liturgy celebrates this divine word in rituals large and small in which the witness of the holy Scriptures to "the word made flesh" comes to life.

Of course, Scripture is more than "code," or *langue*, it is also *text*, an inscription of the foundational events of faith in language. As such, it places a *writing-reading* aspect into the midst of the dialogical relation of the liturgy. This broadens the situation of interlocution to include the distance of history (and the distanciation of hermeneutics), along with the accretions

15. For more on this empathy, see Farley, *Divine Empathy*. According to Farley, divine creativity and the redemptive activity of God in the world are both to be understood as empathetic, i.e., as oriented to "the promotion of the reality, freedom and cooperative interrelation of entities." Ibid., 303.

of historical interpretations—a polyphony of inscriptions, if you will, that extends this code, as sedimentations of "reference" (which is addressed in the next section). In other words, it includes Christian discourse: a long oral and written tradition of the interpretation of this code.

Appropriating this language for purposes of human-divine communication is not a matter of a simple cultural-linguistic enculturation into the semiotic autonomy of this distant or alien text. Rather, the liturgy encourages users of this language and text to approximate a position within *all* language similar to that of the *living Christ*—the pattern by which every code functions properly. Entering into liturgical practice denies us our usual position within everyday language and positions us (through enculturation) in biblical language (calendar, lectionary, prayers, wordings, etc.). Then, as lay readers or clergy take hold of the text and read it aloud, and as preachers begin to engage and struggle with these texts, we are denied a position in that language and are pointed toward the enigmatic position of Jesus as both user of and parabolic presence within that language system. Then, as we will see, liturgical preaching opens up a new position for us within language as a whole through the discovery of timely and inventive language for speaking *with* God (see the next section on the sermon).

These first three liturgical practices within the Liturgy of the Word in the Western church tradition, interpreted from the perspective of the task of human-divine communication, surround preaching with significant assistance in its task—helping us as preachers and worshipers to be (1) in an authentic *relation* with God, (2) *competent* (empathic, intercessory) communicators, and (3) christologically repositioned in relation to *language*. We might say that these three practices establish the unique kind of *intersubjectivity* needed in order to speak now to/with/for/on behalf of God—which is the paradoxism figured by what we commonly call "the sermon."

4) THE SERMON: WHAT SHALL WE SPEAK ABOUT?

The theological Antithesis that emerges at this point, in which the sermon comes under scrutiny, is the *Antithesis of human/divine speech*. This Antithesis has its roots in biblical prophecy, with its introductory formula: "The word of Yahweh came to me, saying, "Go and proclaim in the hearing of Jerusalem . . ." (Jer 2:1). There is, in this type of speech, the inherent notion of what Ricoeur calls a "double author of speech," which links "the notion of revelation to that of inspiration conceived as one voice behind another."[16]

16. Ricoeur, "Toward a Hermeneutic of the Idea of Revelation," 3.

Such speech is bound to "oracle, which . . . is one tributary of those archaic techniques that sought to tap the secrets of the divine, such as divination, omens, dreams, casting dice, astrology, etc."[17]

Karl Barth, who is perhaps *the* theologian of this Antithesis of God speech/human speech, asserts that God chooses to identify with preaching at a point beyond all of the "dialectics" of human speech—and, in fact, God somehow "speaks when he is spoken of" at the point where human dialectic "comes to an end."[18] Barth articulates the revelatory dimension of the paradoxism of preaching well. What he fails to discuss adequately is the *referential* quality of this "double-speech" beyond the simple occurrence of "God speaking." Barth indicates the importance of God speaking, but subordinates the speech of God (as referring beyond itself in a meaning) to the appearance of God in God's speech as "the Word of God." In other words, Barth is more concerned with what Ricoeur calls the "noetic" side of speaking, which connects reference to its (divine/human) speaker, than to its "noematic" side, in which reference is marked not by "utterer's meaning" but by the relatively free-floating "utterance meaning"[19] and the broad possibilities for "meaning" in this situation, now, among *these* interlocutors. The liturgy as human-divine communication, however, invites us to go further—to encounter the inventive, metaphorical, and allegorical referencing of the code/text as "referring" (ontologically) to what *is*.

The liturgical paradoxism that transgresses the God speech/human speech Antithesis is *preaching*, or more specifically, preaching as a historical and liturgical figure of Jesus as proclaimer of the kingdom of God through the events and words of his life, death, and resurrection. In those originary events and words, the creative and always creating God and Jesus the Christ "refer to" something new—"speak" to, with, and on behalf of humanity a new "meaning" or set of meanings. What these words and events "refer to" remains the essential horizon of meaning for the Christian church and its worship.[20]

Preaching enters into the communicative Antithesis of "God speaking/human speaking" as speech that attempts to *refer*, in a secondary way, to what God refers to in the life, death, and resurrection of Jesus—we join in

17. Ibid.

18. Barth, *The Word of God and the Word of Man*, 211.

19. See Ricoeur, *Interpretation Theory*, 12–13.

20. In Trinitarian terms, were we constructive theologians rather than a practical theologians, we might say that the full "meaning" of these words and events were and are only available in any primary way to the second and first persons of the Trinity. These events are, through the power of the Spirit, *their* speaking together, their perfect articulation of meaning, which all secondary witnesses trace.

this human/divine act of reference, speaking together (with God, with one another, with the larger culture, with those who inscribed the text of scripture, and within the historical tradition of those who sought "references" in their own situations) a meaning for that unique reality that exists by virtue of *that* human-divine speaking together. Preaching is an act of reference in which the congregation and God speak together a new and immediate meaning that is a reference, not to God, but to a unique reality *spoken of (referred to) with God*. The goal of preaching is not only the encounter with God speaking in the human words of peaching (the noetic experience of transgressing the human/divine Antithesis in the event of speaking), but to refer together, i.e. *to point beyond this event to its meaning*, and to move, in Ricoeur's words, beyond its "sense" to its "reference."[21]

As with all other liturgical processes, we assume that this dialogical attempt to speak of this unique reality with God/for God/to God/on behalf of God is happening pervasively throughout worship. It is symbolized most powerfully, however, during the ritual called preaching or "sermon." Here, liturgical practice says: "speak," "refer," "mean," "translate," "make sense," "indicate," "point," "gesture toward," "identify," "exposit," "explain," "explore," "illustrate," "discover," etc. At this point, we as worshipers move beyond the intersubjectivity of *relation* (the paradoxism of priest/minister/priesthood of believers), a unique communicative *competence* (the paradoxism of intercessory prayer), and *language* (the paradoxism of Scripture), to *articulate a meaning, a reference*, and thus to implicate human experience now, in this situation, as a locus for such reference.

COMMUNICATION AND SOFT HERESY

Activities of *reference* constitute the capstone elements of communication. According to cognitive psychologist Simon Garrod, communication, "through the interaction, enables interlocutors to align on particular referential expressions (i.e. routines) and to align on particular strategies for reference in relation to the interactive task at hand."[22] In the early church, this kind of "aligning" communication, with regard to what, in fact, Jesus'

21. Ricoeur, expositing Frege's "Uebe Sinn und Bedeutung," identifies "sense" with the "what" of discourse and "reference" to the "about what" of discourse. Sense corresponds to Barth's obsession with meaning that is purely "immanent to the discourse and objective in the sense of ideal." *Interpretation Theory*, 20. Reference, on the other hand "expresses the movement in which language transcends itself" and "relates language to the world. It is another name for discourse's claim to be true." Ibid.

22. Garrod, "Referential Processing in Monologue and Dialogue with and without Access to Real-World Referents," 290.

life, death, and resurrection meant (referred to), was intense, and often conflicted. Many different interpretations or, to use Walter Benjamin's term, "translations" of the original event (as construed in oral tradition and other narrative accounts) were offered to complement (or supplement) the meaning of Jesus' life and teachings.[23] And as Benjamin points out, all such translation is broken or fragmentary, for all translation is, to some extent, allegorical.[24]

According to historian and classicist Marcel Simon, in the earliest church the term *hairesis,* from which came the word *heresy*, simply meant "choice," and specifically the choice of embracing a particular school of thought or world view.[25] According to Simon, in the early church heresies were "in principle, neither good nor bad, since there existed no universally recognized criterion of authority by which to classify them into opposing categories and to distinguish truth from error."[26] Diverse meanings for the life, death, and resurrection of Jesus Christ were proposed, argued, and negotiated. According to historian Harry O. Maier, much of this negotiation took place within household churches. In these household churches, Christian hospitality played a tremendous role in "the promotion and extension of diverse teachings."[27] These household churches welcomed itinerant prophets and teachers who represented various *haireses* (schools of thought) and, although some households were clearly persuaded to adopt very specific views, much to the consternation of the Apostle Paul and other early church leaders, it is likely that many of these churches took the ideas of the wandering prophets and teachers (including Paul) with a grain of salt.

It has been argued that our religious context today closely resembles this pre-Constantinian arrangement in which doctrinally orthodox Christianity (East and West) finds itself on a more level playing field in relation to various *haireses* within the surrounding culture.[28] In this context, communication regarding the referencing or meaning of the biblical witness to the life, death, and resurrection of Jesus Christ is best thought of as the invention of new choices, or *soft haireses,* on their way to truth, rather than as the refutation of hard or closed and doctrinaire *heresy* in rebellion to an orthodoxy maintained as a final authority.

23. See Benjamin, "The Task of the Translator," 71–82.

24. See Benjamin, "Allegory and *Trauerspiel,*" 235. See also Fynsk, *Language and Relation*, 177–89, for an excellent exposition of Benjamin's theory of translation as it relates to the concept of "relation" and the "relationality" of languages.

25. Simon, "From Greek Hairesis to Christian Heresy," 104.

26. Ibid.

27. Maier, "Heresy, Households, and the Disciplining of Diversity," 218.

28. See Wuthnow, *After Heaven*, and Bellah, *Beyond Belief.*

If this is true, and if we are to consider these heresies as "soft," several things are needed in order to refer together in relation to God. In the first place, this situation requires integrity and truthfulness. It requires speakers who have genuine interest in actually coming into relationship with each other and with the God of Jesus Christ. In many respects, this corresponds to the first liturgical paradoxism outlined above. It involves taking up (perhaps strange) roles for God, and for ourselves. And it involves the eventual journey beyond these roles, in favor of as much transparency as possible before God. In other words, it implies engagement with the Antithesis of human/divine relation in order to come into relationship with the God who might speak meaning (refer) together with us.

In the second place, this situation requires what Donald Davidson calls "interpretive charity," such that we believe our interlocutor shares the ability to "triangulate" with us in relation to this divine/human "reference" and "through trial and error . . . solve for the meaning of (each) other's discursive actions."[29] "Reference" here does not mean "mere reference" as it does in the analytic philosophical tradition, nor is it intratextual reference whereby a closed text, like a "language game," is said to "render an agent."[30] Rather, reference, in the event of speaking together *now*, can *only* "refer" as an answer to some prior question or as a solution to some prior problem.[31] In other words, "reference is dependent upon the problematics of the utterance"[32] as it is related to and grows out of immediate human experience, and in our case, immediate human experience in relation to God in a particular context. The need for interpretive charity and triangulation parallels the empathic communicative competence at the heart of the second liturgical paradoxism outlined above—intercession. Intercession is uniquely shaped to mediate discursive forms of reference that respond to deeper spiritual and theological "problematics" in the immediate context.

In the third place, what we are trying to do in preaching that is "on the way to truth" is not to "match our codes" but to "share a similar method of adjusting (our) use of signs."[33] This means coming to some understanding of what Donald Davidson labels as each person's (or community's) "prior theory" (what I believe you think, and what I believe you think I think, etc.). Yarbrough points out that for Davidson, "most of the time prior theories

29. Quoted in Yarbrough, *Inventive Intercourse*, 28 (parenthesis mine).

30. This idea is sometimes conveyed by so-called postliberal theologians. See Frei, *The Eclipse of Biblical Narrative*, and Campbell, *Preaching Jesus.*

31. Yarborough, *Inventive Intercourse*, 31.

32. Ibid. See also Meyer, *Of Problematology*, 235–37.

33. Yarbrough, *Inventive Intercourse*, 32.

will not be shared, and there is no reason why they should be."[34] He goes on to say that "moreover, even the prior theory is quite different from what we call a 'language' because 'an interpreter must be expected to have quite different prior theories for different speakers.'"[35] This "sign-adjusting" aspect of referring parallels the third liturgical paradoxism identified above, the Bible, in which the search for an adequate "code" is paramount. At the heart of this paradoxism, as we have seen, is the constant adjustment of the way signs are used—the constant learning, if you will, of "sign-adjustment"—approximating, as much as possible, the enigmatic christological position from which language itself begins to signify correctly in relation to God.

From the ground of prior theories, referring together with God requires that each party enters a final phase involving the articulation together of a "passing theory" through which we invent an opportune or *kairotic* "adjustment"[36] so that we can "attribute particular meanings to words rather than other possible meanings."[37] A "passing theory" represents a new soft *hairesis*, an adjusted "choice" that exists between us now, and which, in the words of Yarbrough, "is invented on the fly."[38] There are no hard-and-fast rules that regulate this "invention." It is a form of interlocutive heuristics,"[39] designed to pursue and more closely approximate a reference that is "in front" of us as a shared meaning within a larger horizon of meaning. This kind of heuristics is the very heart of the paradoxism called sermon.

Such meaning always contains within it its own undoing, what Blanchot calls "the disaster."[40] This disaster of meaning is inherent in the divine/human Antithesis and the sermon-paradoxism through which all of our prior theories and meanings are negated, new meanings (passing theories, soft *haireses*) are invented, then become sediment within new prior theories,

34. Davidson, quoted in Yarbrough, *Inventive Intercourse*, 33–34.

35. Ibid., 34.

36. In rhetorical theory, *kairotic* refers to what is composed *now*, at this critical juncture or season (*kairos*). It is the opportune (*eukairon*), or a seizing of an opportunity that could only present itself at this moment in time. See Kinneavy and Eskin, "*Kairos* in Aristotle's Rhetoric," 131–42; Carter, "*Stasis* and *Kairos*"; and Miller, "Kairos in the Rhetoric of Science." See also Shivers, "Finding Something to Say."

37. Yarbrough, *Inventive Intercourse*, 33.

38. Ibid.

39. Ibid., 27.

40. See Blanchot, *The Writing of the Disaster*. For Blanchot, this disaster is inherent in "the word's inability to *avoid signifying*" (Fynsk, *Language and Relation*, 234, italics mine), the endless slippage of "meaning," the heresy of all meaning, or, as Christopher Fynsk so aptly puts it: "Mimesis . . . figuring (itself) like a wandering corpse." Ibid., 236. See Ibid., 234–36.

and are negated again—as fragment after fragment, allegory after allegory,[41] pile up, translating new references, yet testifying to the communicability of the originary references as they echoed forth from the (certain kind of) silence of the empty tomb.

WHERE, THEN, IS THE SERMON TAKING PLACE TODAY?

In their recent empirical study of sermon listening in the Danish church context, Marlene Ringgaard Lorensen and Marianne Gaarden report that:

> When the churchgoers were asked about what they have heard of the sermon, they expressed what they had been thinking in relation to the *fragments of the sermon they had actually heard.* It was almost impossible to disentangle what the listeners had heard, which the preacher had actually said, and what the listeners had been thinking, activated by their encounter with the sermon. What the churchgoers remembered and reported was completely interwoven with and inseparable from their own thoughts in dialogue with the sermon. *What remained in the memory of the churchgoers was not what had actually been said from the pulpit, but their personal meaning production, activated by dialogical interaction involving the listener's own life situation and existential reflections.* (Italics mine.)[42]

As a result of their study, Lorensen and Gaarden conclude that there appears to be a "masked agency" in preaching, which:

> can be described as a polyphony of voices, *which is not limited to the liturgical room or the sermon*, but is activated by it. This polyphony *creates a room*, where the churchgoers, through different kinds of dialogical interaction, categorized as associative, critical, and contemplative, create new meaning and

41. According to Benjamin, in *The Origin of German Tragic Drama*, unlike symbol, allegory is forever inventive. It "must constantly unfold in new and surprising ways. . . . Allegories become dated, because it is part of their nature to shock." 183. Allegorizing is involved in "tirelessly transforming, interpreting, and deepening . . ." 231. Like the push toward "meaning," or reference, allegory thrives on abstraction. Like heresy, it resounds with the dangers of "the triumph of subjectivity and the onset of an arbitrary rule over things" 233. It unifies "guilt" (at subordinating the material universe) and "signifying" (naming, evaluating, judging, abstracting). 234. Allegory is self-consciously a "ruin" or "fragment" —showing its hand as merely an interpretation —as the triumph of subjectivity.

42. Gaarden and Lorensen, "Listeners as Authors in Preaching," 30–31.

> understanding. It is *not a room that the listener or the preacher can control or occupy, but a room that both engage in.* (Italics mine.)[43]

It appears that preaching takes place, at least in part, in a parallel "room" to the liturgical room—a room reserved, we might say, for the negotiation of "divine/human" references in relation to lived experience today.[44] The sermon is a liturgical moment, yes—requiring, for its best "referring," a unique relationship, competence, and adjustment within language. But it also connects our liturgical actions (works of the people) to another room of intense conversation, intrapersonal, interpersonal, social, and cultural, in which listeners are, heretically, talking back to preachers, texts, God, and each other—negotiating the meaning of gospel for the here and now.

This, of course, is highly suggestive of a broader definition of preaching that may be useful in this generation, one that is tethered to other para-homiletic forms for the production of religious culture—music, art, social media, salons, etc. The room in which preaching takes place is always the room of *reference*—of exposing and entering the ontological reference for Christian "gospel" in each generation. Such a room is always a much larger communicative space than our liturgical spaces, and larger than our ecclesiastical structures and institutions in general.

It is important, therefore, as we rethink Christian worship and preaching, to redeem the communicative wisdom found in historical liturgies. If we do not need the same (historic) liturgies, as we move forward into the 'post-Constantinian,' postdenominational, postliturgical church, we do need theologically attenuated practices that will facilitate this divine-human communication in ways taught to us by the paradoxisms within the historic liturgies. In short, we need to promote: 1) transparent relationships with

43. Ibid., 28. Similar responses can be found in the massive American empirical study of sermon listening, the Alban Institute's Listening to Listeners to Sermons Project. One analysis of the findings of this study noted that: "Listeners are prone to take even single words and phrases and place them alongside some ordinary experience in their everyday lives . . . [They] are experimenting with theological worlds and worldviews on the spot, trying on metaphors, images, and ideas like garments, adopting some and rejecting others."

44. I realize that I take some liberty with Marianne Gaarden's research by calling this a "parallel" room. Her research analysis focuses on the encounter between situated subjects' experiences and the preacher's words *in worship* creating a room in which the churchgoers generate meaning or a modus of being—this meaning does not exist in advance, but emerges in this room. I agree that this meaning does not exist in advance, but is "invented on the fly" between preacher and hearer. But this room, it seems, is coextensive with a larger "room" filled with intrapsychic and cultural influences—i.e., it is full of many voices, albeit catalyzed by the communicative voice of the preacher.

God, 2) intercessory, or spiritually empathic communicative competence, 3) encounters with the chistologically repositioning language of Scripture, and 4) soft heretical references to the reign of God, which may take place in any number of literal or figurative "rooms."

IMPLICATIONS FOR THE DEVELOPMENT OF HOMILETICAL THEOLOGY

Several very specific implications for homiletical theology have been identified in this essay. To summarize, homiletical theology, from the perspective of a theology of communication, attends to any attempt to engage in human-divine reference, within the distinct form of human-divine intersubjectivity indicated by the Christian liturgy. This means that homiletical theology will attend to any attempt at referring to the reign of God when human-divine relation, situational empathy, and biblical-linguistic repositioning are involved.

Three other larger methodological implications also emerge. The first implication is that homiletical theology is, at one level, a theology of communication. Part of the constructive work of homiletical theology is to theorize and then theologize what I am calling "human-divine communication." Homiletical theology will always ask what theological dynamics are involved in this unique form of communication. And this will include asking: What ways do various kinds of communicative practices undergo modification when communication requires intersubjectivity and "referring" with/to/on behalf of the God of Jesus Christ?

A second implication arrives in the suggestion that it is important to engage in the work of establishing theological and ethical norms for Christian practices of communication. This is implied by the appeal to practices of Christian worship as a way to establish essential norms for softening the heretical activity of theological reference. Such norms for communication, of course, diverge from strictly rational norms, such as those established by H. P. Grice (the so-called "cooperative principle") or Jürgen Habermas (universal pragmatics).[45] Within any theology of communication, it is important to establish criteria for the kind of intersubjectivity that will produce references or "passing theories" that are consistent with Christian witness.

The final implication for homiletical theology is the suggestion that, in fact, homiletical theology is not only situational, it is "portable." Although bound to the communicative norms established by Christian practices of

45. Grice, "Logic and Conversation," and Habermas, *Communication and the Evolution of Society*.

worship and proclamation, homiletical theologians are aware that the business of "communicating with God" is both an ecclesial activity and an activity that is psychically and culturally pervasive. It is entirely possible that the form of intersubjectivity described in this essay, and the type of soft heretical referencing identified, might be instantiated in many contexts and situations outside of the local church. A Christian theology of communication finds within the liturgy and liturgical preaching its normative shape, but not its scope of limitation. Homiletical theologians, therefore, will investigate homiletic practices and artifacts produced in liturgical spaces, and in other "rooms" beyond Christian houses of worship.

—4—

In Our Own Native Tongue

Toward a Pentecostalization of Homiletical Theology

—Luke A. Powery

In his Lyman Beecher Lectures published as *The Holy Spirit and Preaching*, James Forbes states, "The preaching event itself . . . is a living, breathing, flesh-and-blood expression of the theology of the Holy Spirit."[1] Yet, as I have noted elsewhere,[2] there is a paucity of substantive homiletical literature on the Holy Spirit, although theologically, the Spirit is the power of the word, the power of proclamation. For far too long, the field of homiletics has been dominated by the word of God tradition within Protestantism, including a heavy emphasis on Christology; this christocentric emphasis is crucial to the proclamation of the gospel, however, it does not encompass the full scope of what is possible in homiletical theological scholarly reflection. Perhaps many scholars assume the presence and the work of the Spirit, but for the purposes of doing homiletical theology, this is an insufficient approach. In fact, this is not only a disservice to homiletics; this is a disservice to the fullness of the Godhead. Thus, this essay is an attempt to foreground pneumatology for homiletical theology despite the fact it is always a precarious situation to speak about a wind that blows where it wills (John 3:8).

There are numerous pneumatological trajectories or traces of the Spirit in and for the field of homiletics. If one takes the Spirit seriously and even makes the Spirit central to a theological turn in homiletics, this leads

1. Forbes, *The Holy Spirit and Preaching*, 19.
2. Powery, *Spirit Speech*.

to various topoi for conversation. I have named two in previous work,[3] but this paper is an initial step toward navigating the fiery experience of the day of Pentecost as another pneumatic field of fruitful homiletical exploration. Pursuing this particular exploration will keep homiletical theology connected to this age which has been called "an age of the Spirit" by Harvey Cox.[4]

Liturgically, Christians celebrate Pentecost as an end of the Easter season at fifty days, linking the resurrection and ascension of Christ with the sending of the Holy Spirit. Historically, Pentecost is related to the Jewish harvest festival of Shavuot or Feast of Weeks. It commemorated the giving of the Law at Sinai but also celebrated harvesting of wheat. During this festival, people could bring their first fruits to the temple as an offering. Using this historical lens, one might then say that Pentecost is the human experience of the first fruits of the Spirit or the communion of the Holy Spirit with the human spirit. The liturgical or historical significance of Pentecost is not unimportant, however, the focus in this essay, "the pentecostalization of homiletical theology," is not about preaching on Pentecost as a special day in the liturgical calendar. It is also not about Pentecostalism as a Christian movement per se or about Pentecostal preaching within these environs.

Instead, this essay aims to utilize the day of Pentecost as expressed in Acts 2:1–13 as a lens through which to teach and learn about the gift of the Spirit in relation to speaking and hearing the gospel in context. In other words, one may refer to this as a constructive homiletical reading of the day of Pentecost. Undergirding this essay is the belief that Pentecost is fertile soil for critical thinking about homiletical theology; thus it posits the question, "What does the day of Pentecost and the work of the Spirit on that day in particular reveal to us about homiletical theology?" In what follows, I will attempt to answer that question in a preliminary manner; yet what should become clear through this suggestive constructive theological reading of Pentecost is that the ground of homiletical theology is fundamentally a divine gift. After gesturing in a constructive theological manner in relation to the biblical text, I will conclude with some thoughts regarding implications for the further development of homiletical theology.

3. See Powery, *Spirit Speech* and *Dem Dry Bones.*

4. Cox, *The Future of Faith,* 1–20.

HOMILETICAL REFLECTIONS THROUGH PENTECOST

Gift of Speech

To begin with the day of Pentecost already suggests the primacy of the Holy Spirit in the perspective of this essay. At Pentecost what is revealed is that even the coming of the Spirit on this day is a gift. Jesus reminded the disciples of the "promise of the Father" and to wait for it (Acts 1:4). They had to wait to be baptized in the Spirit because the descent of the Spirit is a gift, not something of their own creation. This is further emphasized when Luke writes, "and suddenly from heaven there *came* a sound . . ." (2:2). The sound came. The Spirit came on divine volition. Thus, it is important to remember that the Spirit is God's gift to us, even as it relates to homiletical theology. Divine agency is the prelude to powerful human agency as it relates to being effective Christian witnesses in the world. Because the disciples "will receive power" when the Holy Spirit comes (1:8), the prelude of God's action takes priority in homiletical theology framed pneumatologically.

Linked to proclamation more broadly, we read that "All of them were filled with the Holy Spirit and began to speak in other languages, as the Spirit gave them ability" (2:4). The Spirit gives the people the ability to speak in other languages. As Will Willimon writes, "The first gift of the Spirit is the gift of speech, the gift of speech in different languages . . . the first fruit of the Spirit—the gift of proclamation."[5] As is shown throughout the biblical witness, word and spirit are collaborative. Pentecost is another example of this and demonstrates how the Spirit enables multilingual speech. The gift of speech, proclamation, is a gift of the Spirit. The object of study for homiletical theology, the spoken word, would be nonexistent and most definitely impotent without the Spirit's work in our mouths. The proclaimed gospel is not something of our own creation. Proclamation is a word from outside and beyond us that comes to us and fills us to speak from our particular selves but not about ourselves. This pneumatic speech is for something and Someone greater than us, yet it is expressed in and through distinct cultural ways. It is in us and flows through us but it is given to us by the Spirit. Tongues of fire "rested on each of them" (2:3) such that others might be ignited. Holy fire comes down in order that fire may rise back up through inspired speech. Yet, once again, fire is not a human creation; it is a warm

5. Willimon, *Acts,* 30. The limits of this essay prevent full discussion, but I would be remiss not to mention the apparent link between the filling of the Spirit and inspired interpretation of Scripture as shown in Peter's sermon in Acts 2:14–36, another example of Spirit-empowered speech.

gift, a gift of speech, of tongues, of languages, that comes with a purpose to be understood.

Gift of Understanding

The gift of speech is not given in order *not* to be understood. Proclaimers preach in order to be heard and hopefully understood. As the story unfolds, another gift of the Spirit is obvious—the gift of hearing in one's own language. The gift of ecstatic speech at Pentecost is traditionally highlighted but what is also obviously stressed is how others understand what is being spoken. When disciples are filled with the Spirit and speak in other languages as the Spirit enables them to do so, "Jews from every nation under heaven" become bewildered and amazed because "each one heard them speaking in the native language of each" (2:5–6). The miracle is not the physical ability of hearing but it is the understanding of what is being proclaimed, despite the different culture of the "preachers." Due to their understanding, they have to ask, "Are not all these who are speaking Galileans?"(2:7). The proclaimers were not of the same ethnicity and culture, yet they heard and understood. Homiletical theology in whatever school of thought should necessarily focus on whether the gospel proclaimed is understood. The lens of Pentecost urges one to seek understanding, not mere hearing. This means that a turn to the Spirit in homiletical theology is a turn to the speaker but also to the listener. Understanding is just as important as speaking and both are gifts of the Spirit at Pentecost.

There are two other times this gift of understanding is named (2:8, 11). In one instance, the hearers ask, "And how is it that we hear, each of us, in our own native language?"(2:8). That they "hear them speaking" in their own languages (2:11) is a gift because without understanding, the proclamation may just be a noisy gong, clanging cymbal, or pure white noise. But the Spirit assures that there are receptive ears to the word proclaimed, regardless of cultural makeup. For preaching to be effective there need to be hearers, and the Spirit provides this gift. The audience for the gospel is not void, but filled with the Spirit as well. The Spirit helps us take listeners seriously and to view their role in the preaching event as significant. Proclamation entails both speakers and listeners. The gospel needs a proclaimer and a recipient of the word. However, I would be remiss if I did not point out the fact that in Acts, though others may have heard, they did not always understand. Some were amazed for sure. "But others sneered and said, 'They are filled with new wine'"(2:13).

There was surely ecstasy but also comprehensibility, an ecstatic comprehensibility, or what John Levison calls "sober intoxication."[6] The intoxication comes via inspiration and the infilling of the Spirit that empowers human speech and understanding. One is enabled to hear the word in one's own language, but the hearer does not own the word granted nor is the ability to hear and understand owned by the listener. Understanding is given, gifted to us, in the moment of proclamation, because humans do not have the resources to manufacture it; therefore, without a Giver, we would not receive the gift of understanding. As Nora Tubbs Tisdale writes, "Revelation in preaching can never be earned or deserved or attained by our own human striving. It is always a gift of a God who chooses, in freedom, to reveal Godself to us—to condescend to our *captus* (comprehension)."[7]

Furthermore, understanding is possible because the hearers did not just hear but heard in their "own native language" (2:8), that is, in their own cultural tongue. This suggests that the gift of the word of the gospel is contextualized, revealing a contextual pneumatology of the gospel. The gift of the Spirit who brings the word comes to somewhere, some place, some person. The word is never acontextual if it is to be understood and if it is in and of the Spirit because the Spirit embraces cultures while this pericope also reveals how cultures embrace the Spirit. The word must be "native" to the hearer who stands in a particular culture in order for the gospel to have a hearing. Moreover, "When the day of Pentecost had come, they were all together in one place"(2:1), signifying that the gift comes to a specific place and time as the Spirit facilities the contextualization of the word. Context is inescapable because one can never escape one's own skin or even one's own native tongue. For the gospel to be the gospel it has to land somewhere particular in time and space. In the Spirit, the gospel incarnates through human languages such that people hear in their own particular cultural language the universal message about God's power. As with the incarnation, via the Spirit, God translates the Word into human means that we, humans, may understand and know the gospel in the flesh, in particular ways. To speak to a human world, the word of God or God's sermon had to become human through the gift of the Spirit. The Spirit is the agent of the incarnation, therefore she translates divinity to humanity that the word of God, the gospel, could be spoken and understood in context.

Likewise, on the day of Pentecost, the Spirit takes the initiative to provide a contextual, cultural word for each particular person so that the empowered word can be understood. Once again, the Spirit engages in the

6. Levison, *Filled with the Spirit*, 336.

7. Tisdale, *Preaching as Local Theology and Folk Art*, 36.

work of translation by translating the word into each native language present such that others may hear about God. The gospel needs to be translated in order that "every nation under heaven" can understand it in its own culture. The word is not monolingual. Pentecost represents the Spirit's embrace of cultural particularity and context and promotes "essentially worldwide proclamation."[8] Translation into each language demonstrates a divine care for diverse cultures, ethnicities, and languages. In the Spirit, *diversity* is not a dirty word but a beautiful one in the light of God. If one has problems with diversity, one has to take it up with the Spirit who creates diversity in the first place as the gospel is born in particular contexts, cultures, languages, and bodies, being fully embodied in a material world.

Therefore, one might say that the Holy Spirit communes with the human spirit in order to proclaim an effectual and powerful contextual word. Though the notion of gift prioritizes the work of God, God does not deny or erase human investment in the proclamation of the gospel. Pentecost reveals that human speakers and hearers are needed for "God's deeds of power" to be known. Pneumatology implies humanity, materiality, and the embrace of culture, not the negation of it. The Spirit is life for the human spirit, not death. She ignites and enlivens humanity in such a way that the gospel spreads all over the world. Because of the power and gift of the Spirit, Pentecost suggests the flourishing of humankind and not its destruction. Through the translation work of the Spirit, the gospel of God is proclaimed and heard in the vernacular or what Henry Mitchell calls "the mother tongue" of the Spirit[9] in order for the word to be received and heard as *pro nobis*, or "in our own native language."

One particular cultural case study of this work of the Spirit can be found in relation to the spirituals, musical memorabilia created by enslaved blacks during the crucible of slavery. The spirituals gained their name not only because they were religious folk songs but because they were viewed to be songs of the Spirit from the Spirit for an oppressed community. The spirituals were cultural bearers of the Spirit in the native language of a people for the life of that people. Though these songs, "a tune," or as I call them, musical sermons, were believed to be given by God as a gift, according to the story of High John de Conqueror they were "a tune that you could bend and shape in most any way you wanted."[10] The culture appropriated the musical word to fit the contextual setting and situation of the day, revealing how the Spirit and human spirit worked together for the good of humanity.

8. Welker, *God the Spirit*, 230.

9. Mitchell, *Black Preaching*, 76–87.

10. Hurston, *The Sanctified Church*, 77.

The rhythm, sound, and language were native to the enslaved as affirmation of their humanity that had been denied in slavery. To be gifted with a word to be heard is the affirmation of culture, and that culture expressed the creativity and improvisation of the Spirit within community as a pathway to self-assertion when everything around them attempted to destroy the self. In this cultural and historical example, it was the Spirit's work that saved the black self from annihilation. This word about "God's deeds of power" (2:11) is a gospel of salvation, not only for one particular group, but for the world.

Gift of God-Centered Community

The cultural particularity of the Spirit's gift, as shown at Pentecost and through the example of the spirituals, is not contrary to a universal quality as it relates to proclamation. According to Yves Congar, there is "the catholicity of witness."[11] He further says, "The distinctive aspect of the Spirit is that, while remaining unique and preserving his identity, he is in everyone without causing anyone to lose his originality. This applies to persons, peoples, their culture, and their talents. The Spirit also makes everyone speak of the marvels of God in his own language."[12] The gift of understanding or hearing in context reveals the common message of the gospel: God. Turning to the Spirit is a turn to the human speaker and hearer, but also to God. What the people heard in their native languages was the message about "God's deeds of power" (2:11).

This theocentrism is in fact a gift as it relates to homiletical theology. Preachers do not have to fret about what to preach because the gift of guidance is given—we are to proclaim God. One's stories, illustrations, exegesis, sermon content, and delivery should point to God and God's action. When reflecting on the nature of homiletical theology through a pneumatological lens, one realizes that God is essential to homiletical theology as object and subject. One is given a gift by God through the Spirit, thus one speaks of God. Pentecost privileges the proclamation of God as the universal content of proclamation though through particular cultural means. The end is always God but the means is always particular, holding together the creative relationship between particularity and universality. Both are gifts, yet God is primary as central to pneumatic proclamation. Dietrich Bonhoeffer once preached that people are bored with the church and the cinema appears to

11. Congar, *I Believe in the Holy Spirit*, 44.

12. Ibid.

be more interesting than the church "because we talk too much about false, trivial human things and ideas in the church and too little about God."[13]

The Pentecostal Spirit will not allow us to forget about God because "Through the pouring out of the Spirit, God effects a world-encompassing, multilingual, polyindividual testimony to Godself. In this way God attests to Godself in a process that unites people in a way that causes them both wonderment and fear."[14] Though there is a diverse community, there is unity around the presence of God. Pentecost is a "community-building festival"[15] but it is a distinct community in which God is the center. Cultural specificity is important, as noted already, but in the Spirit it is decentered. God dethrones cultural or ethnic hegemony at Pentecost. But it is also necessary to say that cultural identity is not erased or obliterated either. Cultural identity is fully present and fully inspirited yet the Spirit leads proclaimers to speak about and praise God. The heart of the gospel is God, regardless of the context. The Spirit does not allow us to suffer amnesia on this point, whether in theory or practice.

At the same time, the gift of a word from God about God is that this holy inspiration occurs within and creates a distinct community. Homiletical theology that takes the Spirit seriously must not hide behind or promote God as a way to homogenize the community or homiletics into one totalizing paradigm. Though God-centered, Pentecost reveals the gift of a community that represents boundary-breaking realities across culture, ethnicity, race, and language. In the Spirit there is no room for segregated homiletical theories that suggest homiletical elitism and superiority as if one model is the best spiritual mode. The Spirit works toward integration, collaboration, and mutuality between varied homiletical theological approaches. The Spirit forms community and dialogue. Through this communal interaction, there can be greater understanding about God and even homiletics.

The formation of a global community through the in-breaking of the Spirit breaks humanity out of our proclivity toward homogeneity and moves us to embrace a broad gospel for "the ends of the earth"(1:8). The gift of God opens us toward a hospitable vision in which the Spirit is poured out on "all flesh" (2:17) for proclamation to the ends of the earth. Any culture anywhere can be a conduit of the Spirit, thus there is no limit to whom or where the gospel can be preached. Though a word may be contextual in a particular culture, the gospel is never enclosed or trapped within any culture. The gospel is free and open in the light of an expansive Pentecostal

13. Bonhoeffer, "Ambassadors for Christ," 90–91.

14. Welker, *God the Spirit*, 235.

15. Johns, "Preaching Pentecost to the 'Nones,'" 7.

Spirit who knows no bounds and creates a diverse human community. Pentecost suggests that the Spirit opens us up to the possibility of hospitable relationships across cultures as opposed to closed systems and practices that restrain the full scope of the gospel message of God.

Without the other tongues or languages, the fire of the Spirit might be dimmer, but with one another in the unity of the Spirit, one realizes that the gospel travels across the world into every tribe and nation. The gift of this community is that it is indeed "not a homogenous unity, but a differentiated one."[16] In fact, then, one may speak of homiletical theolog*ies* rather than homiletical theology because it is only through communion with each other that we have a better understanding of the homiletical task. Through unified diversity as evident at Pentecost, it might be that the Spirit reorders our homiletical priorities just as that day was, according to Cheryl Johns, "the beginning of a whole new order of human spirituality."[17] Pentecost may call homiletical theological discourse to a new order but it begins with the recognition that proclamation—as it relates to the community of the speaker, hearer, and God—is an unmerited gift. It is a gift that the fire does not destroy but builds, creates, and invites us to a "common hospitality."[18] This Pentecostal homiletical community welcomes difference and welcomes the divine because of a hospitable pneumatology.

Once again, the cultural musical production known as the spirituals may be helpful in light of this. The spirituals are particular cultural musical sermons from a particular history of oppression in the United States, yet because of the Spirit's influence as songs of the Spirit, they have been dispersed and sung worldwide since the late nineteenth century. These musical sermons have been intoned all over the world in distinct ways by different cultures in order to hear the gospel in a native tongue. These gospel words have been appropriated for different settings and have touched thousands upon thousands as the Spirit translated their meanings in different contexts, including Europe, the home of many historical colonizers. Global humanity has discovered and affirmed a common human experience in the spirituals and this should not be surprising because a main work of the Spirit is to create fellowship. The utilization of the spirituals across the world reveals the fellowship of the Holy Spirit on the earth and provides a concrete representation of what is possible in the light of Pentecost.

16. Welker, *God the Spirit*, 228.

17. Johns, "Preaching Pentecost to the 'Nones,'" 4.

18. Rogers, *After the Spirit*, 205.

IMPLICATIONS FOR THE DEVELOPMENT OF HOMILETICAL THEOLOGY

This constructive homiletical reading of Pentecost presents several implications for the ongoing development of a homiletical theology. First, as homiletical theologians, we stand in a posture of waiting for the gift of the word to come. Thus, the future of a Pentecostalized homiletical theology is the practice of prayer even as that soaked the context of Pentecost (Acts 1). We pray for the gift because one does not know when the Giver will give it. It may not come when you want it but it will be on *kairos* time. In fact, Howard Thurman wisely writes that the practice of spiritual disciplines does "not guarantee that the Spirit will be encountered."[19] This suggests that homiletical theology requires an epistemic humility and a hermeneutics of trust through the posture of prayer. *Epiclesis* is the future of homiletical theology because it grounds theological pursuits in a spirituality discovered and practiced hopefully among a diverse community of thinkers. Pentecostalizing homiletical theology points to prayer and broadly to worship as after Peter's sermon, many are baptized (2:41). The Spirit bridges homiletical theology and liturgical theology. Thus, the future of homiletical theology may even be called "epicletic doxology"[20] because the end of preaching is ultimately the glorification of God.

This connection to prayer may bear fruit for further conversations between Christian spirituality and homiletical theology as well as liturgical theology and homiletical theology, the latter two being separated many times within the academy though they are close cousins. Prayer may offer the possibility of working at the intersection of liturgics and homiletics. Furthermore, the idea of *lex orandi* within liturgical theological literature may challenge homiletical theology to take prayer more seriously and recognize not only the spiritual nature of preaching but that the entire sermon preparation process and delivery is a prayer. As prayer, the sermon, the gospel in human mouths, is a gift received and given, a prayer on the altar of the pulpit offered from the altar of preachers' hearts. Pentecost not only stresses the significance of the Spirit for homiletical theology but it is a call to prayer, thus implying that homiletical theology will only develop with God's aid.

Second, this homiletical reading of Pentecost suggests the importance of cultural embodiment in space and time as necessary to homiletical theological thinking. A turn to the Spirit is also a turn to the human in context with all of her/his breath, voice, body, language, and ethnicity. Homiletical

19. Thurman, *Meditations of the Heart*, 39.

20. Old, *Themes and Variations for a Christian Doxology*, 17–40.

theology should embrace culture and context explicitly because of the material realities associated with sermon-making. Pentecost foregrounds particular cultural diversities as essential to the proclamation of the gospel. In light of this, it would behoove homiletical theologians to clarify the contexts they represent and the contexts for which they write because theological discourse is always contextual, though it may not be stated. Also, the gospel, as it is proclaimed and heard, is contextualized. This means that human bodies are critical in thinking about homiletical theology. The embrace of bodies to do homiletical theology would be an extraordinary counterpoint to the biblical hegemony in homiletics, especially in the face of historical accounts in which biblical texts were used to terrorize bodies. To begin with the Spirit means that one begins with particular cultural bodies and not biblical texts in homiletical theological reflection. The embrace of this Pentecostal vision is the embrace of the Spirit and human body, with all of its cultural diversity and creative productions (e.g. the spirituals).

The Spirit works in specificity and particularity but this does not exclude plurality. This leads to a third implication, which may be thought of as ecumenical openness. Just as the liberating fire of Pentecost surprised and amazed the speakers and hearers, the Spirit refuses to be trapped or imprisoned in any paradigm of homiletical theology, but rather, may ignite new particular ways of sounding the gospel that are different from our own native languages or ideas. My embrace of the Spirit for homiletical thinking (or should I say the Spirit's embrace of me?) frees me even from me, and my own native Powery homiletical theology. As Pentecost reveals, the wind blows where and when it wills, and even though you hear the sound of it, you do not know from where it comes or where it goes (John 3:8). Thus, all frameworks of homiletical theology are provisional and never complete. There is always room for further growth and development, as we only see in a glass dimly, even through scholarship. This suggests that the future of the field of homiletics is always open to new ideas and trajectories and never closes off any particular voice. Every perspective is needed to illumine the mystery of preaching in all of its beauty and agony.

Homiletical theology through the perspective of this pneumatological vision is a gesture toward ongoing, hospitable conversation that is inclusive of many tongues; thus, it is vital to broaden the dialogue about homiletical theology and strive for an ecumenical conversation beyond traditional mainline voices, perhaps even risking to engage marginal voices such as grassroots Pentecostals in Latin America and proponents of the prosperity gospel in this nation and beyond. Homiletical theology cannot develop in a denominational nor national vacuum. The Spirit challenges homiletical theology to push beyond the borders of selfsameness, recognizing that there is always a surplus of meaning when "all flesh" are involved. This may mean a move away from an elitist academic approach toward engagement with those on the fringe with different tongues in theological discourse or for whom no room has ever been made at the academic table. This hospitable gesture may help homiletical theologians to think in more plural ways in considering the impact of their theologies on others.

CONCLUDING SUMMARY

This essay has presented some initial musings on what the day of Pentecost might mean for homiletical theology if one began theologizing through the lens of Pentecost. It was a suggestive, not an exhaustive, attempt to highlight some key aspects of the day of Pentecost as found in Acts in order to begin to explore their fruit for homiletical theology. Three salient themes arose out of this fiery day of proclamation. The first was related to the gift of speech that was sparked by the Spirit. The second had to do with the gift of hearing in context such that understanding came. The third revealed the God-centered community created by the Spirit. Though the day of Pentecost is not explicitly about homiletical theology, if one reads this proclamatory spiritual event as a metaphor, then it may become more transparent what Pentecost offers homiletical theological discourse as noted in the above implications.

It became clear that Pentecost reminds homiletical theology of its roots. That is, that it is grounded in a divine gift. Any idea, formulation, concept, or perspective related to homiletical theology is rooted in a divine gift given by God the Spirit. Speech, understanding, community, and even God, is a gift. All is gift. All of life is a gift. All of homiletics is a gift. That is the ultimate starting point for theological speculation. Any insight received about homiletical theology is a gift, and there have been many insights into the term "homiletical theology," which is why there are many diverse meanings and approaches. Because it is differentiated and varied, one could say it is already Pentecostalized.

However, there is more to the Pentecostalization of homiletical theology than this, especially in light of the notion of gift. As a gift of and in the Spirit, homiletical theology would argue that the giving and receiving of the word is a surprise, at least from the standpoint of the human, because as gift, one never knows when one will receive it or when the Spirit will fall like fire. The pouring of the Spirit or descent of the Spirit is not a one-time event quarantined at the day of Pentecost. It is an ongoing, ever-fresh, ever-moving, ever-rearticulating, never-stagnant, never-entombed-in-tradition movement of God; it is free to ignite, inspire, innovate, instigate and interrogate. The Spirit is free; thus one might expect to be surprised. As we wait for the divine surprise, may we do as they did in the upper room and constantly devote ourselves to prayer (1:14). Let us pray: *Veni Creator Spiritus.*

Homiletical Theology as Practical Wisdom

—5—

The Company of Sages

Homiletical Theology as a Sapiential Hermeneutic

—Alyce M. McKenzie

A PERSISTENT MISCONCEPTION

Several years ago at a faculty committee meeting, we were discussing how to cover courses in homiletics during the semester when both my homiletical colleague and I were to be on sabbatical. A colleague from another field made the remark, "Well, that shouldn't be too difficult. Almost any of us in other fields could teach homiletics for a semester." Not surprisingly the remark led to a lively discussion and a profuse apology! The remark reflected a common misconception about the nature of homiletics as a discipline and its relationship to other fields in theological education. Homiletics, so this notion goes, is nothing more than the application of public speaking techniques to pulpit communication, the content of which is derived from other fields like systematic theology and biblical studies. Homiletics is a derivative rather than a generative, constructive field. My colleague's hastily retracted remark points to the crucial need for this volume of essays dealing with the topic of "homiletical theology." Their collective goal is to provide much-needed clarity and depth in exploring the question, "How can we who preach and who teach preaching convey in a clearer, more compelling way the generative nature of our field?" My essay contributes to the purpose of this volume in its understanding of homiletical theology as the exercise of an inductive, sapiential hermeneutic, which is, at the same time, both practical and constructive. Succinctly put, homiletical theology is the exercise of practical wisdom.

Those beyond our field share a reductionist definition of the term *homiletical theology* as the insights of systematic theology being applied by preachers to the lives of their congregants. By this notion, homiletics—the art of preaching—in its various facets of exegesis, sermon shaping, and communication, is nothing more than a delivery system for the harvest of other disciplines: systematic theology, biblical studies, church history, rhetoric, and communication studies. By this understanding, while these other disciplines are generative in their own right, homiletics is derivative. By this understanding, the process I have my students use in exegeting a text for preaching is backwards. I have them consult with the commentaries only after a rather extensive conversation with the text in which they interact with it in terms of their own experience, knowledge, and congregational context. I have found that if they go to the commentaries first, they preach the commentaries. According to this misconception of homiletical theology, that's the way it should be.

My colleague's remarks only underscored the ongoing relevance of Edward Farley's groundbreaking book *Theologia: The Fragmentation and Reunification of Theological Education.*[1] In that book, which was on the required reading list in our seminar in practical theology at Princeton Theological Seminary in 1989, Farley traced the history of theological education to examine the roots of the fourfold curricular division in theology: church history, Scripture, practical theology, and systematic theology. He sought to recover the meaning of the term *theologia*, as a way of restoring the *telos* or unifying purpose and aim of theology. According to Farley's account, the original connotation of *theologia* was revealed knowledge of God that led to wisdom and a way of living life faithfully he refers to as a *habitus.*

As Farley recounts it, as the centuries rolled forward, *theologia* (theology) became a distinct discipline studied by young male students enrolled in Western medieval universities. The Enlightenment and the rise of science contributed to the relegation of theology to a subject for the training of clergy, with theological education required only for those entering the professional ministry. The understanding of theology as theological reflection for all Christians was gradually reduced to theology as a body of knowledge for professional ministers. The fourfold division of theology that took shape in the late 1800s informs current seminary curricula, with their frequent division into church history, biblical studies, and systematic and practical theology. The reputation of practical theology still

1. Farley, *Theologia.*

suffers from the reductionistic rumors implied in my colleague's dismissive remark: that it is skills for church growth, preaching, leadership, education, and counseling derived from their companion generative disciplines. In *Theologia* Farley bewailed this fragmentation. His book puts forth *theologia* (or theological reflection) as the proper goal of all theological education. He levels a critique at courses that hone ministerial skills but give short shrift to theological reflection. The *theologia* approach he commends and describes for theological education involves starting with situations, reflecting on them in light of theology, reflecting on that theology, and exploring appropriate actions in the world.

Since the publication of Farley's book in 1983, the seminary at which I teach, Perkins School of Theology at Southern Methodist University, as well as many others, have embraced contextual considerations and made them a generative and integral component of courses across disciplines and degree programs. Still, the reductionist understanding of homiletics as public speaking for preachers persists.

The reduction of homiletical theology to a delivery system of systematic theology and biblical studies not only does harm to homiletics, it also reduces systematic theology and biblical studies to resources for preaching. They become preaching's Twitter feed, its *Farmer's Almanac*, its grocery shelf. The preacher works up her sermonic recipe and strolls the aisles of the systematic theology supermarket for ingredients, or crawls through a concordance checking out how many times the word "bread" shows up in a given prophet. Other disciplines are warehouses that hold inventory for sermon points and illustrations. I criticized a colleague in the opening of this essay for a reductionistic remark about homiletics. But I think I made the same mistake recently in a remark at a faculty dinner to a colleague who teaches theology. I quoted Gerhard Ebeling as saying "Theology exists to make preaching as difficult as it needs to be." My colleague was eating a slice of Italian cream cake at the time, and paused with the fork halfway to his mouth to protest: "That's not the only reason theology exists!"

And of course, he's right. Theology, biblical studies, and church history are not just sources of sermon points and illustrations. In the past thirty years, the emphasis on the contextual nature of theological reflection has resulted in systematic theology's explicit acknowledgement of the contribution contextual considerations make to their reflections. Systematic theology and biblical studies are exercises in *theologia* and, as such, integral to one's holistic worship of God. The rabbis had it right when they insisted that study is a form of worship.[2]

2. Rabbinic scholar Dr. Carl Kinbar explains the important difference between study

THE NEGLECT OF WISDOM

Having said that, it remains the case that developments in several fields have contributed to the reduction of homiletics to a delivery system for the insights of other disciplines. Homiletical theory and method through the centuries have aided and abetted this reductionist understanding. Once Christian preaching entered the Hellenistic world, the dominant understanding of the purpose of preaching came to be seen as intellectual persuasion. Three-point sermons reigned as the model of choice in every century up until the third quarter of the twentieth century and the advent of the so-called "new homiletic." The sermon as a series of propositions, each illustrated by a story or anecdote, was a form tailor-made for the purpose of purveying points or propositions. Homiletical method was the opposite of the process I described using in my classes. It meant going behind the scenes early on, finding out a couple of the key truths intended by the original author, and, as a final step, articulating and applying them.

Liberalism's tendency to discern universal moral truths from Scripture and fundamentalism's tendency toward literalism left little room for a homiletical theology built on dialogue with texts in their full-orbed historical, literary, theological identity and congregational context. The biblical theology movement of the 1940s and '50s in the United States, a reaction against both liberalism and fundamentalism, showed promise in its attempt to encounter the Bible as a whole and not as an atomized collection of source documents. However, a key question remains inadequately addressed: Who gets to decide what are the organizing themes of Scripture?

By the time we reach the last third of the twentieth century, theology was viewed in the US as a body of specialized knowledge for the training of professional clergy; the biblical theology movement was busy organizing the study of the Bible around theological themes like covenant, salvation history, and canon, and homiletics' three-point sermons continued their job as a delivery system for the insights of these other disciplines.

In the midst of all of this, a genre of biblical literature (wisdom) was being neglected. Its attendant role (the sage) was being bypassed as a resource for the identity of the preacher, and its implications for the vocation of *theologia* (theological reflection) of all the people of God were being

---

and learning: "Study involves the acquisition and mastery of facts and their interconnections. Because followers of Yeshua are directed to love God with all our heart, mind, soul, and strength, our learning involves more than acquisition and mastery. It involves all four faculties—heart, mind, soul, and strength—and becomes for us a consuming act of love and worship. Learning is an embodied spiritual practice that enables us to cleave to God and one another." Quoted by Rabbi Joshua Brumbach, "Learning as Worship."

ignored. During this time the wisdom literature was relegated to the margins of the canon in biblical studies. It had too much in common with the wisdom produced by cultures surrounding Israel in the ancient Near East, and its modest, situational claims were overshadowed by more sweeping, propositional panoramas. The wisdom literature received little attention in the magisterial works of Old Testament theology of Eichrodt and von Rad. I remember spending a week on it in the Old Testament survey course I took in seminary in the late 1970s, and once I got out into the parish I discovered that the Revised Common Lectionary had little patience with Proverbs.

I suspect that it may be more than mere coincidence that the rise of the new homiletic instigated by Fred Craddock's *As One Without Authority*, written in 1971, corresponded with an upsurge interest in biblical studies in the wisdom literature.[3] The inductive method of preaching Craddock recommended encouraged the development of a homiletical theology understood as arising from interaction with text(s) and congregations rather than imposed upon them. In the last quarter of the twentieth century wisdom has moved from the margins more to the center of interest in biblical studies in both the Old and the New Testament literature. An accompanying development is that the homiletical literature on genre-specific preaching and dialogical congregational exegesis abounded.

THE PREACHER AS A SAGE

In the last third of the twentieth century, the image of the preacher was morphing decade by decade, from prophet (1960s) to therapist (1970s) to church growth consultant (1980s) to CEO and player-coach (1990s) to storyteller (2000–2010) to Bible teacher (2010 onward).

The second decade of the twenty-first century is well underway. In my view, it is high time for the sage, the wisdom seeker and teacher, to have its day as a model for the preacher.[4] The sage is one who is both growing in wisdom and using that growing wisdom to adjudicate the use of existing insights. In the tumultuous postexilic period, as Israel searched for its identity, the sages of Proverbs saw their function as ensuring the *shalom* of a disori-

3. The "new hermeneutic" of Gerhard Ebeling and Ernst Fuchs respected the eventfulness of language, that texts want to do things, not just say things, and it acknowledged the role of the reader in contextualizing that impact. Their thinking influenced Fred Craddock to instigate what came to be called the "new homiletic" with its turn toward the listener in his groundbreaking book *As One Without Authority.*

4. Thomas G. Long's popular introductory preaching text *The Witness of Preaching* identifies four models for the preacher: herald, pastor, storyteller, and witness. The sage is a needed addition to the lineup.

ented people by pointing the young toward behaviors that were conducive not just to their own pleasure, but the harmony of the community. Related goals were fool management and character building.[5] Their hermeneutic was inductive observation, discerning the presence and actions of God in specific interactions in the human and natural worlds. They collected, coined, and collated proverbial sayings, partial generalizations applicable in certain but not all situations. They sought to teach the young how to discern which sayings were an apt fit with the new challenges they were facing in daily life.

The preacher, as one of this company of sages, is not a figure who dispenses knowledge so much as one who models its discovery and its ongoing contextualization. The sages of Proverbs observed multiple situations in daily life. They saw there patterns of cause and effect. Wise and prudent speech, hard work, control of appetites, and respect for the poor led to community harmony. Rash and reckless behaviors and the unbridled pursuit of every appetite led to community chaos. In all of this damage control and wisdom nurturing, there remains an inscrutable aspect of God and of life that we can neither predict nor control. The sages of Ecclesiastes and Job focused on the situations that Proverbs tended to downplay. They asked, "How does the suffering of the innocent fit with traditional 'do good, get good' theology?" They subverted the blanket optimism of traditional wisdom by digging around under its foundations. Jesus, taking a page out of the book of the subversive sages of Ecclesiastes and Job, took it a step further as he both asked and answered the question, "How are we going to respond to the suffering of the innocent?"

AN EXERCISE IN PRACTICAL THEOLOGY

The sages' theological method constitutes a homiletical theology that I'm baptizing a "sapiential hermeneutic." It is an interpretive process that generates theological insights, rather than merely delivering them. Homiletical theology as a sapiential hermeneutic refers to an interpretation of daily life from the perspective of biblical wisdom's inductive approach.[6] Operating out of such a wisdom model of interpretation honors a sequence very much

5. McKenzie, *Hear and Be Wise*, 7–10.

6. Biblical wisdom books and passages include Proverbs, Ecclesiastes, Job, the Song of Solomon, the parables and sayings of the synoptic Jesus, and the book of James. Several psalms have wisdom themes (1, 32, 34, 37, 49, 112, 128). Two apocryphal books also belong to the wisdom genre, the Wisdom of Sirach (or Ecclesiasticus) and the Wisdom of Solomon.

like the *theologia* described by Edward Farley: one is attentive to the specifics of daily situations and interactions and infers general principles/wisdom from them. It is the not the same as applying general principles to specific situations. It is more the discernment of partial generalizations and placing them at the disposal of the community as it encounters new situations. Wisdom (*hokmah* in Hebrew, *Sophia* in Greek) is both a way of approaching life (radical attentiveness to the scenes and images of daily life, looking for patterns of how to live in keeping with God's purposes) and a body of teachings that results from that approach.

Biblical wisdom in the book of Proverbs is built on the essentially positive premise that God has placed the ability to discern wisdom within us, with corresponding clues spread throughout the human and natural world. At the same time, both Proverbs and, to a greater degree, Ecclesiastes and Job, acknowledge the inscrutability of God and the limitations of human knowledge.[7] The dialogue among these three books—Proverbs, Ecclesiastes, and Job—illustrates the operation of this sapiential hermeneutic. The latter two books question and even subvert the optimistic wisdom of Proverbs. This points us toward a crucial feature of homiletical theology as a sapiential hermeneutic—it is not a rigid delivery system. It is both attentive and accountable to new situations and a group wisdom process in which one voice does not dominate. It contains within itself the seeds of its own subversion.

Our task as preachers engaging in homiletical theology is an exercise in practical theology. As we have seen, in traditional depictions of the purpose and structure of theology, systematic theology receives the results of historical investigations; reflects upon their content; tests, refines, and orders them; and transmits the product to the practical fields for implementation. Systematic theology is reflection on God's revelation to the church, and practical theology is its application to the fields of preaching, liturgy, pastoral care, and administration.[8] More recent theological reflection defines systematic and practical theology differently: contextual concerns are not just an afterthought for systematic theology, but are an integral part of its reflections. Practical theology is not a mere receptacle of the insights of other disciplines, but has a role in generating theological insights.[9]

7. The so called "limit proverbs" (16:1, 2, 9; 20:24; 21:30–31) convey these limits to the abilities of human wisdom to predict and order life. See McKenzie, *Preaching Proverbs*, 32.

8. This is the understanding of their relationship most interpreters took from Freidrich Schleiermachers' *Brief Outline of Theological Study* (1811), one that became normative for American theological education in the twentieth century. See Farley, *Theologia*, 84.

9. Wood, *Vision and Discernment*, 51ff.

Homiletical theology as a sapiential hermeneutic acknowledges that, in a profound way, all theology is practical. We bring practical concerns to it from the beginning. We come to the theological task engaging in theory-laden practices. They imply principles and beliefs we need to articulate and understand more clearly. In my work with the wisdom literature for preaching, I have found the structure of theological inquiry put forth by Don Browning in his book *A Fundamental Practical Theology* to be most helpful. He conceives of the enterprise of theological inquiry as an encompassing discipline called *fundamental practical theology*. Within that larger discipline are four submovements of theological reflection: descriptive theology, historic theology, systematic theology, and strategic practical theology.

Taken together, all four of these submovements of theological reflection make up the encompassing discipline of fundamental practical theology. It consists of critical reflection on contemporary practice (descriptive theology) in light of the witness of Scripture and tradition (historic and systematic theology) toward individual and social transformation (strategic practical theology). Its steps involve analyzing and describing contemporary practices; consulting historical, biblical, and theological touchstones; reflecting on their themes and implications; and strategizing appropriate actions.[10]

A sapiential hermeneutic is the operation of practical reason that begins with the first submovement of Browning's fundamental practical theology: descriptive theology.

Descriptive theology is the process by which Israel's sages observed the realms of the inner life, human relationships, and the natural world, and made inferences about harmonious living for individuals and communities. It is also the process by which the subversive strain within Israelite wisdom observed those same realms and made inferences about the limitations of conventional wisdom. Descriptive theology generates theological implications from and for specific situations. According to Browning, it constitutes a form of practical reasoning that operates in five dimensions or levels. They are visional, obligational, tendency-need, environmental, and rule-role.

The first and most encompassing level is the visional. This involves the relationship between the human condition and what a particular practice or genre of human expression views as ultimate in human life. A sapiential hermeneutic is the operation of practical reason that regards the implied ultimate as a narrative about God's creation, governance, and redemption of the world through the life, death, and resurrection of Jesus Christ. This

10. Browning, *A Fundamental Practical Theology*, 47–54.

narrative constitutes the vision that animates and provides the context for the exercise of practical reason.[11]

The second dimension of practical moral reason is the obligational level. It poses the question, "What does the visional level mean for human obligations?" What moral principles ought to order our common life? For the Christian theses obligations center on *agape* love, mutual regard for others, and commitment to justice for all God's children. Recent theological reflection has reminded us that our obligations extend to the natural world: the animal world and the care of the earth.

The third dimension is the tendency-need level. It asks, "What central tendencies and needs of human nature drive this wisdom?"

The fourth is the environmental level. It asks, "What social conditions have contributed to this situation, text, or body of wisdom?"

The fifth and final dimension of practical moral reasoning is the rule-role dimension. Here the question is, "At the most concrete level, what actual practices and behaviors result from living by this wisdom?"

These five dimensions of practical moral reasoning can be expressed as five basic questions about life's meaning and human behavior. When used to interview a given context or body of cultural or biblical wisdom, they bring to life important assumptions that lie beneath the surface.

I call them the "Five Alive" questions: What is most important? (visional). What gets us closer to that ultimate? (obligational). What constitute obstacles to it? (tendency-need). What kind of life-form results from pursuing that ultimate? (rule-role).[12]

The process is reminiscent of Thomas Aquinas's understanding of the virtue of prudence.[13] Aquinas directs considerable attention to the virtue of prudence (or *phronesis*), which, in keeping with the truth and reality of things, is able to judge, arrange, and direct one's words and actions toward the most fitting of all ends: the fullness of communion in love with God.[14]

The sages of Israel, Jesus included, were engaging in practical theology, an expression of practical wisdom or reasoning, what Aristotle called

11. Ibid, 11.

12. I describe these questions in more detail as they relate to biblical wisdom literature in chapter 2 of my book *Preaching Biblical Wisdom in a Self-Help Society*.

13. The *Summa* of Thomas Aquinas serves as an exemplary guide in understanding how knowing and loving God engenders practical wisdom by providing "a clarifying simplification of Scripture for the sake of preaching or confessing, and a clarifying generalization of pastoral experience brought back under the science of Scripture, or the whole of theology." Jordan, *Rewritten Theology*, 153. I am indebted to Michael Pasquarello's responses to my initial paper for these references with regard to Aquinas.

14. See the good summary of Thomas's teaching on prudence in Cessario, *The Moral Virtues and Theological Ethics*, 72–93.

phronesis. Phronesis is reasoning that leads to action. It involves getting clear about our premises in a given situation regarding what we are already doing and what we would like to do.[15]

The sages of Israel approached specific situations with "hermeneutical openness" This hermeneutical openness is an essential feature of the proverb. It allows it to both arise out of specific experiences but apply to others beyond them. For example: "A soft answer turns away wrath but a harsh word stirs up anger" (Prov 15:1). Proverbs are partial generalizations, not universal truths for all situations. Hence the saying, "It takes wisdom to use wisdom." To use the existing body of wisdom appropriately in approaching new situations entails careful attention to the specifics of the new situation, acknowledgment of the limitations of personal knowledge, and the need for group dialogue in discernment and decision-making. This combination of specific origin and more general contextualization is the fundamental dynamic of what proverbs scholars calls "aphoristic thinking."[16] "It takes wisdom to use wisdom" sums up the dynamic of homiletical theology as a sapiential hermeneutic.

TIME FOR A SAPIENTIAL HERMENEUTIC

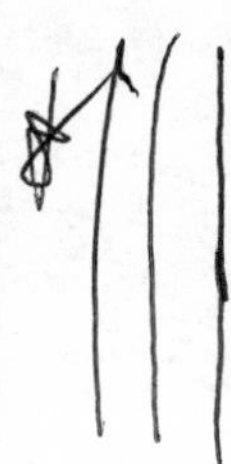

It is by now almost overly well attested that people under thirty are suspicious of religious institutions. Many of them feel that institutional churches want converts and financial contributors, not participants on a pilgrimage of faith.[17] Many young Americans perceive Christianity as seeking mental allegiance to religion, a one-time decision, when what they crave is a process of transformation, a journey.

Another critique of Christianity in America today comes from emerging movements that assert that Protestant Christianity's version of the faith

15. Kruschwitz and Roberts, *The Virtues*, 11.

16. Williams, *Those Who Ponder Proverbs*, 78ff.

17. See Kinnaman and Lyons, *unChristian*. The authors interviewed a representative sample of young Americans aged sixteen to twenty-nine, both mosaics (born between 1984 and 2002) and busters (born between 1965 and 1983). The young adults were what the authors call "outsiders," people who were looking at Christians and Christianity from outside of communities of faith. Many of the perceptions of these young outsiders are negative. One of the six negative perceptions is that Christianity and Christians are too focused on getting converts and not focused enough on inviting people into a transformative experience (12). The other five criticisms were that Christians and Christianity are hypocritical, anti-homosexual, sheltered, too political, and judgmental (29–30).

is individualistic and consumer driven, shaped by the surrounding culture rather than subverting and reshaping it.[18]

Emerging church leaders and participants are suspicious of rigid theological constructs and propositions. They resist what they sometimes call "metanarratives," or universalized accounts of who human beings are and who we should be, on the grounds that theology arises from and needs to prove itself in local contexts and should be open to ongoing critique and conversation.[19] Many are the sons and daughters of evangelicals. As such, they are particularly suspicious of metanarratives that are characterized by the following:

A focus on what we should not do more so than on what we should and can do.

A focus on the salvation of the individual without equal regard for (or at the expense of) the community.

Rigid theological constructions that are not open to the community's conversation and critique.

The values of an individualistic, hierarchical culture that emphasizes personal achievement and fulfillment and tends to reinforce rather than subvert existing structures of power and privilege.[20]

A sapiential hermeneutic is an effective antidote to the legitimate criticisms of institutionalized religion and its preaching. It is dialogical, oriented toward a journey of gradual growth in insight, and it is aware of its own limitations. It emphasizes the *shalom* of the community rather than instant individual gratification. It envisions a group process of wisdom-seeking that is open to criticism and subversion as it remains open and accountable to new situations from generation to generation.

18. The term "emergent church" refers to new forms of church life rising from twentieth century, "modern" churches of America and the UK, as well as other parts of Europe. The emerging church movement is essentially a postmodern critique of a modernist church. Arising from conversations among young leaders in both countries that began in the mid-1990s, it is based on the conviction that if the church does not embody its message and life within postmodern culture, it will become increasingly marginalized.

19. Emerging church leaders do not advocate the adoption of relativism as a philosophical position, but they emphasize the limitations of human knowledge and the need for "biblical humility" in combination with a spirit of robust theological inquiry in a communal context.

20. My thinking on the critique of emerging churches was clarified and sharpened (iron sharpens iron!) by a series of conversations with Dallas Gingles, a graduate student in ethics at Perkins School of Theology, and an active member of the Journey community in Dallas, Texas. His Pentecostal upbringing and knowledge of emerging churches' theologies and community lives equip him to be both critical and appreciative of the contributions of emerging churches in the US.

It is time for such an approach and for such sage preachers. The preacher as sage doesn't dispense the product of the search for wisdom, but rather models a process of discovery of wisdom in daily life, inviting others to join in. The preacher as sage equips listeners to join in the process—by recognition that wisdom is a gift from God, whose search is fueled by radical respect for God the Creator (the fear of the Lord), radical trust in this God, and the observational skills to discern the leadings of God in still, small ways in daily life.[21]

In my book *Hear and Be Wise: Becoming a Preacher and Teacher of Wisdom,* I describe the four virtues of the wise life as discernible in the wisdom literature of the Old and New Testaments. They describe both the dynamics of the sapiential hermeneutic (how wisdom is discerned) and the qualities that take shape in the character of the wisdom seeker and teacher, the sage.

The sage lives a life of three wisdom virtues, which weave like golden threads through the wisdom literature of both testaments. The first is the fear of the Lord or reverence due a gracious, yet ever-mysterious God that is the beginning of wisdom. The second is the acknowledgement of human limitations and an accompanying respect for differing interpretations. The third is the listening heart, a lifelong alertness to patterns of God at work in our experience, that of others, the human sciences, and the world around us. The fourth is the subversive voice, the willingness to challenge and undermine dominant perspectives perceived as unjust.

DOING HOMILETICAL THEOLOGY: PREACHING AND TEACHING FROM A SAPIENTIAL HERMENEUTIC

The sapiential hermeneutic is a hermeneutic with a high tolerance for complexity and ambiguity. Sermons that grow out of the kind of inductive sapiential hermeneutic we have been describing honor the complexity and ambiguity of life.

It is also a hermeneutic of humility. Sermons that grow out of this wisdom process acknowledge the limitations of the speaker with a sense of relief, not embarrassment or frustration. They honor the questions.

Out of honoring complexity and humility comes a respect for diversity. The sapiential hermeneutic is one that honors diversity. It expects, accepts, and respects a diversity of interpretations.

21. See chapters 2 and 3 of McKenzie's *Hear and Be Wise.*

The sapiential hermeneutic is a hermeneutic of listening, of attentiveness. When Solomon in 1 Kings 3:9 prays for wisdom he asks for a *lev shomea*, a "discerning mind" (also translatable as a "listening heart.") So crucial is this faculty of attentiveness to Israel's sages that they attribute it to God. "The hearing ear and the seeing eye, the Lord has made them both" (Prov 20:12).

The wisdom process involves listening to one's inner life through prayer, to Scripture, and to tradition. It requires attentiveness to the congregation, both in the preparation and delivery of the message.

The sapiential hermeneutic is a hermeneutic of courage and adaptability. It requires sensitivity to the particularities of context. It is adaptable and courageous. As needed it will be direct, subtle, risk-taking, challenging, and/or subversive. The sapiential hermeneutic results in wisdom preaching that is intended to foster in those who hear it not just an informed mind, but a transformed identity.

THE SAPIENTIAL HERMENEUTIC AS A COMMUNITY ENDEAVOR: IMPLICATIONS FOR THE DEVELOPMENT OF HOMILETICAL THEOLOGY

The sapiential hermeneutic is also a hermeneutic of community. One of the key insights of biblical wisdom is that wisdom is only wisdom when exercised in community. And so it is with great appreciation that I read the other essays in this volume and connected their insights to my own understanding of homiletical theology as a sapiential hermeneutic. The future development of homiletical theology will occur in the context of a community of reflective scholarship that invites others into the wisdom conversation.

David Jacobsen identifies the unifying thread of these essays as the act of "naming gospel," which, for him, is the starting point for doing homiletical theology. He understands it as a "moment of interactivity between Scripture/tradition and experience/culture. It is this moment of mediation that shapes homiletical theology most profoundly." He names the discrete moment of sapiential inference that, when sustained over time, leads to ethical insights and guidance in human community.

We see this wisdom dynamic in the life, writings, and sacrificial death of theologian Dietrich Bonhoeffer. Michael Pasquarello, in his exploration of the preaching of Dietrich Bonhoeffer, points out that Bonhoeffer's goal was to relate the word of God and the church's testimony to God to the details of the full range of human experience and expression of the word in the world. Bonhoeffer is the embodiment of the boldness and risk involved in doing homiletical theology. What I am calling a sapiential hermeneutic can be subversive and, ultimately, sacrificial.

With examples from Karl Barth, Reinhold Niebuhr, Alfred North Whitehead, and Latin American liberation theologies that arose in the late '70s, Ron Allen describes a sapiential hermeneutic, a homiletical theology that carefully observes, stubbornly critiques, and perennially subverts inadequate expressions of human relationships and communities. He outlines a process that is, in effect, a subversive sapiential hermeneutic in the wisdom trajectory of Qohelet, Job, and Jesus. It consists of a process by which a preacher comes to realize that traditional, conventional theological interpretations may be complicit in personal and social oppression.

John McClure helpfully sets our exercise of wisdom for preaching in its liturgical context. He asks questions like, "What does worship do to transform what we know about human dialogue to make it adequate to human-divine dialogue? What aspects of human-divine dialogue does Christian worship address and seek to transform? How can we keep these aspects alive as we develop new forms of worship and new understandings of preaching?" McClure highlights the human-divine dialogue that is the liturgical context of homiletical theology. Thereby, he reminds us that there is mystery in the exercise of a wisdom that can never fully express the reality toward which it points.

Luke Powery's emphasis on the role of the Holy Spirit in giving the gifts of understanding and God-centered community remind us that the sapiential hermeneutic, while an exercise in human reasoning, is also a divine gift. This is the essential paradox of the Wisdom literature in Scripture—that wisdom is both a lifelong journey of discovery and a gift from God.

Finally, Teresa Stricklen Eisenlohr offers a microcosmic view of the sapiential hermeneutic at work in one pastor's sermon process. She shows us an example of homiletical theology at work, the exercise of theological wisdom by which the preacher encounters the text in the context of the gospel and in the context of the social setting for the preparation and delivery of a sermon.

I understand the future of homiletical theology to be the exercise of a sapiential hermeneutic, a process of radical attentiveness to the particulars of daily life. This faculty is both an exercise in practical reasoning and a divine gift. It leads to community harmony, and, when necessary, subverts superficial harmony in the interest of a deeper, more just *shalom*. It is a naming of gospel, the liberative mediation of Scripture/tradition and culture/experience (Jacobsen). Homiletical theology is subversive (McKenzie, Allen), potentially sacrificial (Pasquarello), liturgically situated (McClure), and Spirit-gifted (Powery). It involves close attention to texts in their multiple contexts (Stricklen Eisenlohr).

A FINAL NOTE ABOUT THE IDENTITY OF THE PREACHER

I said earlier that preaching from a sapiential hermeneutic means preaching to transform the identity of listeners. But before that can happen, the preacher's identity must be in the process of transformation. Preachers are practitioners and embodiments of a homiletical theology understood as a sapiential hermeneutic. They are members of the company of sages. They understand that wisdom is both a gift and a lifelong search. They themselves are in the process of allowing their own identities to be transformed by God the Giver of Wisdom on the path that leads to life.

They incorporate into their own characters the dynamics of the sapiential hermeneutic: respect for complexity and diversity, humility, attentiveness to life within and beyond oneself, and the courage to subvert unjust traditional notions that pass for wisdom.

The goal of the preacher operating out of the sapiential hermeneutic is to model being a sage so that others can join the journey as seekers and teachers of wisdom. The process is *theologia*—theological reflection that grows out of and is accountable to daily life in particular times and places. We are privileged to model a process of discovery rather than run a distribution business, to invite rather than to dictate.

I had a friend who acted as an extra in the 1994 movie *I.Q.*, a romantic comedy set in Princeton, New Jersey and starring Meg Ryan, Tim Robbins, and Walter Matthau (as Albert Einstein). I think my friend walked down Nassau Street wearing a trench coat in one scene. He did not win an Oscar that year. But he was bitten by the acting bug, and paid the dues to join the actors' guild and got a card to carry in his wallet, and was very energized by it all. His wife's comment was, "This is nothing new. He has been acting out for years!"

We can count on our friends and families to tell the truth. The truth here is that we are all living by one kind of wisdom or another, and we are all modeling it for others. Our role as sages is to model biblical wisdom's version of a life lived in keeping with God's purposes and then, through our lives and preaching, to equip our congregations to live this way too. A sapiential hermeneutic is holistic—it describes the shape of the sage's character, the interpretive process by which the sage gleans wisdom, and the message through which the sage invites others to join the wisdom process. When it comes to wisdom, the more sages in the guild the merrier. Our sapiential homiletical motto is not "Misery loves company," but "Wisdom loves company," the company of sages. May our number increase!

—6—

Dietrich Bonhoeffer

On Becoming a Homiletic Theologian

—Michael Pasquarello III

My interest in homiletic theology emerged during twenty years of pastoral ministry in which I attempted, on a weekly basis, to make theological sense of preaching, while at the same time attempting to make homiletic sense of theology. Over time I have come to the conclusion that homiletic theology is a matter of practical wisdom, a kind of "knowing how" that is irreducible to either theory or practice, but rather is integrated within a concrete form of life manifested by those who speak and listen prayerfully in the presence of God.[22] As David Jacobsen states in the introductory essay of this volume, this is "theology on the way." It is an unfinished eschatological conversation; initiated by God, mediated by the sending of the Word and Spirit, enabled by divine grace, and received and answered through the gift of faith. The divine/human conversation we identify as preaching, or "sermon," is understood best by attending to the exemplary lives of others whose experience, practice, and wisdom may yet speak to our contemporary questions, challenges, and concerns.

The work of Rowan Greer demonstrates how the early church maintained a steady conversation between theology and the life and practice of the church. Those who were charged with elaborating technical theology

22. I have attempted to articulate my thinking on what this volume is referring to as "homiletic theology" in Pasquarello, *Sacred Rhetoric*; *Christian Preaching; We Speak Because We Have First Been Spoken*; *John Wesley*; and *God's Ploughman, Hugh Latimer.*

were also preachers in the church whose aim was to articulate and shape the experience and wisdom of ordinary Christians. For this reason, doctrine, Scripture, and practice were integrally related within an ecclesial ethos that was liturgical in its orientation and aim, that is, for the praise of God. The church's worship was not simply an appropriation of the past but was a present, corporate experience of God articulated by the church's faith. The preacher's task was to put into words the wisdom of what the church was being given to apprehend and know; its present appropriation of the crucified and risen Lord as concretely manifested in the world. Faithful preaching of the gospel requires a reconciliation of theology and practice grounded in and demonstrated by truthful witness to Christ, which is manifested in the faith and wisdom of the church: "The Christian vision is meant to be translated into virtue: the faith that apprehends God's gratuitous forgiveness in Christ must be translated into radical obedience to him."[23]

One significant example of such practical wisdom is *De Doctrina Christiana* (*Teaching Christianity*), arguably the most influential handbook for pastors and teachers in the history of the Western church. Its author, Augustine, Bishop of Hippo in Northern Africa (d. 430), affirms the unity of theology as comprising scriptural reading, liturgical participation, and a life of wisdom and virtue. Just as Christ the incarnate Son is fully human and fully divine, and as the crucified, resurrected, and exalted Lord rules at the Father's right hand, so Christ, as head of the church, indwells and invokes the prayer and praise of his body through the Spirit's self-giving love.[24] The church is called to embody the wisdom revealed in the incarnate Word which is replicated by the words of Scripture, proclaimed by its preachers, and echoed in the praise and service of its people. Augustine believed Scripture possessed the capacity to transform the speech and life of preachers and listeners through cognitive and affective love for the triune God who knows and loves creation. This union joins both passion and intellect, generating personal knowledge and wisdom that so habituate one's thinking and speaking to become the praise shout of God's people.[25] As seen from this perspective, homiletic theology is not something that can be learned as a program or methodology, but is a matter of being formed over time through prayerful study, practice, and experience within the ethos and life of a community called church. In other words, homiletic theologians are made rather than born.

23. Greer, *Broken Lights and Mended Lives*, 12.

24. Augustine, *Teaching Christianity.*

25. See the excellent discussion of Augustine's theology of speech in Griffiths, *Lying*.

THE EXAMPLE OF DIETRICH BONHOEFFER

Ebehard Betghe, confidant, friend, and biographer of Dietrich Bonhoeffer, writes of his commitment to preaching: "Preaching was the great event in his life; the hard theologizing and all the critical love of his church were all for its sake, for in it the message of Christ, the bringer of peace, was proclaimed. To Bonhoeffer, nothing in his calling competed in importance with preaching."[26] Following Bethge's assessment, I have read Dietrich Bonhoeffer as a homiletic theologian. From his earliest years at the University of Berlin to his last years of imprisonment, Bonhoeffer's work was increasingly oriented in a homiletic direction and expressed in homiletic form. As an appreciative but critical reader of Karl Barth, and a serious student of Martin Luther, the proclamation of the word by the Spirit that constitutes the visibility of the church in the world was the center of Bonhoeffer's life and work. Just as important is that Bonhoeffer continues to speak to one of the most demanding challenges of our time, which is to relate the center of the word of God and the church's testimony to God to the details of the full range of human experiences, thus lending homiletic discourse to all spheres of life, which is to describe the word in the world.[27]

With this in mind, I would like to begin at the end, with an excerpt of Bonhoeffer's last sermon, which was preached by means of a letter written in 1943 from the Tegel prison camp for the baptism of his godson, Dietrich. His words express a desire for faithful proclamation of the gospel that requires for its credibility the visible, public character of the church. It reflects years of prayer, study, experience, and reflection in the midst of overwhelmingly destructive and despairing conditions and circumstances.

> What reconciliation and redemption mean; what rebirth and Holy Spirit, love for one's enemies, cross and resurrection mean; what it means to live in Christ and follow Christ—all that is so difficult and remote that we hardly dare to speak of it anymore. In these words and actions handed down to us, we sense something totally new and revolutionary, but we cannot yet grasp it and express it. This is our own fault. Our church has been fighting during these years only for its self-preservation, as if that were an end in itself. It has become incapable of bringing the word of reconciliation and redemption to humankind and to the world.[28]

26. Bethge, *Dietrich Bonhoeffer: Theologian, Christian, Contemporary*, 174.

27. Rashkover, "The Future of the Word and the Liturgical Turn," 3–4.

28. Bonhoeffer, *Letters and Papers from Prison*, 389. Hereafter cited in the body of the text as DBW 8.

Bonhoeffer's letter names some of the most significant challenges related to becoming a homiletic theologian. This chapter will focus on Bonhoeffer's years as a student in Berlin, attempting to discern how one is formed to be certain kind of person who is capable of speaking in a manner described by Bonhoeffer. Here I am particularly interested in looking at the theological context of Bonhoeffer's education for ministry at Berlin that was characterized by an "ecclesial turn" that eventually led him out of the academy into the church, a move that he would later describe as a turn "from phraseology to reality" (DBW 8:358). My hope is that by attending to Bonhoeffer's formative years we might find in him a helpful conversation partner in understanding better the practice of homiletic theology.

A significant turning point occurred in Bonhoeffer's life during the spring of 1924 when he and his brother, Klaus, visited Rome. His diary sheds light on his initial experience of Catholic culture and the reality of the church. It is also significant that twenty years later he would convey the importance of his visit to Rome in a letter to Bethge: "I don't think I have ever changed except perhaps at the time of my first impressions abroad. . . . Continuity with one's past is actually a great gift." Bonhoeffer's diary presumably reveals some of the most important impressions made by Rome on his mind. For example, he writes after visiting St. Peter's for the first time, "The first impression was in this case not the greatest—as usual when you paint something with the brightest colors of the imagination. Afterwards it looks much more natural in reality. Nevertheless, at first sight you are immediately overwhelmed." On Palm Sunday he attended mass at St. Peter's. His remarks include a deep sense of admiration for the "splendidly expressive boys' choir, and the distinguished reading of the Passion story." But he was also impressed by how the universality of the church was represented by the variety of religious orders, the singing of the creed, the beauty of the mass, and the procession of the palms, all of which were done with a "certain form of liturgical intentionality." He concludes his diary entry, "It truly seems ideal."

Later that night he attended mass at another church. "It was almost indescribable." He notes how that procession included a large number of women who were preparing for a religious vocation as nuns. The service, Evensong, was sung with "unbelievable simplicity, grace, and seriousness." Bonhoeffer was deeply impressed by the way the young women sang the liturgy without any trace of routine. "Instead it was worship in the truest sense. The whole thing gave one an unparalleled impression of profound guileless piety." He concludes, "The day had been magnificent. It was the first day on which something of the reality of Catholicism began to dawn on me—nothing romantic—but I think I'm beginning to understand the 'concept' of church."

On Ascension Day, Bonhoeffer attended a service at a free church, which he refers to as a sect in the manner described by the work of Ernst Troeltsch. The service prompted him to make a long entry concerning the history of Protestantism, which he thought should not have tried to become an established or state church, but should have remained a large sect. Bonhoeffer surmised that if this had been the case that what he saw happening in Germany during the 1920s, which he identifies as a calamity, might have been avoided. The reality is that the political arrangements that once supported Protestantism no longer exist, so that its appeal to the large majority of people in Germany has dwindled. He describes this state of affairs as really a case of "materialism cloaked under the guise of Protestantism." Its only remaining value is free thinking, but without the kind of freedom envisioned by the Reformers. He viewed the practical, but not formal, severing of church and state in the new German republic as revealing the truth of things; the church had lost its reason for being and was unable to speak and stand in the world on its own. He concluded with a comment that anticipates the theological searching that was to mark his years in Berlin. "It is not the content of the gospel of the Reformation that repels people so much as the form of the gospel, which one still tries to tie to the state. If it had remained a sect it would have become the church the Reformers intended."[29]

A fascination with Catholic Rome would become a permanent influence on Bonhoeffer's thinking upon his return to Germany and enrollment at the University of Berlin, the center of the German liberal Protestantism that he criticized while in Italy. Nor is it insignificant that his most distinguished teachers on the theological faculty were prominent among those who were ideologically driven in support of military expansion in order to return Germany to a position of a leading world political power. At the same time, they also provided this goal with persuasive theological justification. Following Kant and Hegel, their theological orientation was determined by an interpretation of world history that had convinced them God was on Germany's side, that God was active in history for the German people. World War I was seen in apocalyptic terms, an interpretation of history supported by the Protestant-educated classes and the Protestant churches. Those who were opposed, the Social Democratic Party and the Roman Catholic Centre Party, which included the working class, were seen as "vagabonds without

29. Bonhoeffer, *The Young Bonhoeffer*, 88–89, 106–7. Hereafter cited in the body of the text as DBW 9. For a good summary of this important time see Schlingensiepen, *Dietrich Bonhoeffer*.

a homeland."[30] Bethge describes Bonhoeffer's entry into university studies during this critical time.

At the onset of his studies in Berlin, his impetuous thirst for knowledge still lacked direction. The broad horizon of Berlin's liberal and "positivist" school of theology, embodied by its great teachers, opened before him. At the end of this period, Bonhoeffer had proven himself through his own considerable scholarly achievement, and he had completed an incredible amount of work. The decisive turning point occurred in midyear, when he succumbed to the fascination of dialectical theology; he arrived at this by way of literary detour. He was eighteen at the time.[31]

To understand this "turn" it will be helpful to consider some of the key theological aspects of Bonhoeffer's education at the University of Berlin. In *Protestant Theology and the Making of the Modern University*, Thomas Alpert Howard views the development of the modern research university through the lens of theology. It was a theologian, Friedrich Schleiermacher, who served as the principal architect of the first modern German university in Berlin. Howard's narrative shows how the modernization of Germany blurred the lines between church and state and greatly diminished the church's importance as an institution and concrete historical force. Religion was increasingly spiritualized as an immanent power in the general experience of humanity but removed from particular ecclesial commitments and practices, which meant a material loss of social reality and visible coherence for the church.

Since future leaders of society were directed to pass through the university before seeking ordination, the state became more active and controlling of their operation in service of its ideals. This meant that churches and church bodies had little say on the composition of theological faculties. Disciplinary and scholarly criteria were most important for advancement at the expense of confessional identity and fidelity. Above all others, Schleiermacher's work served to transform Protestant theology in the early nineteenth century and gave shape to what would become cultural Protestantism. The role of theology was important for professional training, but not as a science, the subject of critical, orderly, and disciplined study according to methods accessible to all rational persons. Theology was included with the professions of medicine and law since it was viewed as providing material for the training of ministers of the church to do the work of civil servants.[32] Brad Gregory adds that

30. Moses, "Bonhoeffer's Germany," 13–14.

31. Bethge, *Dietrich Bonhoeffer*, 66.

32. Howard, *Protestant Theology and the Making of the Modern German University*,

> The most consequential among these structures and emphases were the sequestration of theology, a commitment to research, an emphasis on the self, and a reliance on the state. . . . The quarantining of theology institutionalized Kant's argument in his *Conflict of the Faculties* (1798) that philosophy—as the expression of autonomous reason and human freedom—should be liberated from the confining constraints of dogmatic theology.[33]

Bonhoeffer's matriculation to the university occurred in the midst of an intense theological argument between Karl Barth, then a professor at Bonn, and Adolf von Harnack, Barth's former teacher at the University of Berlin. The argument revolved around the nature of theology. Harnack thought the ideals underlying theology should be identified with those that gave birth to the University of Berlin—the ideal of humane culture as the aim and context of study which must be objective, in effect the study of history rather than religion. The university served society by producing well-trained, intellectually sophisticated professional clergy who would mediate advanced learning about the essence of Christianity to the people. Barth, on the other hand, contended that historical critical methodology served best when acknowledging its limitations; theology existed in the university just as the church existed in society. The task of theology was not to mirror the norms of culture, but when necessary to confront and even contradict them, since it was a free to pursue its own dogmatic and ecclesial tasks. However, what was necessary was the word of God and faith awakened by God. As Barth wrote, "The task of theology is one with the task of preaching, it consists in the reception and transmission of the Word of Christ."[34] Bethge's comments on the Barth-Harnack debate shows that its significance was not lost on Bonhoeffer during his time in Berlin.

> It was only now that he found genuine joy in theology. It was like a real liberation. The mere fact that the new theology took its start from a task as unmistakable as preaching tore him away from the games of speculation. Bonhoeffer was arrested by the fact that Barth pulled attention away from the facts of humanity that had been laid bare so disastrously in that generation.[35]

I hope to follow Bonhoeffer's path toward becoming an exemplar of homiletic theology focused on the action of the Word in the Spirit that constitutes the public character of the church in the form of Christ. This focus

16–28.

33. Gregory, *The Unintended Reformation*, 348–49.

34. Ibid., 405–15.

35. Bethge, *Dietrich Bonhoeffer*, 74–75.

would remain a constant mark of all his subsequent work. While he was indeed indebted to Barth for recovering an emphasis on divine revelation and human receptivity as a starting point for theology, Bonhoeffer retained his independence in seeking to establish the historical and social reality of revelation—that the freedom of God is committed to the world. The problem as he saw it was with Barth's transcendent ecclesiology, which even in its gains gave away too much: the concrete visibility of the church as the Holy Spirit's work. The practices of the church, the means of grace, particularly word and sacrament, are not only witnesses to the action of the Spirit but embody the Spirit's work in the world.[36]

An additional consequence of Barth's impact that was significant for Bonhoeffer's theological development was that the Protestant Reformers, especially Martin Luther, were taken up and read anew in Berlin. Following the thinking of Luther with the guidance of his teachers Karl Holl and Rudolph Seeberg, Bonhoeffer surprisingly began the theology of his dissertation with the church, a pneumatological ecclesiology that identifies the church's distinguishing mark as "Christ existing in community," which is the work of the Spirit in the present. What Bonhoeffer saw in Luther's work was that worship stands for the mutual interpretive cohesion of pneumatology and ecclesiology. Worship is the activity of the Spirit in the church and the church in the efficacy of the Spirit. The activity of the Spirit is received and learned in worship; the assembly is where the Spirit is promised and can be experienced. Luther insisted on the Spirit's bond with the "external Word," the bodily and sensory practices of the liturgy, the God who communicates himself and converses in "revelatory signs."[37]

A LUTHER RENAISSANCE

Bonhoeffer wrote two seminar papers that help to provide the context for understanding the dissertation *Sanctorum Communio* (the communion of saints).[38] In 1925, Bonhoeffer submitted a seminar paper to Seeberg on the word of God and historical critical research. The influence of Barth's theology of God's transcendence is evident in his treatment of Scripture

36. Rumsscheidt, "The Formation of Bonhoeffer's Theology," 61–64; DeJonge, *Bonhoeffer's Theological Formation*, 36–68.

37. Wannenwetsch, *Political Worship*, 67–68.

38. Bonhoeffer, *Sanctorum Communio*. Hereafter cited in the body of the text as DBW1. For the influence of Holl and Seeberg on Bonhoeffer's study of Luther see Rumscheidt, "The Formation of Bonhoeffer's Theology," 55–61, and DeJonge, *Bonhoeffer's Theological Formation*, 83–128.

as not merely a word about God but God's word itself. At the same time, Bonhoeffer's approach demonstrates a desire to emphasize the location of truth within the historical reality of the world. In a real sense, Bonhoeffer found himself in a mediating theological position between Barth and the Berlin theologians, especially Harnack, since the paper addresses the pneumatological interpretation of Scripture as a historical reality. To establish his approach, he begins with the following statement: "Christian religion stands or falls with the belief in a historical and perceptibly real divine revelation." (DBW 9:285).

The questions taken up in the paper are as follows: history and the Spirit, which refers to the letter and the Spirit, and scripture and revelation, or human words and God's word. According to Bonhoeffer, the Bible is not one book among others but is quite simply the "ultimate book which narrates the most significant of events." He asserts that the problem with historical criticism is in its general principles, which are based on a scientific-mechanistic world view and epistemological methodologies derived from the natural sciences (DBW 9:286). Although he had learned to read Scripture historically and critically he came to judge that, for ecclesial reasons, it was a modest servant but a bad master. As Michael Legaspi observes of the rise of academic biblical studies, "Modern biblical scholarship was preoccupied with the textuality of the Bible, qualification of its authority, a turn to referential theories of meaning, and focus on the world of the Bible, rather than the world as seen through the Bible."[39]

Bonhoeffer viewed this approach as causing the concept of the biblical canon to disintegrate. That is to say, he thought it leveled the content of Scripture and thereby rendered it meaningless by making it match historical knowledge. On the other hand, when revelation is discovered "the extraordinary enters and its power is self-evident." Following Luther, Bonhoeffer insisted that revelation is found only in Scripture where God is pleased to speak and where God's word is heard, experienced, and proclaimed. He clarifies this point further, stating that Scripture is not revelation. Instead, it is a document or fragment that gives witness, but which cannot be objectified by rational science or it is silenced. Scriptural understanding of Christ, as the word of God, is not a priori and interior to human understanding but rather is created by the Spirit of God. Christ appears in verbal form, the Spirit in personal form, and the past becomes present. Scriptural understanding is therefore dependent upon the work of the Spirit who inspired its writers, disclosing to them that revelation could be found in Jesus, who was fully human within the framework of ordinary events (DBW 9:292–93).

39. Legaspi, *The Death of Scripture and the Rise of Biblical Studies*, 25.

Bonhoeffer again echoes Luther, viewing the words of Scripture as written down proclamation, or "good tidings and report." The written words of Scripture, which are of the Spirit, mediate understanding of the facts as incarnate images of Christ, the word which is present as revelation, judgment, and will. The measure of biblical exegesis is "what drives toward Christ." He concludes, "Because God speaks to people by means of the authentic witness of historical revelation, God must personally also have spoken in historical events." These events are embedded in the faith of the prophets, apostles, and the historical person of Jesus Christ. This means the empirical church, the church as a historical reality, will have the word of God as its source of truth and norm. Even theologians are dependent upon the Spirit in their work, since every attempt at interpretation, every attempt to speak God's word with human words remains a prayer, a plea for the Holy Spirit who grants understanding, preaching, and hearing, a plea which begins, *Veni Spiritus*: come Holy Spirit !(DBW 9:296–98).

Bonhoeffer is describing preaching as a liturgical practice that springs from prayer and praise, reverent attention to God speaking in Jesus Christ who is attested by the whole of Scripture and embodied in the faithful obedience of the church. Praying and reading Scripture with the assistance of the Holy Spirit is a profoundly practical activity as well as an intellectually rigorous one. As an act of worship, moreover, preaching is the work of the whole church that is constituted by the Spirit in grateful response to the presence of the risen Lord in word and sacrament. In other words, the saving knowledge of God is received in worship. Awakened by the gift of divine grace, the church is summoned by the astonishing goodness and love of the triune God.[40] The proclamation of the word acclaims God's glory for the salvation and sanctification of creation, which is the evangelical witness of the church through its participation in the life of God.[41]

Heiko Oberman writes of Luther's desire to see prayer and study, worship and thinking, piety and knowledge reunited to overcome divisions created by the medieval universities. "For Luther this model of theological study in the liturgical context of prayer was the ideal and remained so even after he renounced his monastic vows."[42] In Luther's theology, there is reciprocity between the subject matter of theology and its methodology, which becomes evident in Bonhoeffer's work as well. Luther wove together the intellect and affections, spirituality and scholarship, praying and thinking. On the other hand, he stood in monastic life, with its liturgical theology

40. Brueggemann, *Israel's Praise*, 26–28.

41. Behr, "The Trinitarian Being of the Church."

42. Oberman, *Luther*, 172–73.

grounded in the divine service of God. At the same time, he studied in the university with its tradition of scholastic disputation. However, it is monastic theology, a life of prayer that pervades all human activity, and which is most explicitly focused in corporate worship, that provides the content of theology that academic practice regulates by ordering and reflecting on its subject matter. This is the pathos of the word, in that the affections are central. In the presence of God, it is God who is acting and speaking and the church that is receiving and hearing. Theory and practice are, for Luther, grounded in the pathos of the word which sees human receptivity, or faith, as the divine work of God who wills to have communion with human creatures.[43]

While the preacher is called to the ministry of speaking, he or she does so within a community of listeners whose life is constituted by participating in a conversation initiated, sustained, and completed by God through the ministry of the Word and Spirit. Moreover, this "listening" is of a particular kind; the disposition of prayerful attentiveness to the presence of Christ, the living Word, through the grace of the Holy Spirit in the reading and speaking of the whole biblical message in the midst of the church's worship. For Luther, proclamation is the center of all the church does and the central point of its theology and mission. The oral address of the gospel, in both divine and human form, communicates God's gracious promises in Christ for the salvation of the world. In this particular form of Christian speech, derived from Scripture and enlivened by the Spirit, Christ gives himself and his gifts, the "joyful exchange" of his righteousness for human sinfulness that opens the "gates of heaven" for all the continued gracious workings of the triune God.[44]

The preaching of the gospel is the message of the cross and resurrection that is heard and appropriated through faith that comes by hearing the word of Christ. This is the message of Christ and what he has done, which by the work of the Spirit turns and snatches listeners away from themselves to participate in the gracious reign of the One who has acted on their behalf.[45] Luther's commitment to the oral, sacramental nature of the word was such that he devoted himself with single-minded purpose to breaking open the words of Scripture so that the gospel, the voice of God speaking through the risen Christ in the power of the Spirit, might become a shout of praise

43. Bayer, Silcock, and Mattes, *Theology the Lutheran Way*, 15–33.

44. See the discussion in Meuser, "Luther as Preacher of the Word of God"; Lischer, "Preface"; Gerrish, *The Old Protestantism and the New*; Pelikan, *Luther the Expositor*; and Bonhoeffer, *Communio Sanctorum*.

45. Sauter, *Gateways to Dogmatics*, 124.

in the church, reaching not only the mind but the very heart and soul of its listeners: faith that comes only by hearing the word.[46]

Luther considered such confidence in speaking of God as a gift of the Spirit received in prayerful attentiveness to the words of Scripture within the life of the church. The path that leads to truthful speech requires submission to the pathos of transformation; one must learn to be attentive and receptive to God's word; to stand under Scripture in order to be interpreted rather than to stand over scripture as judge. Luther's preface to *A Brief Instruction on What to Look for and Expect in the Gospels* provides a concise summary of the gospel narrative:

> Gospel is and should be nothing less than a discourse or story about Christ. . . . Thus the gospel is and should be nothing less than a chronicle, a story, a narrative about Christ, telling who he is, what he did and what he suffered, . . . For at its briefest, the Gospel is a discourse about Christ, that he is the Son of God and was made man for us, that he died and was raised, that he has been established as Lord, of all things.[47]

The gospel is a book of promise; when it is opened, read, and proclaimed Christ himself comes to listeners while listeners are led to Christ. Robert Jenson comments on this conviction: "For the preaching of the gospel is nothing less than Christ coming to us, or we being brought to him . . . Christ speaks in preaching; and it is in rendering the person of Christ, the living Word, that God is his own Word, the 'good things' in God's Word are God himself; moreover, we are the 'good things' we hear in the gospel, by attending to them with faith we are shaped to what we hear."[48] Luther saw the most fitting response to the grace and gift of Christ—who is both the sacrament and example of salvation—as the obedience of faith that loves one's neighbors in the same manner God has dealt with humanity in sending his Son.

FOLLOWING LUTHER AS EXEMPLAR

Significantly, in the fall of 1926 Bonhoeffer wrote a seminar paper focusing on the Holy Spirit and the theology of Luther (DBW 9:325–69). For this he drew primarily from two disputations written by Luther between 1535

46. Steinmetz, "Luther and Formation in Faith"; Lazareth, *Christians in Society*, 31–57; Oberman, "Preaching and the Word in the Reformation"; O'Malley, "Luther the Preacher"; and Webb, *The Divine Voice*, 141–46.

47. Luther, "A Brief Instruction on What to Look for and Expect in the Gospels (1521)," 104–5.

48. Jenson, "Luther's Contemporary Theological Significance," 283.

and 1545: "Theses Concerning Faith and the Law" and "The Disputation Concerning Justification." The background of these two disputations was Luther's desire to provide fundamental understanding and clarity concerning the gospel in light of attacks from theological opponents whom he viewed as antinomian. The important elements, according to Bonhoeffer, are justification, law and gospel, faith and love. He describes Luther's way of approaching the matter of the Holy Spirit as following Paul and the early church, rather than the metaphysics of medieval scholastic theology. In other words, Luther begins with the Holy Spirit and humanity, the means and experience of grace, and arrives at God, rather than beginning from systematic and metaphysical approach that works its way down to human faith and experience of divine grace (DBW 9:326).

Reflecting on Luther's work, Bonhoeffer asserts the desire of God for sinners, that the gift of the Holy Spirit and the reason for grace is all of God. Thinking from a starting point within the action of the Spirit, he traces its workings in law and gospel, in putting sinners to death, and in bringing forth new creatures in Christ. Christ is given and received through faith, which is the work of the Holy Spirit. Through the action of the Spirit, which is faith, Christ is grasped as being for us as well as in us. He notes, "So, faith from the Spirit, Christ in faith, the Spirit from Christ, and therefore in faith, Christ gives the Spirit." In faith the Holy Spirit creates a new person, a new self and new will, and a new heart that truly and personally desires what the Spirit desires (DBW 9:336–38; quote 338).

Here we see Bonhoeffer, who by reaching back to Luther in order to find his way forward, was taking important steps toward becoming a homiletic theologian. He proceeds to discuss the medium of human words and the capacity of human understanding, through which "the Holy Spirit speaks the word of God as a gift, as the effective reign of God" (DBW 9:357). Continuing the line of thinking established in the seminar paper on the spiritual interpretation of Scripture, he concludes the need for the interpreter, preacher, and hearers to be read or changed in worship by the subject of interpretation, by the work of the Spirit who is God's gift and power.

This spiritual interpretation can only originate from the word. Therefore, faith arises only from the spiritually understood word. This, however, assumes faith, Spirit out of faith, faith out of Spirit, since like can only be understood by like. God only knows the Spirit, hearing the word or receiving faith can only be an effect of the Spirit (DBW 9:357).

This conclusion leads Bonhoeffer back to the place of Scripture, whose meaning is a gift of the Spirit and faith, and thus of Christ himself, which constitutes a "holy circle." This means preaching Christ is the meaning and criterion of Scripture. This also leads Bonhoeffer to assert that the efficacy of preaching occurs only because it pleases God, who in the ministry of word and sacrament bestows the Spirit and allows it to grow and bear fruit. Preaching should be seen as a duty, a calling, and as a ministry of the word, the power of the word that is the Spirit who moves hearts when human words do not. In addition, preaching is an office; its purpose is to give the Spirit, active in the word, to establish the church. Here Bonhoeffer moves to a particularly important point that will play a prominent role in his dissertation work. The activity of the Spirit in the word is the "cement" that builds the church-community and which mediates between the invisible holy church and the visible sinful church. This reality is recognized through faith, revealed by the Spirit, and confessed: "I believe in the Church" (DBW 9:363–65).

Bonhoeffer interprets Luther's reflections on the work of the Spirit in the reading of Scripture and preaching of the word as springing from the gospel itself. He writes, "We should not live in fear of poor preachers and should not rely too heavily on good ones." Wherever the word is, through it the Spirit is effective, and there is the church. He concludes by summarizing Luther's doctrinal presentation, "God the Father, in God's integrity, sends the Son and the Holy Spirit as gifts (in the larger meaning of the word)." Biblical interpretation, theology, preaching, and hearing are subject to the life-giving activity of the Spirit through prayerful attentiveness to the word; forms of active receptivity that are the divine work of God in the church (DBW 9:367–68).

SANCTORUM COMMUNIO: THE ECCLESIAL TURN

Bonhoeffer's dissertation, *Sanctorum Communio*, which was written under the supervision of Rudolph Seeberg, presents an amazing study of the church as a theological community that embodies God's will and purpose for humanity in history. Although it was written in his student years, this work manifests what is arguably Bonhoeffer's enduring and central concern: the church is the space created by God in the world where the rule of the incarnate, crucified, and risen Christ is made visible. Ecclesiology is constituted by the Spirit through the word and sacraments and is the concrete expression of Christology. This was an attempt by Bonhoeffer to develop a specifically Christian sociology as an alternative to the liberal assumptions of his Berlin teachers. In developing this approach Bonhoeffer challenged and rejected the categories established by Ernst Troeltsch—church, sect, and mysticism—to reclaim the concrete visibility of the church. In other words, the church is neither a voluntary association nor a compulsory organization, since both categories fail to take into account the reality of the Spirit and the essential relation between the Spirit and church-community.[49] As someone close to Bonhoeffer commented on the dissertation, "There will not be many who really understand it, the Barthians won't because of the sociology, and the sociologists won't because of Barth."[50]

For Bonhoeffer, homiletic theology is inseparable from this ecclesial turn, in that the visibility of the church, "Christ existing in community," is essential for interpreting Scripture as the proclamation and embodiment of God's self-revelation in Jesus Christ. Although Bonhoeffer's christological starting point reflects Barth's emphasis on revelation, so that revelation occupies space in the world through the work of the Spirit, Bonhoeffer's thinking also addresses the concerns of his Berlin teachers regarding historical and social realty. The church is not a religious organization or association, nor is the founding of Christianity a new religion among other religions; it is the renewal of humanity as a divine realty in the humanity of Christ. Its life principle, therefore, is the gratuitous, self-giving love of Christ; being with others and being for others in the same manner of Christ's freely being in the world.

To support this vision of the church, Bonhoeffer drew from an early treatise by Luther, "The Sacrament of the Body and Blood of Christ," which states, "In this sacrament, therefore, one is given through the priest a sure sign from God himself that he or she is united with Christ and his saints and has all things in common with them, that Christ's sufferings and life are one's own, together with the lives and sufferings of all the saints." The treatise serves to highlight the sacramental nature of the church as it is constituted by and embodies the vicarious action of Christ in the world.

> See to it that you give yourself to everyone and by no means exclude anyone in hatred or anger. For this sacrament of fellowship, love, and unity cannot tolerate discord and enmity. You must take to heart the infirmities and needs of others, as if they were your own. Then offer to others your strength, as if it were their own, just as Christ does for you in the sacrament. This is what it means to be changed into one another through love, out of many particles to become one bread and drink, to lose one's own form and to take on which is common to all.[51]

49. Green, "Human Sociality and Christian Community," 113–23; For a good discussion of the importance of this work see Green, "Editor's Introduction," and Soosten, "Editor's Afterword" in *Sanctorum Communio*.

50. Cited in Bethge, *Dietrich Bonhoeffer*, 83.

51. Luther, "The Blessed Sacrament of the Holy and True Body and Blood of Christ, and the Brotherhoods," 245, 251.

What is often overlooked in Bonhoeffer's "theology of sociality" is its strong emphasis on the liturgical and sacramental reality of the church, a theological matter which was central for Luther. Thus the last part of *Sanctorum Communio* is an extended discussion of the empirical church. As Bonhoeffer writes, "The whole theological reflection thus far not only leads to the discussion of the sanctorum communion, but is possible and meaningful only from the perspective of the sanctorum communion." His approach is neither exclusively historical nor sociological, but embraces both. Most important, however, is that his approach is grounded in the reality of God and God's revelation that is to be either believed or denied, a methodology that can be acknowledged only by one who stands inside the church. There the Spirit speaks through the word to a plurality of hearers to create a visible sign which takes place in history—the empirical form of the church: "The church of Jesus Christ that is actualized by the Holy Spirit is really the church here and now; Christ existing as church-community" (DBW 1:122, 216).

Bonhoeffer's final dissertation chapter draws from the seminar papers we have already discussed. One particularly important matter related to the ministry of the word and sacraments is the gap between the empirical church and the essential church, the difference between a disfigured, sinful church and a pure, spotless church. These two churches, which include both devout and nominal members, are made one in the word that is the unity between possibility and reality. Because the German state church was formally open to all people, its strength was in its empirical form, although this characteristic was often overlooked by its despisers. As interpreted by Bonhoeffer, proclamation is a liturgical act in the public life of the church, so that the word becomes the bearer of the social activity of the Spirit, even though as human words it is fraught with contingency, imperfection, and sin. The source of the church's life is the freedom of the Spirit and the charismatic significance of preaching; the theological and sociological principles by which it is built up. In the practice of the assembly the means of grace are forms by which the church-community expresses itself publicly *and* embodies the effective and purposeful actions of the Spirit as a theological community; the church is both a means to an end *and* an end in itself. Bonhoeffer writes, "God makes the divine self the means to God's own end" (DBW1:229).

The final sections of *Sanctorum Communio* offer a number of practical judgments regarding the significance of the church in relation to particular challenges in that time. Bonhoeffer addresses the church's purpose of offering the gospel to all people and the church's nature as a concrete manifestation of God's gracious will for the world. This will entail tradition and loyalty to the past, a conservatism justified by the Reformation roots of Protestantism. On the other hand, the church's appreciation of history will also give rise to the need for wrestling with the present, for the principle of progress, and for the urgency of hearing and preaching the gospel as a responsibility of the whole church. This may require innovation, such as learning from the younger generation and even listening to voices outside the church. However, this is also a kind of vitality, a give-and-take that is healthy because it seeks a proper conservatism and proper progress.

Bonhoeffer was primarily concerned with the established church, the German state church that in theory was available to all, but in reality was a church that had lost its center to become rigid, empty, and harmful to its members and repulsive to many nonmembers. On the other hand, Bonhoeffer was also concerned by the rise of a popular-cultural church in Germany that was built on being "new and progressive"—but without sufficiently honoring the wisdom of the past. As he saw it, there was a great need for the unity of traditional and popular churches to create an integrity that would be a particular manifestation of God's gracious will for humanity in the world.

Here it is important to note that in Bonhoeffer's time the state church had lost access to ordinary people because of its failure to bring the gospel into contact with the conditions of their lives. He viewed this weakness as a consequence of the failure to give appropriate attention to the great numbers of German people who were afflicted by isolation and seeking comfort in a community life with others, a condition comprehended by many of the social and political movements in Germany, even if the church was silent. A Swiss pastoral friend, an avid reader of Barth's theology, wrote to Bonhoeffer concerning this dilemma.

> The church as it is today is based on two classes, the middle class and the farmers, the people of the land. . . . I belong neither to the middle class nor to the people of the country. Instead, I belong to the intellectual class. . . . The world to which I direct my talk and out of which I speak does not go to church. . . . [But] the sermon is, after all, a dialogue. But a dialogue between an intellectual and a middle class person or a farmer is not possible. Neither one understands the other. . . . As an intellectual pastor I am condemned to solitude (DBW 1:156).

In Bonhoeffer's judgment this problem is homiletic in nature, by which he means *how* the church proclaims the gospel, the same observation he had made about Protestantism during his time in Rome. The gospel must be proclaimed concretely, both for those who have remained within the church and for those who have rejected the church. Homiletically speaking, the problem was that sermons during this time were aimed at the bourgeois, whom Bonhoeffer describes as civil servants, skilled workers, and merchants. In his opinion, such sermons tended to focus on people who lived "relatively securely and comfortably, in orderly families and circumstances, who are relatively educated and relatively stable morally" (DBW 1:273). These were people who came to church expecting to experience something beautiful, learned, and moral in the form of a speech delivered by a university-trained pastor whose status in Germany was that of a civil servant. The aim of this preaching was to ground the sermon in a manner that displayed the preacher's literary expertise so as to connect with the (self) interests of the audience (DBW 1:265–69).

It will be helpful to consider in more detail the state of preaching in Germany during Bonhoeffer's years in Berlin. In an illuminating study of shifts in theology and preaching during this period, Angela Dienhart Hancock provides a summary of the homiletic landscape in Germany that helps us to understand better Bonhoeffer's relation to Protestant preaching.[52] Hancock shows how preaching of the gospel and political propaganda became invariably related. A new "holy history" emerged, "a salvation story with a distinctly German cross and a radiant political messiah."[53] There was an established Protestant homiletic tradition that shaped sermons and provided a dominant understanding of the purpose of preaching.

The influence of Schleiermacher was still very important, in that German homiletics was established in relation to the other disciplines of theological study in the university: philosophical theology and historical theology, with preaching being part of practical theology. Because the study of theology was to produce leaders for a church that would be capable of serving a modern society, the practical disciplines were constituted by principles and rules of art, or "theories of practice." From within this theological framework, the mediation of the "essence" of Christianity was to be communicated through preaching. Schleiermacher's work was thus influential for the study of homiletics during the nineteenth century for the three main traditions in Germany, "Enlightenment rationalism, Lutheran Orthodoxy, and pietism." He identified the preacher's God consciousness as the subject of the sermon, which invited the community to dialogue with both the preacher and the Bible. The preacher, however, was central, "a species of virtuoso, akin to an artist or poet."[54]

52. Hancock, *Karl Barth's Emergency Homiletic.*

53. Ibid., 138.

54. Ibid., 143.

Hancock's excellent discussion offers an illuminating narrative of reactions to Schleiermacher's vision of preaching. Perhaps more important, however, is the homiletic reformation that occurred at the turn of the twentieth century, which was marked by economic, social, and theological changes. A crucial element was the "emancipation of the culture from the church."[55] The primary concern, therefore, was that preaching had lost contact with the hearers of that time. What emerged from a number of perspectives was a kind of preaching known as "modern." This "modern" approach sought to identify with listeners more closely, to place more emphasis on the personal witness and honesty of the preacher, and to make the content religious in the sense of practical liberal Christianity. Since the church was formally open to all people, it was assured that listeners were not necessarily a believing audience. In addition, Scripture was read in lesser amounts due to the effects of historical critical methodology and a history of religions approach. Most important was that sermons should be life oriented and practically applicable, able to touch the happenings, feelings, and experiences of people. Topical preaching, while not necessarily religious or focused on Christian topics, was popular. The aim was that preaching would help the church to recover numerical and political influence in German culture, a hope shared alike by liberal Protestants, orthodox Lutherans, and pietist pastors. Hancock writes,

> The 1920's began with a Protestant church in crisis. More than ever it needed to assert its relevance, slow the tide of defections, and preach Christian values to the nation even as it worked to bind up the wounds of those mourning fallen sons, the lost monarchy, and the now distant spirit of 1914. Many Protestant preachers undertook these tasks using the homiletic ethos that came with "modern preaching." . . . Indeed, in many ways it was well suited for the needs of the day.[56]

As a theological student and pastor in training, Bonhoeffer arguably would have been influenced by the homiletic concerns of the day. However, his work points to a unique independence in thought and practice that gave rise to a homiletic theology oriented by God's revelation in the word by the Spirit for its social manifestation in the world. The influence of Barth, combined with his serious study of Luther, may have been a major contribution to Bonhoeffer's resistance to increasing pressure to fuse the gospel and German culture in preaching. Many "political theologians" and nationalist Protestants wanted preaching to identify the new republic and its system of

55. Ibid.

56. Ibid., 165.

social democracy as a threat to the old unity of the Protestant church and German people. Many believed the church should use preaching to establish its "relevance" in the new Reich by preaching a gospel that was tied to "common blood, nationality and culture."[57]

Bonhoeffer's university work does not point to the "modern" preacher as described in Hancock's work. It is true Bonhoeffer's dissertation expresses a concern for people, their capacities to hear the gospel, and the need for preaching to engage the concrete affairs of life in order to embrace all classes of people in Germany. On the other hand, Bonhoeffer sought to address these concerns in light of the gospel, the revelation of God through the work of the Spirit in the word that builds up the visible life of the church as Christ's presence in the world. According to Bonhoeffer's emerging theological vision, for which preaching was an integral and inseparable expression, because the church exists to serve the reign of God it cannot seek to proclaim and establish German nationalism. This homiletic problem was both theological and ecclesial in nature, symptomatic of a church that had lost its identity as a theological creation and visible, social reality. Bonhoeffer saw a potentially fruitful way of addressing this problem by opening theological education to people from all social classes, a move that would also serve to expose theological students to others from all walks of life. But even more important was that "Serious reflection on the gospel and a keen eye for the present are the forces from which the living church is born anew" (DBW 1:273).

The final pages of Bonhoeffer's dissertation entail a "sociology of worship" in which he discusses the actual liturgical practices of Lutheran congregations. His suggestions for change sought to maintain continuity with the theological past while also drawing contemporary congregations into the reality of worship. His reasoning was that many congregations were not sufficiently mature in faith to engage fully in the liturgy of the church. To address this need he suggests Scripture should be prominently read early in the order of worship as is done in the English *Book of Common Prayer*. He believed this change would serve to familiarize people with the Bible as the book of the church and the book on which the church is built. Here we see the practical wisdom of a homiletic theologian being formed in conversation with the word, the church, and the world. For Bonhoeffer, the church, or "Christ existing in community," is both centered and open, both traditional and innovative, both a divine revelation and a social reality (DBW 1:275–76).

57. Ibid., 164–65.

IMPLICATIONS FOR HOMILETIC THEOLOGY

Sanctorum Communio demonstrates an ecclesial turn in Bonhoeffer's search for the social intention of revelation as the Spirit's activity in the word that effects human transformation in the world. In a letter to Bethge ten years after Hitler's rise to power in Germany, Bonhoeffer reflects on how his way of seeing the world has changed. "It remains an experience of incomparable value that we have for one learned to see the great events of the history from below, from the perspective of the outcasts, the suspects, the maltreated, the powerless, the oppressed and reviled, in short from the perspective of suffering" (DBW 8:52).

I want to conclude this essay where it began; with Bonhoeffer's last sermon, which was written from prison on the occasion of his godson's baptism. "Our church has been fighting during these years only for its self-preservation, as if that were an end in itself. It has become incapable of bringing the word of reconciliation and redemption to humankind and to the world" (DBW 8:389). Commenting on Bonhoeffer's concerns, Rowan Williams suggests the problem was one of integrity; the language of the church becomes empty and even destructive to faith when it is isolated from a lively and converting worship and spirituality that is not afraid of silence and powerlessness. There is a need to recover the strangeness and generative power of words in a conversation that has become all-too familiar and detached from life.[58]

Williams continues by discussing the formation that is necessary if our lives are to be shaped by discipline and consistency in relation to the word of God and in forming a reflectively consistent speech for God. He notes this activity, which engages all Christians and not just theologians or pastors, requires a self-awareness that asks if our language is really talking about what it says it is talking about or is serving other ends or purposes.[59] Christian discourse may lack integrity because it conceals its true agenda and forecloses the possibility of genuine response by stepping back from the risk of conversation, from recognizing its unfinished quality, and from the possibility of correction. To the degree that Christian discourse is honest, it will show in its workings what is involved in bringing the complexities of our human world to judgment before God, and will enable, without illusion, a vision of what it has set out. Williams writes,

> Christian reflection takes as normative a story of responses to God in the world and the world in God, the record of Israel and

58. Williams, *On Christian Theology*, 40.

59. Ibid., 6.

> Jesus. . . . The biblical record . . . is the kind of record it is because it weaves together history and liturgy: the God perceived in the life of Israel is constantly addressed as well as talked about. . . . The language of worship ascribes supreme value, supreme resource or power, to something other than the worshiper, so that liturgy attempts to be a giving over of our words to God as opposed to speaking in a way that seeks to retain distance or control over what is being spoken of . . .[60]

Williams notes that the overall canonical shape of Jewish Scripture puts readers in this place of worship before God, just as the New Testament portrays the life, death, and resurrection of Jesus as the shape of God's activity in history, thus opening a direct and clear language for prayer and praise. For this reason, language about God has integrity to the extent that is directed toward God. In other words, it is in prayer, in giving ourselves to God, that who we are and what we do and say are one.[61]

Williams's comments on Bonhoeffer urge us to consider the manner in which language about God, including the language of preaching, or homiletic theology, is kept honest to the degree that it turns on itself in the name of God and so surrenders itself to God. He writes,

> Speaking of God is speaking to God; in prayer our language is surrendered to God in repentance, in exposure to the judgment of God, by confronting and naming its own temptations to self-deception and self-love; of its own falsehoods and self-interests: in other words, we must study the workings of our own speech, not with a sense of our own self-importance but in penitence, as a sacrifice of praise that acknowledges that we are answering to a reality, the living God, who is neither possessed nor controlled by our words, and that our speech is dependent upon the generative power of something irreducibly other than ourselves.[62]

In considering the implications of Bonhoeffer's student years for homiletic theology, it is significant that, while seeking to recover the social visibility of the church through the preaching of the gospel, he began also to discover the character of the world as God's redeemed creation. By attempting to describe the word in the world, Bonhoeffer was also calling the church to allow its witness to divine revelation to necessarily include its engagement with the world.

60. Ibid., 7
61. Ibid.
62. Ibid., 9.

Bonhoeffer's return to Luther was also a significant move in reorienting his judgment of Germany's religious life and for demonstrating the capacity of homiletic theology grounded in the word to link its discourse to all spheres of existence. He looked to both knowledge of the word and a keen eye for the world to perceive the full range of human experience in light of the word, especially the experience of suffering, failure, limit, and need. Rather than asking with his Berlin teachers how the word must be translated into categories acceptable to the world, Bonhoeffer's theological approach to preaching and his homiletic approach to theology pursued a different question: how can the word engage the world as word without sacrificing itself to the language of other forms of knowledge, engaging these realities for the sake of the redemption of the world?[63]

Bonhoeffer's developing practice of reading Scripture and preaching was situated within a "pneumatological ecclesiology" that sought to join the word of God to the world by extending the movement of the Spirit and the power of the gospel into the depths of human language and experience. His assessment and criticism of the church in his day points toward the need for homiletic theology to be a public witness rooted in prayer, reflection, and discernment, or an expression of practical wisdom. The practice of reflection and discernment cannot be separated from the language and wisdom of prayer in that it renders faithful encounter with the world possible—the word encountering the world, but also the world encountering the word.[64] Oswald Bayer writes of this Lutheran vision: "We are still in the world, and we enter into a new worldliness. The 'new creation' is a return to the world, not a retreat from the world. The new creation is a conversion to the world, is a conversion to the Creator, hearing God's voice speaking to us through his creatures."[65]

Moving contrary to the liberal theological arrangements that had separated word and world, theology and church, Scripture and preaching, liturgy and mission, Bonhoeffer perceived the nearness of the word in preaching and sacrament, in praise and repentance, but also in contending with the range of conditions and circumstances in all spheres of human behavior and expression. He discovered that the church may come to discern its foundational scriptural narrative in the acts and hopes of others, a "re-conversion" of the church, which, in turn, is able to bring those actions,

63. Here I am indebted to the fine essay by Rashkover, "Introduction: The Future of the Word and the Liturgical Turn," 4–5.

64. Ibid., 10.

65. Bayer, *Living by Faith*, 28.

experiences, and hopes in relation with Christ for their fulfillment by the grace of God.[66]

This chapter has attempted to show how Bonhoeffer came to this judgment in prayerful reflection on the scripturally mediated word in the church while also having a keen eye for the world in order to discern the surprising activity of the word. He believed the church is addressed by God to become what it is through the preaching and hearing of the word and celebration of the sacraments, a living encounter with the gospel in which it is transformed by the Spirit to perceive and live in the world more humbly but wisely. Such perception of the church's mission in the world, and the world's place in the word, occurs through the practice of corporate wisdom within a conversation generated by reading, speaking, hearing, believing, and living: "Christ existing in community." This conversation may be called homiletic theology.

66. Williams, *On Christian Theology*, 38.

Homiletical Theology and Method

—7—

Preaching as Spark for Discovery in Theology

—Ronald J. Allen

I am both honored and perplexed to contribute a chapter to a full-scale work focused explicitly on homiletical theology as method, content, and practice. I am honored to be part of an early wave of thinking about a promising topic. However, I am perplexed because, while I have heard the expression 'homiletical theology" for about twenty-five years, I have not known exactly what it means.[1] I confess, with some embarrassment, that I am still not entirely sure what to make of this notion. However, I am in good company. The contributors to this book use the expression "homiletical theology" with different nuances in regard to its nature, methods, content, and function.[2] It seems that we are still at the point of sorting out a common understanding of homiletical theology.

1. I first noticed the notion of "homiletical theology" in Buttrick, *Preaching Jesus Christ.* In his many works Buttrick often appears to use the term *homiletic* in the same way that the term *homiletical* occurs in the present book.

2. I have long thought that using the word *homiletics* and its cognates works against the basic purposes of preaching when the former is used in public discourse. Few lay people in the church—and, I imagine, even fewer people outside the church—know the meaning of the term *homiletics.* Instead, I think we should use language more directly associated with "preaching" to speak about the subject and work of preaching. The language of "preaching" is much closer to the life of the church than is the language of "homiletics." Nevertheless, from time to time in this essay I employ the language of "homiletics" since it is the lingua franca of the discussion in this book.

Not long ago, many theologians and preachers regarded preaching as a consumer discipline. In this framework, formal theology—biblical scholarship, history, systematic theology, ethics, and others—produced the heavy-duty theological content that scholars of preaching funneled towards the preaching task and that preachers applied to the congregation in sermons. Creativity on the part of the preacher came mainly in how preachers utilized methods, insights, and content from these other sources. The traffic flowed one way on this bridge: from formal scholarship to the preacher.

Scholars of preaching today have almost universally rejected the consumer viewpoint, and now think of preaching, from start to finish, as a theological act with preaching's own theologically creative dimensions. Scholars of preaching and preachers seek to give a theological interpretation of all aspects of preaching, from übertheological perspectives on preaching (e.g., theology of preaching) through giving theological accounts of all aspects of the preaching event. Indeed, homiletical theology embraces the first movement of electricity across a brain synapse beginning sermon preparation through articulating the theological content of the message and embodying the sermon to the long (and often unnamed) effects of the sermon.

While the precise definition of homiletical theology may still be under consideration, we can certainly say that homiletical theology moves in this latter stream. This chapter hopes to make a modest contribution to the emerging discussion about the nature and function of homiletical theology by envisioning homiletical theology as a spiral movement relating the different modes of theology involved in preaching—especially systematic theology, constructive theology, practical theology, and other modes of theological awareness. I am especially interested in naming how theological reflection in connection with preaching can spark change in theological conviction not only in the preacher and congregation but also in constructive and practical theologies, as well as in other theological modes.

The goal of homiletical theology is to help preachers become aware of ways in which all theology is ever and always present and at work in preaching (even when unrecognized by the preacher or congregation) and in which all aspects of preaching can contribute to the total theological understanding of preacher and congregation. The preacher as homiletical theologian enters into conversation with others in which each party may be changed by interaction with the other.[3] While the most obvious conversation partners may be systematic theology, constructive theology, and practical theology, the partners extend to the full range of real-life experience.

3. For example: Allen, McClure, Allen, eds., *Under the Oak Tree*; Allen, *Preaching and the Other*; Allen, *The Homiletic of All Believers;* McClure, *Other-Wise Preaching.*

From this point of view, homiletical theology is a not a categorically different way of doing theology nor is it a completely distinct theological content.[4] Homiletical theology is theology in connection with all phases of preaching. As the heart of this chapter notes, the practice of homiletical theology can be a source of an altogether fresh theological perspective that has not previously been part of the theological world.[5]

The chapter begins by reviewing many basic elements included in homiletical theology. The core of the chapter portrays homiletical theology as a continuously moving theological spiral. We note that homiletical theology typically takes place from the perspective of the constructive formulations of the particular theological family of the preacher and/or congregation. Theological reflection in the practice of homiletical theology can cause the preacher and/or congregation to rethink aspects of their theological world views. Four case studies demonstrate how theological reflection in a preaching context can lead to the emergence of new theological households. The chapter offers criteria for the preacher and congregation to keep in mind when assessing the promise and theological possibility for an idea that

4. From this point of view, academic theology and homiletical theology are not different animals housed in different cages in the ecclesial zoo. Academic theological formulations (having to do with both content and method) are precipitates of theological formulation arising from theological reflection prompted by the interaction of the Bible, doctrine, and life experience. Academic theology, especially as it comes to expression in systematic and constructive theology, organizes perceptions about God, Christ, the Spirit, the church and the world in ways that make sense of a people's interaction with the Bible, tradition, experience, and reason, and that give the preacher and congregation accessible and convenient ways of talking about God in relationship to life. We might think of systematic and constructive formulations in their academic expressions as compressed experience. Academic formulations are others with whom the preacher and congregation have conversation in the practice of homiletical theology. The relationship between academic theology and life is reflexive: academic theological perspectives can help preacher and congregation interpret life theologically, while real-life experience can lead academic theologians to reconsider their theological formulations. Later in this chapter we picture interaction with academic theology as a moment in the theological spiral of homiletical theology.

5. "Constructive theology" is similar to "systematic theology" in that both attempt to give an overarching account of the formative beliefs of an individual or community. In particular, such theological formulations construe the nature and purposes of God, how God relates to the world (and appropriate responses), and engages in ministerial/congregational practice from the perspective of that theology. Proponents of constructive theology think that "systematic theology," as a genre, sometimes calls for preachers to think in artificial categories or to force an artificial logic among the various elements of doctrine. While not always explained this way, systematic theology may be seen as a modern effort whereas constructive theology is more postmodern in the way in which it allows for diverse elements while still seeking a faith that is coherent overall. For a leading work in this vein, see Jones, Lakeland, and Workgroup, *Constructive Theology*. For an approach to preaching and systematic theology, see Allen, *Preaching Is Believing*.

appears to be a fresh theological discovery. We end with implications for the development of homiletical theology, and with a brief plea for humility.

ELEMENTS AT WORK IN HOMILETICAL THEOLOGY

The elements that go into the work and content of homiletical theology are similar to those in any other theological expression. While I list these elements individually, in actual homiletical practice they interpenetrate. A mature homiletical theology offers a comprehensive theological interpretation of the nature of these things, their functions and purposes, and how they actually relate with one another:[6]

- The world view of the preacher, congregation, Christian movement, and larger population within which the sermon comes to life
- The sources on which the preacher and congregation draw in order to help interpret the world and God's nature and purposes: the Bible, Christian tradition and doctrine, philosophy, the arts, the various sciences, manifestations of human experience, etc.
- The nature and purposes of the cosmos
- The nature and purpose, and present condition, of human beings (as understood in their various contexts and cultures) involving such things as how we know and how we make decisions
- The deepest convictions of preacher and congregation concerning the nature of God, God's purposes, the extent of God's power, and how God works in the world, in particular how and why God exercises divine power
- The criteria and method by which to come to an interpretation of God's presence and purposes in the congregation and its various contexts
- What we can count on from God, what God offers, what God asks, what we can expect when participating in God's purposes and the consequences of turning away from those purposes

6. Of course, each ecclesial community formulates its understandings of these things from the standpoint if its own context, presuppositions, values, and practices. In the postmodern ethos, preachers and scholars of preaching cannot speak blithely of universals, such as "*the* human condition," but should respect the otherness of the views of specific communities.

- Criteria by which to gauge the degree to which a sermon is consistent with the deepest purposes of God as discerned by the preacher and the congregation
- Criteria by which to determine whether a congregation can truly believe the sermon within the context of the congregation's current world view (or the degree to which a sermon may challenge the congregation to change its world view)
- The nature, purposes, and mission of the church
- The purposes of the sermon within the service of worship
- The purposes of the sermon within the larger life and mission of the congregation
- The purposes of the sermon within the public sphere beyond the congregation
- What happens when the preacher speaks and the people listen
- The dynamics of how listeners interact with the sermon
- The nature and function of the preached word,
- The form or genre of the sermon as theological expression
- The embodiment of the sermon as theological incarnation
- Appropriate responses to the divine presence and purpose (as interpreted in the sermon) on the parts of individuals, households, the congregation, and the larger world
- How the preaching of the sermon relates to the preaching of the congregation
- How God (through the Holy Spirit) is present and working at each moment of sermon preparation, in the embodiment of the sermon, and in the continuing effects of the sermon in the congregation
- The points and degrees at which discoveries made in the process of homiletical theologizing might call into question dimensions of deepest theological conviction

One must say two things about this list. First, it is partial. Other elements play into theology as an act of preaching (or preaching as an act of theology). Second, while scholars and preachers may discuss each element separately, in actual theological practice they are an organic whole in which the parts function in relationship to one another.

HOMILETICAL THEOLOGY IN SPECIFIC THEOLOGICAL FAMILIES

As noted earlier, in my view, in the strict sense, homiletical theology does not stand alone as a theological family the same way that we speak of theological families that have distinct theological presuppositions, methods, and views, such as evangelical theology, neoorthodox theology, or liberation theology.[7] As I see it, each major theological family has its own homiletical theology. As I think of it now, homiletical theology is a way of doing theology in preaching through particular theological families in light of the presuppositions, content, methods, and aims of those specific theological households.[8]

To be sure, preachers and congregations may find it complicated to identify their particular theological identities since preachers and congregations often combine historical and contemporary dimensions in their theological families. The major historical theological households include familiar names still found on many church buildings around the world:[9]

- Orthodox
- Roman Catholic
- Lutheran
- Anglican and Episcopalian
- Reformed
- Anabaptist

7. From this point of view the designation "homiletical theology" may be initially confusing in current theological discourse as a preacher could take it refer to a distinct theological family such as liberation theology or postliberal theology. A more familiar, and often analogous term, is "liturgical theology," by which we often mean giving a theological account of the liturgy. Liturgical theologians sometimes point out that the liturgy can be a source for theological reflection (and a source of theological insight), and can thereby contribute to the larger understanding of God on the part of the preacher and congregation.

8. Other contributors in this book take a different viewpoint, seeing homiletical theology less as a function of particular theological families and more as an effort in its own. I welcome this dialogue as a step on the path to coming to more common understandings of homiletical theology.

9. For a taxonomy of historical and contemporary theological families in relationship to preaching, see Allen, *Thinking Theologically*. Given the perspective in homiletical theology articulated in this chapter, *Thinking Theologically* may be a kind of unintended prolegomenon to homiletical theology in exploring how theology shapes preaching by pointing to how the characteristics of particular theological families call for sermons with resonant characteristics. *Thinking Theologically* does not directly consider how preaching might shape theology.

- Wesleyan
- Society of Friends
- Pentecostal

The major contemporary theological families include the following:

- Liberal theology
- Theology in the mode of mutual critical correlation
- Process theology
- Fundamentalism
- Evangelical theology
- Neoorthodox theology
- Postliberal theology
- Liberation theologies
- Confessional theology
- Radical Orthodoxy
- Theologies of otherness
- Racial and ethnic theologies

A preacher is often a member of both a historic theological family and a contemporary one. Thus a preacher might be a member of the Reformed tradition who interprets that tradition through the lens of liberation theology. Another preacher might be a Lutheran-confessional preacher or a Wesleyan-process preacher.

In the case of each family—both historic and contemporary—the homiletical theology of the preacher ought to manifest the characteristics of that particular theological configuration because each theological household has its conceptions of the sources of theological insight, the nature and purposes of God, the nature and mission of the church, the nature and aim of worship, and the nature and mission of the sermon within the service, the congregation, and the larger world.

The preacher engages in homiletical theology within this larger framework of theological perception. To continue the examples, above, one might then speak of a Reformed-liberation-homiletical theology or of Lutheran-confessional-homiletical theology or of a Wesleyan-process-homiletical theology.

Homiletical theologians should also be alert to the theological possibilities for the immediate context and for larger patterns of conviction that come to light in any and all phases of homiletical practice. Indeed, as we note in the following sections, the practice of homiletical theology may spark fresh discoveries in theology that then change perceptions of and within all expressions of theology.

HOMILETICAL THEOLOGY AS THEOLOGICAL SPIRAL

A spiral is a serviceable image for homiletical theology in action. A spiral implies movement from one place to another. The movement, however, is not simply linear. While the general movement is forward, the preacher goes back over where the preacher has been and reflects upon it. This process continues, literally, until the end of time. This spiral way of thinking and acting brings together emphases from systematic or constructive theology, as well as practical theology as reformulated by Edward Farley, Don S. Browning, and others.[10]

For heuristic purposes we can describe this movement as follows.[11] The preacher arrives at the point of beginning to prepare a new sermon with a working homiletical theological vision that includes a theological vision that can be described in systematic or constructive theological terms. The preacher engages in the practice of preaching in light of this vision. The preacher encounters the biblical text (or other starting point for the sermon) in its frame. The preacher identifies what the text (or other resources) invite the congregation to believe and do. The preacher analyzes the context in which the preacher will bring the sermon to life. The preacher works out a relationship among the context, what the text asks the congregation to believe and do, and the preacher's core theological convictions. The preacher formulates a sermon whose purpose, content, and genre should be consistent with the preacher's homiletical theology. The preacher embodies the sermon in a way that is supposed to be consistent with the preacher's animating theological vision, while attending to the congregation and the movement of the Spirit, both in the moment of preaching and in the congregation's response to the sermon afterward.

10. Through much of the twentieth century, many figures in the church conceived of practical theology as applied theology. That is, ministers learned skills that enabled them to put their theology into practice (e.g., preaching, planning worship, counseling, running a Sunday school). Such applied theology sometimes lost its theological roots and became *techne*. See the classic works by Browning, *Fundamental Practical Theology*; Farley, *Theologia;* and Farley, *Practicing Gospel*, 1–70.

11. I describe this process as if it unfolds in a sequence of steps. From preacher to preacher, and from week to week, in actual practice these things sometimes take place in quite different orders.

At points along the way, the preacher doubles back on what the preacher is doing, and reflects theologically on (1) the sermon content that is emerging, (2) the process of sermon development itself, and (3) the adequacy of the preacher's overall theological vision to interpret the present moment. Along the way, the preacher asks questions such as these: Is the sermon moving in a direction that is appropriate to the preacher's deepest theological convictions? Are the claims that are surfacing in the sermon consistent with the experience of the congregation? If the claims of the sermon are inconsistent with the congregation's experience, the preacher can sometimes ask, how does the congregation need to interpret its experience in the world, possibly changing what the congregation believes or does, in order to be consistent with the congregation's theology? At other times, the contrast between the convictions of the preacher and the situation of the congregation are such that the situation of the congregation causes the preacher to ask whether the congregation truly understands its convictions, but in some theological families the preacher can take the next step and consider whether the convictions themselves are adequate.

The preacher, then, does not simply adopt Barth, Tillich, Gutierrez, Cone, Suchocki, Dube, Koyama, or Keller, and then apply that theologian's vision to the preacher's congregation and world. Homiletical practice can prompt evaluation and possible reconsideration of the theological convictions of preacher and congregation. This aspect of homiletical theology occurs within the preparation of an individual sermon, sometimes several times. It continues from week to week, and from season to season.

In this model all modes of theology exist in ongoing dialogue. Systematic, constructive, practical, and constructive theology continuously talk with one another. In overarching homiletical theology, the relationship between theological conviction and the development of the sermon is reflective: each can help shape the other.

FRESH THEOLOGICAL DISCOVERY IN THE THEOLOGICAL SPIRAL

Preachers often modify their homiletical theologies. Changes occur across the arc of a preaching life. Something comes to the preacher's attention that prompts the preacher to think afresh about her or his theology in part or in whole.

The preacher comes upon an issue in regard to the immediate process of sermonizing or in übermatters (such as the theology of preaching or core theological convictions) and finds that her or his present theological awareness does not adequately explain the issue. The preacher then searches for a more adequate interpretation. For example, the preacher may come face-to-face with a text in the Bible or an affirmation in Christian doctrine or an ethical command or a life experience for which the preacher's existing theological position does not offer a satisfying theological perspective. The preacher then takes steps toward theological resolution, making changes as necessary.

Preachers typically make changes in their theological perspectives along three lines. In each case, reflections in the context of preaching spark theological discovery.

Changes within the Preacher's Existing Theology

First, preachers often make emendations within their existing theological perspective. When encountering a question or issue in the way raised above, they turn to their theological family and find something they did not know, or recover something forgotten, or clarify, or amplify. Indeed, preachers sometimes discover hidden resources that were at their fingertips all along but that had escaped the pastor's notice. The preacher then modifies her or his immediate theological operations by supplementing them from within her or his theological house without completely relocating from one house to another.

Changing from One Theological Family to Another

Second, in a more far-reaching theological development, some preachers move from one theological family to another. A preacher is no longer satisfied by the ways in which an existing theological world view leads her or him to interpret the Bible, or doctrine, or particular manifestations of world view or actual life experience. The preacher, seeking a more adequate interpretation of the relationship between what the preacher believes (or would like to believe) and experience, looks at other theological families, and discovers that another family has more explanatory power.

In parallel fashion, a preacher may find that ideas in her or his theological world view come into conflict with ideas from another theological world view with such intensity that the preacher seeks to clarify what she or he most truly believes. In this case, what actually happens in life or in some other aspect of interpretation challenges what the preacher believes. The preacher becomes aware of interpretations that are different enough that they cannot both be true at the same time.

For example, a preacher who grew up in an evangelical theological tradition may come to think that certain evangelical principles no longer square with important aspects of the scientific world view. The preacher may then find that another theological viewpoint that provides both a theistic core with a rich personal spirituality that is essential to the preacher while taking account of contemporary developments in the wider scientific world. The preacher moves from one theological house to another.

Creating a New Theological House

Third, from time to time the preacher cannot simply modify a theological world view or exchange one theological system for another. The preacher reviews existing theological systems and does not find one that makes adequate theological sense. Something more is needed: a theological perspective that is articulated for the first time. The preacher builds a new theological house. This option is illustrated in the next section.

EXAMPLES OF PREACHERS AND OTHERS WHO HAVE GENERATED NEW THEOLOGICAL FAMILIES

We turn now to representative examples of preachers and others who came to fresh conclusions through preaching or broader life consideration: Karl Barth, Reinhold Niebuhr, Alfred North Whitehead, and liberation theologians. Because of limitations of space, these discussions are simplified.[12]

The reader may think, "But these are all well-known theologians. How can they be examples to me?" To this one replies, "But they were not well-known theologians when theological discovery came upon them. They were engaged in preaching or other life activities that raised questions for them that could only be resolved only by fresh theological points of view." A preacher in Poplar Bluff, Albuquerque, Indianapolis, or Tipton could make such discoveries.

12. I have critical reservations about the theologies of Barth, Niebuhr, and the liberation theologians. However, the emphasis here is more on calling attention to how theological discovery takes place and less on probing the adequacy of particular theological content.

Karl Barth

Karl Barth's essential theological insight came while he was preaching in a congregation in Safenwil, Switzerland, from 1911 to 1920.[13] Barth had been educated in the liberal movement that itself sought to rethink important aspects of Christian faith from the perspective of the Enlightenment. Liberalism sought to liberate people from superstition and from arbitrary external authorities.

The liberal movement viewed the Bible and other religious statements as products of human reflection on experience. Some liberal theologians in Germany and elsewhere placed a low emphasis on sin and took an optimistic view of human progress that led to a close alliance between religion and culture. A number of liberals in Germany supported German involvement in World War I in the name of preserving superior German culture.

Barth the preacher could not reconcile the optimistic spirit of liberalism in the hands of the German nationalists with the violence of the war and the social chaos that followed.[14] For Barth, liberalism's God was little more than an image of that group's cherished values.

Barth sought a notion of God that was beyond cultural limitation. In particular, Barth sought sources for a view of God and the religious life that could not be co-opted to serve particular groups in the way that liberal theology allowed its interpretation of God to bless the violence epitomized by World War I. Barth came to think that the Bible presents a view of God as wholly other. For Barth, even the highest expressions of Christian doctrine and theology, including those that acknowledge the transcendence of God, do not fully understand or represent God. God cannot be co-opted. Indeed, Barth's God exposes how every human enterprise is compromised and falls short of God's hopes for the lives of individuals, communities, and nature.[15]

For Barth, the word of God through preaching creates a crisis in the congregation in which listeners should recognize the ways they fail to embrace God's purposes, while offering the congregation the grace necessary to turn away from the idolatries of modern life (including liberal theology) and to turn toward the coming world of God.

13. Gary Dorrien offers an exceptional exposition of Barth's theological pilgrimage in his *The Barthian Revolt in Modern Theology*, 14–80.

14. One can argue that Barth, like Niebuhr, caricatured liberalism. For Niebuhr's caricature, see the analysis by Daniel Day Williams in note 17 below. By focusing on the particular misuses of the liberal tradition in German theology in connection with the First World War, Barth threw out the baby with the bathwater.

15. It is worth noting that any notion of God can be co-opted, even the notion of a God who is wholly other. All construals of God are culturally conditioned.

Scholars debate the degree to which Barth succeeded in both his criticism of liberalism and in formulating a satisfactory theological alternative. For now, it is enough to note that as a preacher, Barth did not set out to make a theological discovery. But when his existing theology did not offer an adequate interpretation of real-life experience, he did not simply repeat inherited clichés but sought more meaningful perspectives.

Reinhold Niebuhr

Reinhold Niebuhr was serving as a minister in a congregation, Bethel Evangelical Church in Detroit, Michigan, when his theological reflection followed a movement similar in structure and content to that of Barth.[16] Niebuhr completed his theological study and began serving Bethel in 1915, staying there until 1928. Like Barth, Niebuhr began as a liberal.[17]

As in the case of Barth and many others, Niebuhr's optimism foundered on World War I. His frustration deepened as the Allies compounded the tragedy of the war for Germany by imposing tremendous penalties at the treaty signed at Versailles. His hope for the human prospect was further challenged by realities of urban life such as the mistreatment of workers in the auto industry.

Niebuhr's optimistic theology implied that an event of the carnage of World War I should not happen, nor should workers be brutalized. Individuals should have acted on behalf of love, justice, and community to have prevented the war. But the war did happen. A significant gulf opened between the promises of his optimistic theology and actual experience.

What could Niebuhr say to the congregation that was theologically credible in light of their experience? He revisited the doctrine of sin and found sin much more pervasive and powerful than liberalism allowed. At heart, sin for Niebuhr is pride, especially pride of power: the human attempt to establish security in the face of fear of insecurity. That is why people go to war and exploit others. Life is not essentially optimistic but tragic. The

16. For overviews of Niebuhr's theological odyssey, see Stone, *Reinhold Niebuhr*, 35–53, and Stone, *Professor Reinhold Niebuhr*, 22–43.

17. Niebuhr gave his own summary of six important themes of liberal thinking: injustice results from ignorance and can be corrected by education; human civilization is inevitably progressing morally; the behavior of the individual is the key to a just world; people will ultimately respond positively to calls to love, be just, and live in community; wars are foolish, and result from people who are more foolish than the people who realize that wars are foolish. See Reinhold Niebuhr, *Does Civilization Need Religion?*, 153. Williams points out Niebuhr's misrepresentations of liberal theology in its mature form in Williams, "Niebuhr and Liberalism."

effects of sin are expressed not on only as the suffering of individuals but also through social systems.[18]

Niebuhr continued to rethink his positions throughout his life. For example, in response to World War I, he became a pacifist. When the world was threatened by Nazism, he moved away from pacifism and took what he considered a realistic position: Such monstrous evil could only be defeated by force. These changes remind the preacher to be alert to the possibility of rereading the relationship between the preacher's theology and experience in the church and world.

Alfred North Whitehead

Alfred North Whitehead was not a minister but a mathematician who became a philosopher. His insights have been expanded and made accessible by preachers.

Whitehead's perspectives stand out against (1) the backgrounds of traditional philosophy and theology as well as (2) a Newtonian view of the universe. Traditional philosophy was concerned with being, and held that reality is made up of substances that exist over time. When change occurs, it is secondary and incidental. Traditional theology interpreted God in similar categories. God is unchanging (immutable), not affected by the world (impassable), and all-powerful (omnipotent). Classical theology held that God was simultaneously altogether loving, altogether just, and altogether powerful. For his part, Newton thought the universe operated according to immutable laws. Newton's world is mechanistic: it operates mechanically according to laws. It is reductionistic: one can explain the universe by reducing it to its most basic parts. It is deterministic: the laws determine what is going to happen. It is individual: every event has a specific cause.

A machine is a useful model of Newton's view of the world. The parts all have particular functions that they perform again and again.

To my knowledge, Whitehead never recounted in a formal writing how he came to his essential theological discovery. By Whitehead's lifetime, the Newtonian world view had begun to come apart when scientists discovered that atomic and subatomic particles did not behave according to Newtonian laws. Many people, often in conjunction with quantum physics and the theory of relativity, came to believe the universe is more open and less deterministic than Newton portrayed. Here a scientific discovery called into question larger life assumptions.

18. Stone, *Reinhold Niebuhr*, traces the many changes in Niebuhr's theological lifetime.

One of Whitehead's children was killed in World War I. His friend Bertrand Russell remembered, "The pain of this loss had a great deal to do with turning his thoughts to philosophy and with causing him to seek ways of escaping from belief in a merely mechanistic universe."[19]

When traditional philosophical, theological, and scientific categories failed to offer adequate understanding, Whitehead sought a more satisfactory interpretation. Quantum physics and the theory of relativity helped open the door to a more open view of the material world. Beyond that, Whitehead noticed in his own life that he was ever taking in new stimuli, reflecting on them, retaining some while turning away from others, then releasing the self of that moment into the continuous flow of life so that the same process recurred moment after moment.[20] His basic philosophical category shifted from being to becoming: reality is constant process.

Whitehead came to regard God as "the poet of the world, with tender patience leading it by [God's] vision of truth, beauty and goodness."[21] Whitehead's God intends for every situation to manifest optimum experiences of satisfaction and love. God adapts to how love might be appropriately expressed in each emerging situation. Moreover, Whitehead holds that while God is more powerful than any other entity, God is not omnipotent in the classic sense. God does not have the singular power to do anything God wants at any time. God's power is expressed through persuasion, lure. God, then, does not singularly cause evil events, nor could God singularly prevent them. Evil occurs when participants in a moment do not respond to the highest visions available to them. Yet, even when people do evil things, God does not give up on them, but offers them possibilities that are relevant to the choices they have made and their emerging circumstances.[22]

19. Russell, *Portraits from Memory*, 93.

20. Whitehead, *Modes of Thought*, 228.

21. Whitehead, Griffin, and Sherburne, *Process and Reality*, 346.

22. By way of truth in advertising, I am a member of the process theological family. My journey into this identification follows the structure of theological discovery outlined in this paper. I was troubled by the tensions among the traditional Christian claims that God is omnipotent (that is, God can do anything God wants any time God wants), that God is love, that God is just, and the manifest suffering in the world, especially the suffering of the innocent. Moreover, as a preacher I found it hard to explain to faithful people how such a God related to their immediate suffering when they would pray for such things as healing, restoration of relationships with children, employment, and yet their situations would not change, and would sometimes get worse. Traditional explanations, such as "God knows things that we do not know," seemed vacuous. I could not, with integrity, commend traditional views of God. While process theology resolves this particular tension, I am fully aware that it raises other questions. I continue to think that the gains with process are greater than the questions and losses.

While Whitehead was not a preacher, he sought a way of thinking about God and God's relationship to the world that is true to actual life experience. In doing so, he hit upon a theological discovery that reframed, for him, foundational Christian perceptions about the nature of the world and the nature and extent of God' power.

Liberation Theologies

Latin American liberation theology was the first household to emerge in what became a family of liberation theologies. In the case of each liberation impulse, preachers find that conventional theological interpretations are complicit with personal and social oppression. Preachers who become liberation theologians effectively ask, "Is repression God's purpose?" Rereading the Bible and elements of Christian tradition with this question, they conclude that Scripture and theology contain resources for understanding God as liberating from oppression. The pulpit itself is transformed from an instrument of repression into a witness for liberation.

In the 1950s, the Roman Catholic Church in Latin America emphasized individual sin and forgiveness, and gave relatively little attention to corporate implications of biblical teaching and Christian doctrine. Moreover, the church was identified with the existing social order with its hierarchy that ascribed social power to the upper classes. Preachers in the Roman Catholic Church effectively found themselves reinforcing existing social structures that benefited the wealthy at the expense of the poor, often accompanied by political repression and violence.[23] While the Protestant churches were not as strongly identified with existing social hierarchy, Protestant preaching tended towards maintaining the social status quo.

Some preachers and other church leaders, prompted in part by revolutionary impulses in the broader culture, grew dissatisfied with repression and poverty. By drawing on the Bible and the deeper reaches of Christian theology such thinkers came to believe that liberation from oppression is one of God's fundamental purposes.

In the United States, the Eurocentric church often formally and informally supported not only the separation of Eurocentric and African American communities but also supported the exploitation of the latter by the former.[24] For black liberation theologians, the experience of racism raises

23. For the emergence of Latin American liberation theology see Boff and Boff, *Introducing Liberation Theology*, 66–77, and Sigmund, *Liberation Theology at the Crossroads*, 28–39.

24. Dwight Hopkins recounts the emergence, themes, and practice of African

the question of whether God desires people to live in such brutal ways. Black liberation theologians came to perceive that God seeks to liberate people of color from Eurocentric repression, and seeks for all peoples to live with justice, dignity, respect, freedom, self-determination, and access to the resources for a good life.

For millennia, many expressions of the church assumed, consciously or unconsciously, that males were superior to women.[25] Such attitudes led not only to inequality but to injustice and abuse. The experience of repression because of gender prompted preachers in both Eurocentric circles and communities of color to consider whether gender repression is God's aim. As in previous instances, re-engaging the Bible and Christian tradition turned up resources for believing that God opposes oppression and wants the genders to live in egalitarian ways.

The church long held that intimate relationships between people of the same gender did not fulfill God' purposes.[26] Not only has the church often opposed such relationships but at times the church actively persecuted such folk. Pockets of change began in the church only when gay, lesbian, bisexual, transgendered, questioning, and asexual people claimed that their sexual experience could fulfill God's hopes for covenantal relationships. Dissatisfaction with conventional ecclesial teaching prompted theological discovery in this arena of sexuality.

These are only examples of a much wider phenomenon. In each case a person or group noticed a disjuncture between an existing theological tradition and the experience or world view of a particular community. This disjuncture prompted a search for a more adequate theological interpretation. Such discovery can happen to any preacher in any context.

CONSIDERATIONS IN MAKING THEOLOGICAL DISCOVERIES

A preacher almost never wakes up in the morning and thinks, "I am going to try to find or invent a new theological perspective today." As noted previously, the possibility of theological innovation typically presents itself

American liberation theology, including womanist theology, in his *Introducing Black Theology of Liberation.*

25. An exceptional overview of feminist theology is Russell, "Introduction to Feminist Theology." This anthology contains many feminist classics. For homiletical implications of feminist, womanist, and Mujerista theologies, see Bond, *Trouble with Jesus.*

26. A concise introduction to gay, lesbian, bisexual, transgender, questioning and asexual theological concerns is Cheng, *Radical Love*, 25–42.

when preachers experience theological tension in the course of preparing to interpret a biblical text, doctrine, or life situation from the perspective of the theological family to which they subscribe. At the same time, preachers can heighten their consciousness of the possibility of theological change and can have in mind criteria and patterns of thinking to help make their way in theologically responsible ways through the possibility of theological innovation.

Questions for Preachers to Keep in Mind

While a preacher may not set out to make a theological innovation, preachers might be more aware of the possibilities of theological discovery if we would periodically ask questions such as the following:

- To what degree do I *really* believe what I invite people to believe and do in the sermon?
- To what degree do I find evidence in experience to support what I preach?
- To what degree am I confident the congregation can count on God to act in the ways I suggest in the sermon?
- Are there discrepancies between what I say in the pulpit and what I observe in real-life experience?

When answers to such questions create tension in a preacher's theological house, a preacher needs to bring the theological tension to the surface so the preacher can look for meaningful resolution. Typically, the preacher would look in the Bible, in Christian history, theology, and ethics, in philosophy, in the arts, in the physical and social sciences, and in community life.

When turning to these individual sources, the preacher begins by looking through the lens of the issue or question that prompted the search. If the lens proves unsatisfactory, the preacher can test other lenses to see if they are more satisfactory. If existing lenses are not adequate, the preacher can grind a new lens. In each case above—Barth, Niebuhr, Whitehead, and the liberation theologies—theological reflection led to theological reconceptualization. Feminists, womanists, and mujeristas looked again at biblical texts with the question, "Can this text legitimately be interpreted in such a way as to empower egalitarianism and other movements towards liberation?" While fresh theological perspectives do not require rereading such sources from fresh standpoints, it is noteworthy how often theological renewal has involved a reappropriation of the Bible and Christian tradition.

Criteria for Theological Discovery

Given the fascination of many people in North America with things that are new, a preacher may be tempted to regard a fresh theological point of view as a kind of theological flavor of the month. A preacher needs criteria by which to gauge the degree to which new possibilities are truly promising. The following criteria are useful when considering alternative theological approaches.[27]

1. The new perspective should be in recognizable continuity with elements in the Bible and Christian tradition. Such continuity should take account of: the world as the gift of the God of Israel who continues to be a living presence involved in the world for the good of the world, ways in which the life of Israel point to God's purposes, an understanding of how Jesus Christ relates to God's purposes; the Holy Spirit as an ongoing agency of God in the world; God's purposes for the church and the world, and how to respond faithfully.

2. The new perspective should be at home in the world view of the preacher and the congregation. It should make sense in the framework of how the preacher and community think the world operates, and it should not require the congregation to suspend their normal expectation of how things happen and do not happen in the world. In particular, the new perspective should be one which the preacher can fully believe. This is a matter of integrity. The preacher and congregation need to believe that God really acts in the ways assumed in the new model. People need to know what they can count on from God and what they cannot. The same is true of human response.

3. The new perspective should be logically consistent. A theology that contains elements that contradict one another is self-contradictory and ultimately self-nullifying.

4. The new perspective should address the issue that created dissatisfaction with the previous theological viewpoint.

5. When making the change from the old theological view to the new, the gain should be greater than the loss. Every theological perspective has strengths and weaknesses. When making a trade, the preacher wants a new theology that is true to life, coherent, and compelling.

6. The preacher should be prepared to do the homework needed to understand the new perspective. Few preachers today have at arm's

27. Of course, in today's pluralistic theological world, different Christians would offer different takes on these criteria, and some Christians would offer different criteria.

> length the breadth and depth of knowledge of the Bible, Christian history and theology, philosophy, the arts, and the sciences (physical and social) that may be necessary to fill out a new point of view. Whether physical or virtual, the preacher may need to go to the library.

One of the most pervasive themes in contemporary theology is the importance of conversation in community. The preacher should seek the counsel of a wider community in trying to assess the strengths and weaknesses, as well as the gains and losses, that would accrue from the revised theological point of view.

OBSTACLES TO THEOLOGICAL DISCOVERY

One of the biggest obstacles to theological discovery is that preachers often continue in theological ruts without paying real attention to the relationship between what we say in the pulpit on Sunday morning and what happens in real life or what we otherwise unreflectively assume to be true. In other words, the preacher's commitment (sometimes unconscious) to their existing theological point of view often prevents the preacher from thinking outside the preacher's existing theological box.

A preacher who in the past identified various theological options and made a critical choice of theological house may have difficulty being open to a fresh theological point of view. When faced with tension between a theological belief and life experience, or tension among different theological perspectives, the preacher who has made such an effort may be inclined to defend her or his theological position without considering the gains and losses that come with theological alternatives. Indeed, preachers sometimes try to explain away challenges.

Another obstacle to theological discovery may be a preacher's lack of awareness of other theological possibilities. Most students arrive at seminary with an embedded theology, that is, a theological view they have picked up along the way but which they have not examined critically. They assume this embedded theology even if they cannot say what they find persuasive, especially in comparison to other theological perspectives. Of course, embedded theology is sometimes fully filled out, especially if the student comes from a church marked by preaching from a particular doctrinal perspective. However, many students have more or less cobbled together some theological beliefs from scraps of the Bible, slogans in popular piety, and ideas they happen to recall from official statements of faith. Preachers who operate from such theological bases are seldom aware of other theological possibilities, and seldom take initiative to seek broader perspectives. Such preachers often pass warmed-over theology from sermon to sermon and from congregation to congregation.

Such preachers would do well to make a conscientious decision to be open to considering fresh theological points of view. Even if preachers visit other possibilities only to return to their original theological location, the act of considering other viewpoints can have the effect of clarifying why they continue to be at home in the place they started.

IMPLICATIONS FOR DEVELOPMENT OF HOMILETICAL THEOLOGY

It is exciting to be part of a fresh wave of interest in homiletical theology. At this point, I note four implications of the current essay for further discussion regarding homiletical theology.

Matters of Definition: What is Homiletical Theology?

First, the discussion around the definition of homiletical theology needs to continue. As far as I can tell, scholarship in preaching does not subscribe to a single definition of homiletical theology. This essay poses a minimalist understanding of homiletical theology: homiletical theology is a not a categorically different way of doing theology, nor is it a completely distinct theological content. Homiletical theology is theology in connection with all phases of preaching. The practice of homiletical theology gives a theological account of all aspects of the preaching event while simultaneously being a potential source of theological reformulation and theological discovery. Whereas this chapter operates out of a minimalist approach to homiletical theology, some of the other contributors to this volume claim more for homiletical theology.

Homiletical Theologies (Plural)

Second, we should probably speak less of the singular "homiletical theology" and more of various "approaches to homiletical theology." As in so many theological matters these days, we should recognize a pluralism of homiletical theologies in a way analogous to recognizing a pluralism of liberation theologies. The move to the plural would not simply accede to the postmodern recognition of diversity in nearly all things, but would acknowledge the fact of significant theological differences in regard to interpreting the sermon and its homiletical world.

In this vein we should talk about such phenomena as "homiletical theology in evangelical theological families," "homiletical theology in the mode of mutual critical correlation," "postcolonial homiletical theology" or "homiletical theology in theologies of otherness." Going a step farther, we should recognize plurality within different homiletical theological families. For example, we could think not only of "postcolonial homiletical theology" but of Asian postcolonial homiletical theology and African postcolonial homiletical theology. And, of course, there are differences in homiletical theology within both Asian and African postcolonial theological worlds.

Thick Description of Homiletical Theologies Related to Particular Theological Families

A third implication is especially related to the approach to homiletical theology articulated in this chapter. Preachers and scholars of preaching need to provide more thick descriptions of homiletical theology in the historical and contemporary theological families as well as in the distinct amalgams of historical-contemporary-homiletical theologies.

At present, we have detailed understandings of the theologies of preaching associated with most historic theological families. We have pretty comprehensive understandings of the theologies of preaching in some contemporary families, especially evangelical, liberal, neoorthodox (especially Barth), and postliberal. We have a clear grasp of the content of liberation theologies (and liberation practices of exegesis and theological social analysis), though less awareness of the theology of preaching inherent in liberation theologies. We have developing insight into theologies of mutual critical correlation, process theology, racial and ethnic theologies, theologies of otherness, and Radical Orthodoxy. But we do not have the fuller accounts of homiletical theology as it might come to expression in connection with these families.

Case Studies of Homiletical Theology in Action

Fourth, we need case studies of homiletical theology in action. We would have a better idea of what we actually gain as preachers, church, and academic community if we could see how homiletical theologians put homiletic theology into practice in relationship to specific biblical texts, particular

Christian doctrines, and particular situations pertaining to individuals, households, congregations, and the world beyond the congregation. In this book, for example, Michael Pasquarello provides a model for such thinking by focusing on the development of Dietrich Bonhoeffer as a homiletical theologian.

The Preaching of the Community

A fifth implication does not develop specifically from this chapter but from more general ecclesiological reflection. We need to think towards a homiletical theology for the congregation as a preaching community. David Schnasa Jacobsen surfaces important themes in this regard by calling for more attention to the congregation as community of theological reflection and the congregation as preacher. While it is true that the preacher is a local theologian, in the priesthood of all believers, the preacher's theological calling is not to think theologically for the congregation but to help the congregation as a community engage in theological reflection. In this regard, the preacher is a kind of player-coach. While the preacher preaches in the congregation, the congregation preaches in the larger world. One purpose of the sermon is to coach the congregation for its preaching beyond the property line of the church building and grounds.

These communal tasks are hard. Theological education, at least under rubrics of European origin, continues to be heavily oriented to the minister as individual. One of my purposes in Introduction to Preaching, for instance, is to help students find their particular, typically individual, voices. This is all good and well, but it stops short of the bigger and more important step of helping the preacher figure out how to help the congregation find its theological voice, as well as helping the congregation figure out where and how to preach. Homiletical theology is in an ideal place to help preachers and congregations broaden our perspectives and practices on these matters.

A CLOSING PLEA FOR HUMILITY

I close with a plea for humility in homiletical theological discourse. Virtually all theologies are centered in a God of love who seeks for all people to live together in love. A bitter irony in some theological discussion today occurs when theologians, preachers, and pew Christians speak with one another in ways that fall short of love. Indeed, Christians sometimes speak in caricature about viewpoints other than their own, and behave in ways that are dismissive, arrogant, rude, angry, and otherwise disrespectful towards Christian who subscribe to other theological perspectives.

To be sure, Christian conversation needs to be clear and straightforward. This sometimes means saying and hearing hard things. But Christian perspectives and Christian community are undercut by contradiction when we profess to witness to a God of love but are unloving towards other witnesses whose testimonies differ. Homiletical theology needs to move forward by not only advocating a God of love but by relating to all involved in loving ways.

In this spirit, David Schnasa Jacobsen rightly says, "Within [the] eschatological frame, we must all concede that our best accounts, in an age of theological construction, remain provisional and thus unfinished this side of heaven."[28] Needless to say, the reader would expect a contributor who subscribes to process theology to regard the task of homiletical theology as ever and always unfinished, or, as Professor Jacobsen more poetically implies, ever and always beginning afresh. From a process point of view, preacher, theologian, congregation, and God are always in process with respect to seeking an adequate interpretation of God, God's purpose, and appropriate responses. While time may not "make [all] ancient good uncouth," new occasions call forth fresh perceptions.[29]

From where I sit, all homiletical theological perspectives are *interpretations* with certain strengths and weaknesses. They have a provisional character. We cannot have full and uninterested access to God until we see God face-to-face. Until that day, everything we say about God should be draped in humility and spoken in love.

28. Jacobsen, chapter 2 above, 46.

29. The reference is Lowell, "To Us All, to Every Nation."

—8—

The Way and the Way of Homiletic Theology

—*Teresa Stricklen Eisenlohr*

In recent decades the term *homiletic* or *homiletical theology*[1] has been bandied about without much consensus about what it is. David Schnasa Jacobsen nicely categorizes recent uses of the term to show that we vary in how we conceive of it, suggesting, too, that these variances are due to larger differences around how preaching and theology are related.[2] What we also need to consider is how the theologies of preaching out of which we do our work require examination of how God speaks to human beings and how we know that it's God and not the anchovy pizza we just had talking back. Although this is a task for another day, it is important to note at this juncture that questions of discernment, God's word, human language, ecclesial traditions, Scripture, cultural contexts, rhetoric, communication theory, biblical exegesis, hermeneutics, epistemology, pedagogy, narrative theory, perception, and theological dogma—all issues that comprise homiletic theory—are also issues with which systematic or constructive theologians must contend. Thus, in trying to define homiletic theology we are doing nothing

1. Because *homiletical theology* is a term that has been used in former centuries to refer to an academic discipline, I prefer the term *homiletic theology* in order to avoid any more confusion than we already have.

2. Jacobsen, "What is Homiletical Theology?," chapter 1 above.

less than beginning to carve out a discipline, which Paul Scott Wilson called for more than two decades ago.[3] So let us begin!

My attempt at defining homiletic theology will proceed by looking at how and why we define anything, which requires a kind of clearing away of what homiletic theology is not. After creating theoretical space for homiletic theology to exist within its wider field of operational connections, I will then go on to define homiletic theology as the theological thinking required for preparing to preach the gospel in any given sermon at any given time and place.

CARVING OUT THEORETICAL SPACE: WHAT HOMILETIC THEOLOGY IS NOT

When we try to define something, what we really do is make distinctions. We create categorical space from out of the mix of several factors in order to discern the general shape or characteristics of one thing or phenomenon over against something else with which it appears. Hence, one of the ways we define something is by saying what it is not. In order to define homiletic theology, we have to distinguish it from the other things with which it appears—preaching, homiletics, academic theology, and a theology of preaching. In actuality the tasks and issues of homiletic theology are intertwined with all of these—and this needs to be kept in mind even as we make some distinctions. What we are attempting to describe is a dynamic mix of several somewhat variable factors at play in various preaching situations in strange and wonderful and ultimately mysterious ways. With this caveat, then, we proceed.

Homiletic theology is not preaching.

Although homiletic theology is done for the sake of preaching and ends with preaching, it is not preaching per se. Preaching is the actual public event of delivering the sermon, which involves not just what the preacher is saying verbally and nonverbally, but also what hearers are hearing. In whatever venue it occurs, preaching is the public announcement of the gospel of what God is up to, which, as seen through the Scriptures, is pretty much the same as what God's always been up to—creating, calling humanity into communion, loving, judging, redeeming, healing, reconciling, blessing. Preaching continues Christ's ministry of announcing that God's reign is drawing near

3. Wilson, "Is Homiletics Academic?"

even now, inviting people to live in communion with the divine through repentance and belief.[4] Thus, Christian preaching publicly encourages us to answer God's invitation to live more fully in concert with the divine Way of Christ. Because the purpose of preaching is to proclaim the gospel, every sermon that seeks to fulfill its purpose requires homiletic theology.

After all, anyone who has listened to preachers preach out of the same biblical text knows that no preacher just preaches the Bible. As hermeneutics tells us, some sense of the whole governs how we interpret any given text. What this whole is is the gospel. However, as Edward Farley argues, the gospel is not a static formula, but a living reality. As such, it defies our attempts to fix it into any one configuration, as the Bible shows us, for the good news is that in Christ our God accommodates Godself to us for the purpose of redeeming and blessing creation.[5] The task of preaching the gospel, whose dynamic facets shine differently depending upon the contexts of history and human need, is what our Lord has called us to do (Matt 28:18–20). Because this dynamic gospel is the whole through which we read any given scripture and because our social location bears upon our interpretation of any given text and the gospel itself, preaching ultimately has to be a thoroughgoing theological task in order to be more than mere rhetoric in a religious context or mere literary criticism of a biblical passage. The theology that preachers do involves discerning the living word from the living Lord that longs to be spoken into specific contexts at particular moments in time. This is homiletic theology.

Homiletic theology is also not a homiletic or homiletics.

A homiletic is a *general* theory of preaching. In actual practice a homiletic, like homiletic theology, should grow naturally out of a theology of preaching, though too often it is not clear how a homiletic and theology of preaching are related, for these implicit assumptions are not always made explicit.

A homiletic is to be distinguished from homiletics, which is the academic study of preaching. Although *homiletical theology* is a term that has historically been used to denote the field of homiletics within the theological curriculum, we need to be careful here. How preaching and theology are related academically is important, for educational theory is responsible for splitting the preaching of the church from theology.[6] As a field of inquiry, homiletics includes not only the various theories of preaching (i.e., vari-

4. This is the essence of the gospel that Jesus preached, as we see in Mark 1:14–15.

5. Farley, "Toward a New Paradigm for Preaching," 71–92, 87.

6. Stricklen Eisenlohr, "Preaching and Theology in Light of Theological Education."

ous homiletic-s) and the communication theories, contextual analyses, and philosophies they draw from, but also an examination of the theologies out of which homiletics and various homiletic-s emerge.

Homiletic theology is not a theology of preaching.

As suggested above, homiletic theology draws from a theology of preaching but is different from a theology of preaching. A theology of preaching articulates what God's got to do with preaching, and how God's word comes to us through language and, possibly, other communication media. A theology of preaching underlies all of the work we do in homiletics as the background assumptions out of which we do our work. It has a more universal, finished quality than the specific ad hoc theological judgments a preacher makes during sermon preparation. As such, a theology of preaching functions like one's own background does in the shaping of his present-day life. In its preparation of any given sermon, homiletic theology works out of some configuration of a general theology of preaching as it makes specific judgments about what God's living word would speak into the preaching situation at hand.

Homiletic theology is not academic theology.

Generally, when we use the word *theology* we think of the subject learned in academic institutions—the study of God. Preachers must know various academic theologies and work with them in crafting sermons. While academic theology is certainly crucial for the task of preaching, this is too narrow an understanding of theology, which is more than just an academic discipline. So let's be clear: a theology is not the same as theology. In truth, many (most?) academic theologians understand theology as a dynamic *way* of thinking about God, not a finished product. With this understanding of theology, we can say, then, that preaching is an act of theology in its own right. It just looks different from the theology learned in academic institutions due to its differing rhetorical contexts and purposes.[7] (See Figure 1.)

7. Wilson makes this observation in *The Practice of Preaching*, 67: "systematic theology and preaching for the most part have different audiences and purposes, and therefore different rhetorical goals and strategies for achieving those goals."

FIGURE 1: RHETORICAL COMPARISON OF PREACHING AND ACADEMIC THEOLOGY

RHETORICAL FACTORS	ACADEMIC CONSTRUCTIVE THEOLOGY	PREACHING AS HOMILETIC THEOLOGY
Purpose	Outlines a communal portrait of God in such a way that explains who God is and what God is about.	Gives a communal picture of God in such a way that not only explains who God is, but invites us to be a part of the picture.
Context	Usually the academic community or theologically educated clergy in mostly a published form or an educational forum.	Usually ritual where we're "genred" into symbolic ways of seeing the divine at work through ritually charged words and activities. Even if preaching is public, it is connected to the liturgical practices of the ecclesial community.
Time/Space Considerations	Limited in writing only by publishing concerns, but the time and space is exponentially greater than that of a sermon. Limited in the classroom by curricular constraints.	Limited by liturgical traditions, which vary, and by communal expectations. In public, street-corner preaching, virtually unlimited except by various ordinances. On radio and TV, limited by show time.
Audience	Mostly other academic theologians or theologically educated clergy.	Mostly ordinary folks of mixed educational backgrounds and ages.
Linguistic Media	Mostly written, which affords the technical clarity of conceptual thought in linear logic.	Predominately oral even if delivering a written manuscript, which means concepts and images must work together to form meaning for people.

The primary category out of which homiletic theology, preaching, and homiletics itself work is rightfully theology, then—not rhetoric, hermeneutics, biblical exegesis, or communications theory. To see preaching as anything other than an act of theology renders it a mere human endeavor equivalent to any other human words, which is a denial of the Christian assertion that a preacher's words are to be more than mere human speech. In the Holy Spirit, they may indeed become God's words addressing us as a living word from the living Lord.

OUT OF THE VIA NEGATIVA, A WAY FORWARD

Since preaching is a theological act, and we are trying to define homiletic theology, we need to articulate our understanding of theology itself. If what we are trying to do is homiletic theology, with theology being the hard noun, we have to be clear about what theology is.

What is theology?

Theological thinking arises from an obscure and ambiguous sense of the presence of a transcendent Other we call God who comes to us through immanence, through such things as the church's testimonies, words, and actions; the Bible; worship; conversations and interactions with others; dim intuitions; reflections upon the beauty of creation; philosophical ponderings; music; logic; etc. Theology begins with an awareness of Something More at work through the ordinary stuff of this world that has a personal character as an Other beyond the manipulations of our consciousness and perceptions and that through which the divine is manifest. Through participation in the practice of faith and dancing in its symbolic world of texts, traditions, and faith acts that testify as to what God and God's Way in Christ is like, we begin to glimpse something of the Reality to which all God-words point. We start to see for ourselves that there really is some Other upon which the whole world is dependent. And our fascination with this glimpse is enough to keep us engaged in seeking to be more closely related. Thus, theology begins as curious wonder that goes forth to find out more about God. Theology is faith seeking understanding of who God is and what the divine intentions are toward us.

This experiential, intuitive way of knowing God was included as part of the early definition of the word *theology*, or *theologia*. In its earliest usages, theology included contextual discernments about who God is and what the divine will is in specific lived realities. Growing out of the interpretive tradition of discerning God's will in specific cases in light of the Torah, *theologia* is a more dynamic concept than static legal statutes. Just as Torah included not only the written laws of Moses found in the Pentateuch, but also past interpretations and judgments and stories attached to those laws,[8] so *theologia*

8. Torah is basically the way of living in covenant with the Creator and creation. The ancient Pharisaical understanding of Torah that became the rabbinic tradition, which Jesus worked out of, saw Torah as the way of being in covenant with God and one another. It included the law of Moses written in the Pentateuch as well as the oral interpretations of the written Torah. The Sadducees, on the other hand, believed only the Torah written in the Pentateuch was authoritative for Jewish life. See Schiffman,

included discerning the Way of God in particular lived experiences in accord with past precedents. The early Christian church, however, borrowed the Greek term *theologia* to talk about discerning the way of God. *Theologia* was an ancient Greek term used to designate the work of both (1) poets who gave us mythological explanations of the world and (2) philosophers who thought about what the poetic language meant in order to construct suppositions about reality at large.[9] *Theologia* was an integration of both symbolic and conceptual logic with a component of prudent wisdom that knows how to act (*phronesis*) as a result of immersion in faith's ways of being in the world (*habitus*). As Edward Farley describes it, *theologia* is a kind of practical wisdom that results from being immersed in faith.[10] Understood as the perpetual task of faith, not as finished product, *theologia* deals with both past and present evidences for God's perpetration of goodness in the world in order to discern how best to follow in accord with this divine Way. This is the understanding of theology homiletic theology works out of. It is more than just studied analysis and book knowledge, though this is certainly a part of it. However, the sources of *theologia* go beyond the book knowledge about God to include any references to God—Scripture, liturgy, spiritual perceptions, ecclesial practices, stories, images, confessional statements, as well as ecclesial dogma.

Theologia is the best way for preachers to understand theology because we don't just deal with Scripture in our preaching; we also sift through stories, metaphors, images, history, people's lives—virtually anything—in order to seek out where the risen Lord might be lurking. We do this because it is our job as preachers to be those who, having been found by Christ, give testimony as to where we've seen him so that others might come to know Emmanuel.

Although it is important for the church to be able to articulate what it believes in its more settled doctrine, thinking of theology as *only* a body of knowledge perverts the relational knowledge of God that faith's *theologia* is designed to foster. Indeed, understanding theology as a thing, a body of knowledge we are to learn, ultimately makes the living God captive to our knowing. This also perverts the nature of faith's knowing, which is more relational. Reducing knowledge of God to a body of knowledge about God renders theology into a finished product that we simply apply like a medicinal salve to any given situation.[11] Rendering theology as a body of

---

From Text to Tradition.

9. Congar, *A History of Theology*, 32–33.

10. Farley, *Theologia.*

11. This is exactly what happened in homiletic theory, as Crowe shows in his book

knowledge that has set God's having spoken in the past as a fixed known places us in the God position whereby we judge and manipulate truth. This actually hinders the healing movement of God's word coming through our *theo-logia*/God-words by placing us outside God's speaking whereby we stand in the divine position as arbiters of truth, as opposed to those who discern truth as coming to us through relationship with the Lord whose be-ing is manifest incarnate here and now, as in the past. Defining theology as *theologia* keeps us honest as to where we stand with our limited, partial human perspectives, reminding us that live and move and have our being from within God's speaking that addresses and embraces us within our human finitude.

Understanding homiletic theology as *theologia* means that the preaching of the church participates in the same issues involved in what theologians call theological prolegomena, which includes matters of revelation, philosophies of language, epistemology, hermeneutics, Scripture, tradition, etc. What theological prolegomena actually is, though, is a question of *how* we can do theology at all. *Theologia*, then, becomes a way of doing theology, or what theologians call theological method.

What is homiletic theology, then?

Most simply, homiletic theology is a way of thinking theologically through the preparation of any given sermon. Like academic theology, it stems out of *theologia*, but it is not limited to rational ways of thinking and expressing the faith, though it includes consideration of various doctrines and academic theologies. In its reflections, homiletic theology seeks to track the way of God in the world, searching along past known travel routes of Scripture and ecclesial traditions only to find the Holy One sneaking up on us to surprise us with divine goodness suddenly shining through the ordinary stuff of human life here and now as in olden days. With the church's insights of this Other who loves all of creation beyond our comprehension, our homiletic theology is done out of a theology of preaching, which is born of our divine commission to continue to preach what Jesus himself preached, died, and was raised to rule—namely, the *basileia* of God who is at work in the world

Theology of the Christian Word. The living Word of God became associated with orthodox doctrine in the late patristic era. It is no wonder, then, that one of the earliest works on preaching, Pope Gregory's sixth-century *The Book of Pastoral Rule*, encouraged preachers to apply the good medicine of the gospel like a doctor assesses what is wrong and applies a salve for healing. See St. Gregory the Great, *The Book of Pastoral Rule*, 161.

to bring creation into its intended *shalom*.[12] We preach this basic, dynamic gospel in Christ, through Christ, and with Christ in the unity of Holy Spirit, in accord with the beatific desires of a God who, as we know in Christ Jesus, accommodates Godself to humanity, coming to us incarnate in the ways we need in order that we might receive the invitation into the way of blessing that God has for all. This, of necessity, includes judgment of our current harmful ways, which requires our repentance. True repentance, though, ultimately includes belief (i.e., trust) in God's sovereign way as we turn from our old ways to point ourselves in God's direction—i.e., the Lord's purpose in creating and redeeming the world, which is symbolized as the eschatological vision of God's reign. Until God's reign comes in all its fullness, we can only experience it in part in fragmentary ways.

With our best discernments of divine intentionality for a particular people in a particular time and place, then, homiletic theologians design sermons that they present as an offering for God to use as God so pleases to continue the work of redemption and blessing in the world. These words are ours, yet with our *theological* offering in the Holy Spirit, we pray that through them the living Christ might draw near and call others to come participate in God's *basileia* way of life to the glory of God and the benefit of humanity and creation. This rendering of homiletic theology is done out of a particular theology of preaching that sees the purpose of preaching as being that of preaching the gospel of God, as Christ did, as the apostles did, and as a long line of other preachers down through time have. While the gospel often comes through Scripture, it cannot be reduced to Scripture,[13] which may be why the mainline church has continued to decline: we've been preaching discrete snippets of Scripture and/or its structured meanings, sometimes to the detriment of proclaiming the gospel.

Clear about the purpose of preaching as being the call to continue proclaiming the gospel, homiletic theology is a deliberate way of thinking theologically through the process of preparing to preach any given sermon in such a way that its words are open to the Word. Unlike the public nature of preaching, homiletic theology involves the mostly private struggle of preachers as they seek to discern the exact form the gospel needs to take for a particular sermon in accord with the overall aim of preaching. It involves the moments of sermon preparation whereby the preacher combs Scripture, engages in contemplation, analyzes the preaching situation in all

12. It is important to note that *basileia*, often translated as kingdom, actually denotes the reigning *activity* of God. The good news is that God is at work in the world to bring creation under God's dominion, which is characterized by *shalom*, harmonious right relationship where justice and love and peace and health and wholeness rule.

13. Farley, *Practicing Gospel*, 87.

its cultural and congregational complexities, receives insights, and thinks pastorally and prophetically about how to preach on any given Sunday. Sometimes even as he preaches, a pastor is engaging in homiletic theology as he changes a sermon on his feet in response to something happening in the preaching moment itself. Because of these on-the-spot decisions that are hopefully done with some theological wisdom, homiletic theology can't be fully finished until the sermon is over.

In short, then, homiletic theology is the theological reflection that occurs as one prepares a sermon. It is the reflection that occurs as preachers look at the world and the human situation, tracing the *basileia* movement of God through it all. We use the tools of Scripture and ecclesial practices through time to do this, much as a detective uses a magnifying glass, so that we can track what in the world the Lord is up to so that we can invite others to come and see for themselves (John 1:35–46). Discerning the Lord at work even now, homiletic theology results in a sermon that gives testimony as to what we have seen and heard,[14] reiterating God's proclamation that in Christ Jesus we have been set free from our bondage to sin. In publishing these glad tidings, we are inviting others to live as though this emancipation proclamation is indeed in effect even though there continue to be forces that try to thwart the divine dream.

HOMILETIC THEOLOGY AS WAY OF TRACING WAY[15]

Although a sermon and a work of theology look very different, in fact, the theological reflection that leads to the production of each work partakes of the same *theological* movement whereby (1) faith questions are raised in real-life situations; (2) they are submitted for analysis afforded by a more distanced reflection in order to make judgments regarding truth and what it is we are called to be and do in relation to this truth; (3) they are communicated to particular rhetorical audiences who hopefully (4) take the theological insights back into lived existence in faithful engagement with the world.[16] This also generally describes the theological method of Ed Farley, whose work informs my own thinking about homiletic theology.

14. Florence, *Preaching as Testimony*.

15. See Farley, *Ecclesial Reflection*. This section (with some alterations) previously appeared in my "Analgesic Jesus and the Power of God for Salvation."

16. This is a basic description of the hermeneutic circle, thus recognizing that all of theology makes interpretive judgments about God.

Of course, one might object: aren't you just applying the work of an academic theologian to the task of preaching, thereby rendering all said so far about the nature of theology and homiletic theology null and void? Ah, you clever readers! My response? I think of my work not as an application of a product like an analgesic cream,[17] but rather as more akin to fishing in the same stream of thought. After all, as David Tracy says in his explication of Longergan, theological method is not a set of rigid rules that we must follow but "a normative pattern of related and recurrent operations."[18] After considering various works on theological method,[19] I choose to follow Farley's phenomenological understanding of theological method for a few reasons, the primary one being that it is more in accord with the tasks, needs, and purposes of the preaching of the church and its proclamation of the gospel in concrete situations. It seeks to describe what decisions theologically discerning preachers make in preparing sermons, and it offers a touchstone that helps us see whether or not our words are in accord with God's Way. This method takes seriously that those to whom we preach are an admixture of both doubt and faith. Believing with Gadamer and other homileticians before me that a method needs to emerge out of the work itself,[20] Farley's method is critical, flexible, yet structured enough to provide a viable theological process for thinking through sermon preparation as it actually occurs. Partaking of *theologia's* way of theological reflection, sermon preparation can also occur with more depth of insight and earn the respect of academia's critique of preaching, thus improving the church's proclamation and bridging the gap between the church and the academy.

According to Farley, *theologia* is comprised of four basic movements that sometimes overlap with simultaneously occurring operations: (1) comparisons of faith's testimonies of our ecclesially shaped being-saved experiences to create a sketchy portrait of the One who is behind these experiences; (2) the emergence and coalescence of universals and their intentionalities; (3) judgment regarding the truth of the various items in play in any given situation in order to discern the degree to which they are in accord with faith's ultimate intentionality—*basileia*—which functions as critical norm; and (4) return to the lifeworld with theologically deliberate being, word, and deed. We heuristically refer to these moments as (1) portraiture; (2)

17. See Stricklen Eisenlohr, "Analgesic Jesus and the Power of God for Salvation."

18. Tracy, *The Achievement of Bernard Lonergan*, 235.

19. These include Bevans, *Models of Contextual Theology*; Hodgson, *Winds of the Spirit*; Kaufman, *An Essay on Theological Method*; Lindbeck, *The Nature of Doctrine*, Schreiter, *Constructing Local Theologies*; Tracy, *Blessed Rage for Order*.

20. See Gadamer, *Truth and Method*. Davis, *Design for Preaching*, is credited as the first homiletician to call for an organic method whereby form and content merge.

emergence of universals; (3) judgment; and (4) appropriation for gospel ends.

1. Portraiture

Theology begins by examining linguistic portraits of ecclesial faith—not just the language of Scripture, but also of ritual and the utterances of the communion of saints of all times and places. We also add places in the world through which we see the light of Christ shining through—in art, stories, the news, people's lives, history, etc. To be honest, as a Reformed theologian, I usually weight Scripture more heavily among all these words, for these have classically been proven to offer the clearest view of God's ways in the world.[21] We gather these fragments together to form an ever-changing mosaic pattern in a kind of kaleidoscopic swirl of images and understandings. Then we look into them in order to see what it is that moves them and enables us to see divinity shining through all their fragmentary expressions.

2. Universals' Emergence

As we compare these fragmented, fluid portraits of faith's testimonies, certain recurring patterns, or what Farley calls "ecclesial universals," emerge. With theologians of yore, we can see that God is creative, beatific, communal, holy, judging, redemptive, promoting of human flourishing in communities of justice and care. God is what ultimately is beyond the vicissitudes and failures of our lived existence. And God is seen most clearly shining through Jesus Christ's way of offering self to live in accord with God's sovereignty over all of life and through his way of insisting that social existence reflect God's intentions for creation—a way that he embodied in healing, forgiving, feeding, teaching, demanding justice, and conquering the powers of death with love. Indeed, Jesus embodied God's *basileia* way of life he preached in such a way that his way of being in the world in submission to God's rule continues to live as the Way into the *basileia* of God that is happening in part among us now as God works to redeem and heal and fully establish the divine justice of love. It is this Way of God that we preach, a Way that is learned, however imperfectly in this world of sin, through the words, symbols, and actions of the church that mediate that elusive Divine Presence that holds us in its relativizing grip.

21. For a pertinent discussion of a classic, see Tracy, *The Analogical Imagination.*

For academic theologians, these ecclesial universals resulted in the classic loci of the faith (such as Christology, eschatology, ecclesiology, pneumatology, etc.) that continue to exert influence on the theology that is done in academic institutions. Theological loci became knowledge about the nature of God, abstracted out of the quotidian world. They were originally conceived of as *loci communes*, or common places, where one could go to learn about the nature of God in the world. In the university setting, though, students are examined on what they can remember, so the commonplaces lost their connection with everyday life as students studied them as mere heuristic devises apart from their lived realities.

Theologia, though, seeks out God not only among the theologies of books. It also sets out to discover universal patterns in relation to God that emerge out of a specific context that includes awareness of having been shaped by the church, society, individual histories, and academic theological traditions. This is why it is usually done by those who have more experience with faith's traditions; their training allows them to be better God detectives as they know how to correlate all the gathered data. *Theologia* understood in this more ancient way is a method well suited to the needs of the preacher, for in each sermon preparation a preacher has to examine not only the doctrines of the church, but other places as well, including the current life of the ecclesial community, both local and universal, with its Scriptures, testimonies, histories, and practices; the cultures in which people live; the individual lives of those who come seeking a word from the Lord; the liturgy and its openness to the divine realm; others' reflections of life and faith; art; what is happening in the community; etc. Out of all the places where they catch glimpses of God in the portraiture moment of sermon preparation, preachers form their own kinds of universals in the form of "what keeps coming up" for their attention as they prepare to preach on any given day.

3. Judgment

Not everything that keeps asserting itself for our attention is of God, though. We must test the spirits as we prepare to preach. Therefore, the next moment in theological discernment, according to Farley, is judgment. Examining the intentionalities of faith's ecclesial universals ultimately points us in the same direction that Jesus' whole life tended toward—the sovereign beatific activity of God in the world, symbolized by the sovereign reigning of God (*basileia*/kingdom). This eschatological beatific vision is life as it was meant to be from its beginnings—a world without the ravages of sin; a world characterized by *shalom* and its holistic justice, peace, health, wholeness, harmony, and love; a world in which God reigns supreme. In short, it is a world centered around God, structured by God's Way. As the trajectory of all our stories of Emmanuel, the *basileia* of God is the referent of the gospel we preach in the midst of a sin-shaped world. Ecclesial faith affirms that the *basileia* of God is among us even now in part through Christ, for we experience its first fruits as appetizers of the feast of God's full reign coming. This *basileia* entelechy of Christian faith itself also provides us with a touchstone by which we measure not only the truth claims of religious language and practices, but also the very nature of reality itself. The degree to which something is in accord with the aims of God is the degree to which something is of God and good.

This critical norm of the divine *basileia* gives preachers seeking to encourage a particular congregation to follow the Way of Jesus Christ a way of judging between possible concrete options before us as we prepare to preach. We can test the nature of the powers operative in situations and texts to discern what of these powers is in accord with this horizon of divine intentionality toward which all of ecclesial existence points.[22] This involves a certain hermeneutic of suspicion whereby the corruptions of ideological power that are attendant with and perpetuated through the linguistic historicality of human existence are exposed and thus able to be resisted in accord with the normative qualities of God's sovereign activity. But judgment also involves a hermeneutic of trust whereby we look for future possibilities that are distinguished by ecclesial refection upon the gospel of God's sovereign activity. Similarly, this *basileia* norm enables us to discern what is true and good among all the things crying to be said in any given preaching event (i.e., Bible, gospel, church year meanings, the rhetorical occasion, the meanings of the rhetorical situation at any given moment in a church's history, the rhetorical expectations of parishioners, the co-opting desires of sociocultural ideological idolatries, denominational demands, hallmark, etc.). In order to test truth, then, judgment is done in accord with God's *basileia* norm to discern what is of God in the midst of sin's corruptions.

4. Gospel Appropriation

After soaring into the stratosphere of rigorous thinking, theology turns toward home to splash down into the situation out of which it arose in order to best address and embody what needs to be said and done in accord with the aims of God. For preaching, this means actually structuring a sermon.

22. Farley, *Practicing Gospel*, 29–43.

Because the nature of all our God talk is inherently metaphoric and rhetorical, preaching will be a form of poetic rhetorical theology[23] structured with a communication strategy required for public discourse in that culture so that people can hear the gospel and come to know the Holy One. Exactly how each sermon proceeds, though, should be determined by the nature of the gospel itself so that the Word might become incarnate in any given preaching event.

SO WHAT DOES HOMILETIC THEOLOGY LOOK LIKE IN ACTUAL PRACTICE?

This sounds more complicated and regimented than it is in actuality. An example can illustrate as we consider a preacher examining Scripture and its language, allusions, contexts, theologies, and imagery; world history and current events; church life; theology; people's lives (past and present); popular culture; and people's sinful resistance to the gospel.

Background

Homiletic theology works within and out of a theology of preaching that understands the purpose of preaching as an essential part of the church's mission to proclaim the gospel. Preaching seeks to lead a people to be more open to the work of God for blessing and redemption in the world. Therefore, preachers work like sherpas or wagon train leaders encouraging and guiding a varied group of people who come from different places with different ways of navigating the world who are nonetheless united in wanting to go to a mysterious place of promise. A preacher leads people in ministry from where they currently are (Point A) toward the omega point of God's reign.[24] The best each sermon can do on this journey is lead people one step deeper into kingdom territory, which is to say more open to the sovereign activity of God in the world in patterns of blessing, redemption, and shalom. The territorial analogy breaks down because of the kingdom symbol's historical collusion with colonialism, but the journey motif is nonetheless helpful in enabling preachers to understand the limited effects of any given sermon that can only move people from Point A (where they are) to Point B (a little less attached to sin and more inclined toward the Way of Christ). The *basileia* omega point of all our preaching gives us what the whole of the

23. See Buttrick, *Homiletic*.

24. See Teilhard de Chardin, *The Future of Man*, 115–16.

ministry of the church aims toward, knowing that on our own power we will never get there but nonetheless trusting that our Lord is indeed coming again with the fullness of the divine reign, as promised. In that hope, we preach.

Starting Place.

Pastor Pauline is preparing to preach a Christmas Eve sermon at a Presbyterian Church (U.S.A.) in a transitional neighborhood where immigrants from Sudan and Mexico have recently settled. Folks from the neighborhood have recently joined other longtime members who now mostly drive in from the suburbs. Wanting to serve the community in which they live, the church has decided to do something different this year. Instead of two services, they will have one big celebration that will include more traditional Mexican and Sudanese festivities. A *los posadas* is scheduled to begin at 6 p.m. through the neighborhood, ending at the church with the entourage finally welcomed into a traditional Sudanese feast. Afterwards, a piñata will send children scrambling for candy before Santa will pass out sheet sets to each household (a Sudanese tradition) and toys to the children. Drums will then lead all up into the poinsettia-filled sanctuary for a candlelight Christmas Eve service. Some of the older members are grumbling about not being able to do family celebrations at home. Others are grumbling that they want the beautiful silence of an 11 p.m. service with the rowdy children going to an earlier service. Some of the grumbling has to do with power issues and the old guard having to relinquish their control of the church to younger, different generations. It's quite the rhetorical situation. And Pastor Pauline is tired, questioning her call to that grumbling congregation.

Portraiture

After all these festivities, Pastor Pauline will be preaching in the midst of a late liturgical service celebrating the incarnation. New banners will be hanging in the sanctuary. Their design makes it clear that all of creation is coming to gather around the Christ child. The sanctuary will be decorated with a plethora of candles celebrating the light of the world that no darkness can overcome. Stellar music will celebrate Emmanuel. Luke's nativity story and John 1 will be read, and holy communion will be served. They will sing "Silent Night" and pass the light of Christ from candle to candle until the darkness becomes light.

Pauline knows that the assembling of the body of Christ happens as the people of God gather for worship in a ritually charged space open to divine dimensions of reality. She contemplates standing with the eternal communion of saints praising the Lord. She decides to wear her white robe with the silvery white stole that she got on eBay from the estate of a priest's family, imagining what that priest would have preached to her congregation. Then she imagines what the Christ child himself would have preached from the womb, if he could have, when Mary and Joseph were anxious about finding a birthing place. She contemplates whether the whole story is more like Brueghel's *The Fall of Icarus,* with divine things happening right in front of everyone while they went about their lives too busy to notice;[25] that would be like human beings. She meditates upon the profound mystery of the incarnation and puzzles yet again over Christ's nature as fully human and fully divine as she visits the nursing home and hospitals. In the middle of the week, she laughs when she hears one of the church's preschool teachers comment that the place is a zoo during the children's Christmas program in which the preschoolers are dressed as animals who have come to see the baby Jesus. In their version, giraffes, zebras, and elephants appear! And in the audience, Pastor Pauline notes all the different peoples from across the globe who are gathered to support their children during that program. People from warring countries unite around their children.

Last week she had sequestered herself to assiduously study the Scriptures she will be preaching and noted the literal meanings of the text. She learned about *kataluma* in the homes of the day and that shepherds were rather shady characters at that time. She remembered that there is no record of a census that early in other historical texts and wonders if this is a metaphor for God taking account of humanity and providing a way for all to be set straight, as prophesied previously. She has been thinking about the theological implications of each part of the Scriptures and their contemporary analogies as she heard news about yet another Herod killing off his own people in Africa in order to consolidate power. Knowing her congregation well, she realizes where they will have trouble believing what the text is saying and thinks about responses to their doubts. She has continued to mull over the images of the text. As she sees the clerk in the grocery store treat an elderly Hispanic man rudely before graciously waiting on her, a young white woman, she wonders if the biblical phrase was emphasizing that there was no room for *them* in the inn. She remembers giving birth. In short, she has been pondering all these things in her heart about what the texts have to say to us as individuals and as a society.

25. Brueghel, *Landscape with the Fall of Icarus.*

In addition to all of the meanings and symbols at play in the larger liturgical worship service and Scripture, Pastor Pauline considers what's been happening in the community—the crime stalking the neighborhood, the ethnic tensions, children raising themselves with parents having to work two and sometimes three minimum-wage jobs just to provide the family food and shelter, the new community center program on parenting. This leads to her pastoral concern for Rita, who's been trying to leave her abusive family behind by earning a scholarship to college only to find herself pregnant. She wonders what's happening with those she doesn't see but a couple times a year. She thinks about the children who will be hopped up on sugar and dancing on their weary parents' last good nerves. She hopes George will be okay this first Christmas without his beloved wife of forty-three years, whom Pastor Pauline buried last month.

Pastor Pauline notes all of these musings and starts clumping like things together. Not all of these things that she is examining are overtly biblical, but she intuits their relationship and articulates the connections, working like an impressionist painter laying down bits of paint, building up individual brush strokes until some things start becoming clear.

Universals

When she does, she sees that the various characters in Luke's narrative (along with the magi in Matthew's) are like the different animals in the world, who, with the whole planet, are coming to worship the Christ. However, there are those who try to thwart the power of love, like Herod or those who have no room for *them*. But the Christ child is born. Darkness cannot overcome light. Out of all the different characters in the story, she wonders where we place ourselves in the messiness of life. With the messengers of God by spreading the joy of the good news that Christ comes to all? With the shepherds who come to Christ to worship despite our feeling that we don't belong in the presence of the holy? With Joseph who in our nativity sets always seems to be making room for others to come to Christ while he stands watchful in the background? With innkeepers who side with the economically and politically powerful and shut the door against those we deem a threat to our place in the world?

Judgment with the touchstone of the gospel.

What emerges in looking at what keeps coming to her attention out of all the thinking done earlier is a protosermon or two (or four). Indeed, other sermons could also arise out of the portraiture admixture. The question now is whether or not these are in line with the gospel of what God is longing to say to the world through her words here and now. As Pastor Pauline contemplates her sermon notes, she sees that what she has so far is in line with God's call to live in accord with the divine reign. It is honest about God's rule demanding our allegiance and encountering our resistance that is judged, not to condemn ultimately, but to bless. She reconsiders whether or not she should include her comment that the rowdiness of their celebrations tonight actually fits better with the way God works in the world than do the hushed tones of the silvery deep silence of midnight candlelight services. Is that true, or does she just want to lambast those who are getting on her last good nerves with all their grumbling? When she examines this further, she realizes that she, too, will miss the quiet beauty of that later service, but she knows that her initial conclusion is correct. God seems to work in the midst of this zoo of humanity, and our attempts to beautify the muck of redemption can be attempts to weave an aesthetically pleasing false security blanket that allows us the comfort of our illusions that *we* are in control, not the wild God of the jungle. That might preach, she thinks.

Rhetorically shaping a sermon.

Out of all this, Pastor Pauline knows that with everything going on that night, she needs to limit the sermon to ten to twelve minutes. From communication theory and her own experience, she knows that it will take two to three minutes for hearers to be able to grasp each main concept of her sermon, and that there's no point in preaching if the sermon can't be taken in by its hearers. Knowing that the purpose of a sermon is to move people one step deeper into God's kingdom territory on this journey they're all on toward the New Jerusalem, she starts with where they are by naming the magic and discomfort of trying to get all these different cultures to cohere on this sacred night, admitting that it's been a little "zoo-ey" tonight. Then she'll tell the story of the preschool pageant, morphing into the truth that the characters in the nativity story gathering around the baby Jesus were like animals in a zoo that would have had trouble getting along in the wild. After picturing the various groups like animals on the savannah, she'll note that in the background ethnic and political forces are stalking like a hungry lion, similar to what we see in Sudan or even the grocery store of our own neighborhoods today. Then she will ask where we are in this scene and where we want to be, noting that there may be a part of us that so prefers the silent windswept hills among the pretty sheep with quiet angelic music that we don't want to leave the glowing firelight of the stars to join the smelly animals at the manger. But when we hear the news of Emmanuel, the question becomes how we'll respond. Will we ignore it and go about our business as usual? Perhaps we'll align ourselves with those forces in the world who don't want God's new life because we want to be the Lord of our lives. Or will we choose to be with the giraffes and elephants and, yes, skunks worshiping the new thing that God is doing in the most unlikely of ways?

The sermon strategy is a raw sermon outline with flaws, but, like the gospel itself, it requires orientation toward Christ as Lord of all of creation, acknowledging where we are while urging us to lay aside sin's false barriers to go deeper into God's sovereignty. With further prayer that her gifts be inspired by and accepted in the Holy Spirit, Pastor Pauline starts composing the sermon in earnest.

IMPLICATIONS FOR THE DEVELOPMENT OF HOMILETICAL THEOLOGY

What's at stake in thinking through the issues of theological method with regard to preaching is truth and God's revelation to the world through preaching. The truth of God's disclosure as living Presence to the world is what actually attracts disciples—not our institutional church programs, glitzy worship services, or nice pastors. People come to church seeking a living word from the living Lord, not a commentary on life from another Garrison Keillor or the sales pitch of a snake oil salesman. People come seeking God's *alétheia*—truth, the reality that lures us to follow its ways of resurrection with joy even in the midst of crucifixions. Truth is not something we fling at people from the pulpit, but a Presence disclosed in mysterious ways beyond our control through even the likes of us sinful human critters, and it is the church's job to be devoted to watching for our Lord's coming. We are also to test to spirits to determine what of the new life we are experiencing together is of God or our own idolatrous ideological delusions. Before this Truth-Presence all our human measures of truth fall short. God's Way doesn't always make sense; it is incoherent by rationalistic standards. Like Jesus, God's truth is sometimes inappropriate by human social standards. And the truth of the cross bears pragmatic problems. But underneath all our judgments regarding the characteristics of truth and the norms we determine it by (i.e., appropriateness, coherence, pragmatism), there is a deeper Truth that preaching bears witness to, a Presence[26] that all words ultimately fail

26. See Farley, "Sacred Rhetoric," in *Practicing Gospel,* where he notes, "What the Gospel is takes on specific content in specific situations but no specific content contains

to do justice, a Presence that suddenly lights up our fragmented sermons' testimonies so that the gift of God's grace overtakes us with the glory of redemption. It is a Presence beyond preachers' manipulations or attempts to methodologically lasso and harness for our own ends, but one that is more likely to come to us as we seek it though the spiritual discipline of diligent, faithful sermon preparation.

This Presence is the power of God that we homileticians know we cannot fully account for even as we do our best to encourage our students to preach coherent, appropriate sermons that work. Defining homiletic theology as theological method gives preachers a way of *theologically* pursuing the elusive truth of this Presence that flashes forth with redemptive glimmers of revelation in human history, so that our meager words of testimony, offered to God for divine use, might, God willing, be helpful in carrying out divine purposes. If all we do as homileticians is teach preachers how to shape language without robustly attending to homiletic theological discernment, then the preaching of the church may work as an infomercial that sells Jesus like some kind of magic elixir, but it is not likely that it will be God's power for salvation.

For all its specificity of method, homiletic theology acknowledges the mystery of the Spirit's inspiration as the preacher thinks theologically through the task of preparing any given sermon. What we are doing is unfinished, ad hoc theology along the Way. Homiletic theology defined as method gives preachers a process to follow in sermon preparation that helps them think more deeply about their important task of preaching and explore not only Scripture, but also liturgy, what's going on in the church, individuals' lives, the community, society, history, and cultural artifacts, in order to discern what in the world the Lord seems to be up to here and now and invite people to participate in God's mending of the broken world, which includes our own individual lives. This is particularly important in an era where the church is changing from an institutional Christendom model to a more missional one where preaching needs to issue God's invitation to become part of the divine mission of reclaiming and blessing the world. Preachers can't do this just by preaching the Bible and applying it to our lives today. They need to do the deeper work of seeing where God is active in the world in ways that are like those of old, looking through Scripture into the *basileia* reality of God's activity in the world.

This deeper work of theological discernment can result in sermons that are more appealing to those who disdain a televangelistic paradigm for preaching a gospel that is so pat that it's easily parodied. Similarly, teaching

the totality of the world of the Gospel" (87).

this method that takes the task of doing theology seriously in the midst of ministry can result in an improved relationship between the preaching of the church and academic theology. This, in turn, can help bridge the gap between the church and the academy. This is important because if preaching is denigrated within the academy, we are dooming the preaching of the church to a catch-as-catch-can education that is often not theologically rigorous, perpetuating the gulf that exists between the church and the academy. It is important that preaching continue to be taught in theological education, and it needs to be taught with the critical rigor of the academy that honors it as an important ecclesial activity. As such, homiletic theology can help clarify homiletic theory that demonstrates what a complicated theological activity preaching actually is.

Moreover, homiletic theology teaches students to value what they learn in theological education so that they come to understand that all of ministry is *theologia*. If students leave seminary or divinity school thinking that theology is a finished body of knowledge that they can use as a tool for ministry, problems ensue. The pragmatism of the American culture tells us that only tools that are useful should be used. If they're not, they can be easily tossed aside. What was learned in theological education can be seen as useless in light of the latest, more accessible self-help/business management tools, leading pastors to chuck not only theology, but serious biblical exegesis, translation, and history as well. Ministry, including preaching, thereby easily becomes co-opted by the larger culture, reduced to just another human activity among others, with God being a nice, but usually suspect, authority or proof in a rhetorical argument that is not that convincing of anything. Indeed, in this scenario, a sermon is to be endured as a traditional activity for the sake of tradition, but no one really expects the living Lord to show up.

Homiletic theology that understands its tasks as emerging out of a theology of preaching that sees God as alive and well and still inviting us through the preaching of the church into divine communion can keep its center in the living reality of the living Lord. Probing reality for the divine, it can offer our best human words as a place for the Holy One to be heard without any illusions that we are God. And in the Holy Spirit, Christ just may speak into the depths of human experience to do the convincing that is beyond the capability of any rhetorical technique. Preachers can understand their preaching as part of God's *basileia* activity that they can only experience as fragmentary and partial, like the Grand Canyon's beauty that was slowly carved out by little bits of water over time. Each sermon can thus matter while also being relativized, keeping us appropriately apprised of the homiletic situation. Preachers are not saviors, as many seminary students secretly suspect; they are only one in a long line of colaborers in the gospel.

Homiletic theology is thus something we need to do as preachers, not homileticians. Homileticians can teach homiletic theology as the process of sermon preparation that thinks theologically through the mystery of shaping a sermon for a particular moment in history. But homiletic theology cannot just be the theological analysis of our preaching after the fact, as worthy as that exercise is.[27] Similarly, it can't be considering what type of academic theology it falls under.[28] Nor can it be one category among others that we consider alongside language, ecclesial symbols, Scripture, and culture.[29] Both preaching and homiletic theology can be subject to theological analysis and should be, but academic theology is not the final arbiter of a sermon's truth. Whether or not its *theo-logia* becomes God's word of transformative power is what ultimately determines a sermon's truth, so *theologia* and its connection with God's word has to be the primary category under which all aspects of the sermon and its preparation occur. This is also true of the discipline of homiletics and homiletic theory in service to the preaching of the church, and careful distinctions need to be made in order to negotiate the institutional and societal changes that are occurring. A history of preaching and theology shows that homiletics has had a tendency to pick up the latest innovations in rhetoric, communications, culture, biblical studies, and/or theology and run with them instead of thinking theologically about the whole of our field, including the place of the discipline and how preaching is taught in academia. What homiletic theology gives us is a way to integrate the complexities of preaching in such a way that our best thoughts and intuitions about the One who reveals out of protective concealment, spoken by broken people in fragile, beautiful, yet corrupt words, can nonetheless become God's word for us and for our salvation in whatever incarnate circumstances we live, which, at the end of it all, is nothing short of a divine miracle.

27. Cooper and McClure, *Claiming Theology in the Pulpit.*

28. See, for example, Hall, *The Future Shape of Preaching,* and Allen, *Thinking Theologically.*

29. McClure, *The Four Codes of Preaching.*

Bibliography

Alban Institute. Listening to Listeners to Sermons Project. http://www.alban.org/conversation.aspx?id=2110.

Allen, O. Wesley. *The Homiletic of All Believers: A Conversational Approach to Proclamation and Preaching.* Louisville: Westminster John Knox, 2005.

Allen, Ronald J. *Preaching and the Other: Studies of Postmodern Insights.* St. Louis: Chalice, 2009.

———. *Preaching Is Believing: The Sermon as Theological Reflection.* Louisville: Westminster John Knox, 2002.

———. *Thinking Theologically: The Preacher as Theologian.* Elements of Preaching. Minneapolis: Fortress, 2008.

Allen, Ronald J., John S. McClure, and O. Wesley Allen. *Under the Oak Tree: The Church as Community of Conversation in a Conflicted and Pluralistic World.* Eugene, OR: Cascade, 2013.

Andrews, Dale. "Response." In *The Renewed Homiletic*, edited by W. Allen, 96–99. Minneapolis: Fortress, 2010.

Augustine, Saint. *On Christian Doctrine.* The Library of Liberal Arts. New York: Liberal Arts, 1958.

———. "Teaching Christianity: De Doctrina Christiana." Translated by Edmund Hill. *The Works of Saint Augustine: A Translation for the 21st Century*, part 1, vol. 11. New York: New City, 1996.

Barth, Karl. *Homiletics.* Louisville: Westminster John Knox, 1991.

———. *The Word of God and the Word of Man.* Harper Torchbooks. New York: Harper, 1957.

Barthes, Roland, and Honoré de Balzac. *S/Z.* New York: Hill and Wang, 1974.

Bartow, Charles. "Homiletical (Theological) Criticism." In *The New Interpreter's Handbook of Preaching*, edited by P. Wilson, 154–57. Nashville: Abingdon, 2008.

———. *The Preaching Moment: A Guide to Sermon Delivery.* Abingdon Preacher's Library. Nashville: Abingdon, 1980.

Bayer, Oswald. *Living by Faith: Justification and Sanctification.* Lutheran Quarterly Books. Grand Rapids: Eerdmans, 2003.

Bayer, Oswald, Jeffrey G. Silcock, and Mark C. Mattes. *Theology the Lutheran Way.* Lutheran Quarterly Books. Grand Rapids: Eerdmans, 2007.

Behr, John. "The Trinitarian Being of the Church." *St. Vladimir's Theological Quarterly* 48, no. 1 (2004) 67–88.

Bibliography

Beker, J. Christiaan. *Paul the Apostle: The Triumph of God in Life and Thought.* Philadelphia: Fortress, 1980.

Bellah, Robert N. *Beyond Belief: Essays on Religion in a Post-Traditionalist World.* Berkeley, CA: University of California Press, 1991.

Benjamin, Walter. "Allegory and *Trauerspiel*." In *The Origin of German Tragic Drama,* 159–232. London: Verso Books, 2003.

———. *The Origin of German Tragic Drama.* London: NLB, 1977.

———. "The Task of the Translator." In *Theories of Translation: An Anthology of Essays from Dryden to Derrida,* edited by John Biguenet and Ranier Shulte, 71–82. Chicago: University of Chicago Press, 1992.

Bethge, Eberhard. *Dietrich Bonhoeffer: A Biography.* Minneapolis: Fortress, 2000.

———. *Dietrich Bonhoeffer: Theologian, Christian, Contemporary.* London: Collins, 1970.

Bevans, Stephen B. *Models of Contextual Theology.* Rev. and expanded ed. Faith and Cultures Series. Maryknoll, NY: Orbis, 2002.

Blanchot, Maurice. *The Writing of the Disaster.* Translated by Ann Smock. Lincoln, NE: University of Nebraska Press, 1995.

Boff, Leonardo, and Clodovis Boff. *Introducing Liberation Theology.* Maryknoll, NY: Orbis, 1987.

Bond, L. Susan. *Contemporary African American Preaching: Diversity in Theory and Style.* St. Louis: Chalice, 2003.

———. *Trouble with Jesus: Women, Christology, and Preaching.* St. Louis: Chalice, 1999.

Bonhoeffer, Dietrich. "Ambassadors for Christ." In *The Collected Sermons of Dietrich Bonhoeffer,* edited by Isabel Best, 87–94. Minneapolis: Fortress, 2012.

———. *Letters and Papers from Prison.* Edited by Christian Gremmels, Eberhard Bethge, Renate Bethge, Ilse Tödt and John W. De Gruchy. Dietrich Bonhoeffer Works, vol. 8. Minneapolis: Fortress, 2010.

———. *Sanctorum Communio: A Theological Study of the Sociology of the Church.* Edited by Clifford J. Green; translated by Reinhard Krauss and Nancy Lukens. Dietrich Bonhoeffer Works, vol. 1. Minneapolis: Fortress, 1998.

———. *The Young Bonhoeffer: 1918–1927.* Dietrich Bonhoeffer Works, vol. 9. Minneapolis: Fortress, 2003.

Brown, Sally A. *Cross Talk: Preaching Redemption Here and Now.* Louisville: Westminster John Knox, 2008.

Browning, Don S. *A Fundamental Practical Theology: Descriptive and Strategic Proposals.* Minneapolis: Fortress, 1991.

Brueggemann, Walter. *Israel's Praise: Doxology against Idolatry and Ideology.* Minneapolis: Fortress, 1988.

Brueghel, Pieter. *Landscape with the Fall of Icarus.* Royal Museums of Fine Arts, Brussels, Belgium, 1558.

Brumbach, Rabbi Joshua. "Learning as Worship." Yinon Blog. http://www.messianicjudaism.me/yinon/2013/02/18/learning-as-worship/.

Buttrick, David. "Foreword." In *Homiletics,* by Karl Barth, 7–11. Louisville: Westminster John Knox, 1991.

———. *Homiletic: Moves and Structures.* Philadelphia: Fortress, 1987.

———. *Preaching Jesus Christ: An Exercise in Homiletic Theology.* Fortress Resources for Preaching. Philadelphia: Fortress, 1988.

———. *Speaking Jesus.* Louisville: Westminster John Knox, 2002.

Campbell, Charles L. *Preaching Jesus: The New Directions for Homiletics in Hans Frei's Postliberal Theology.* Eugene, OR: Wipf and Stock, 2006.

Carter, Michael. "Stasis and Kairos: Principles of Social Construction in Classical Rhetoric." *Rhetoric Review* 7, no. 1 (1998) 97–112.

Cessario, Romanus. *The Moral Virtues and Theological Ethics.* Notre Dame, IN: University of Notre Dame Press, 1991.

Chan, Simon. *Liturgical Theology: The Church as Worshiping Community.* Downers Grove, IL: IVP Academic, 2006.

Chapell, Bryan. *Christ-Centered Worship: Letting the Gospel Shape Our Practice.* Grand Rapids: Baker Academic, 2009.

Cheng, Patrick S. *Radical Love: An Introduction to Queer Theology.* New York: Seabury, 2011.

Christopherson, D. Foy. *A Place of Encounter: Renewing Worship Spaces.* Worship Matters. Minneapolis: Augsburg Fortress, 2004.

Clayborn, Patrick. "A Homiletic of Spirituality: An Analysis of Howard Thurman's Theory and Praxis of Preaching." PhD diss., Drew University, 2009.

Collins, Kenneth J. *A Faithful Witness: John Wesley's Homiletical Theology.* Wilmore, KY: Wesley Heritage Press, 1993.

Congar, Yves. *A History of Theology.* Garden City, NY: Doubleday, 1968.

———. *I Believe in the Holy Spirit.* 3 vols. New York: Seabury, 1983.

Cooper, Burton Z., and John S. McClure. *Claiming Theology in the Pulpit.* Louisville: Westminster John Knox, 2003.

Cox, Harvey Gallagher. *The Future of Faith.* New York: HarperOne, 2009.

Craddock, Fred. *As One Without Authority.* 4th ed. St. Louis: Chalice, 2001.

Crichton, J. D. *Understanding the Mass.* New York: Continuum, 1992.

Crowe, Frederick E. *Theology of the Christian Word: A Study in History.* New York: Paulist, 1978.

Davis, Henry Grady. *Design for Preaching.* Philadelphia: Muhlenberg, 1958.

Deeg, Alexander. "Disruption, Initiation, Staging: The Theological Challenge of Christian Preaching." *Homiletic* 38, no. 1 (2013) 3–17.

DeJonge, Michael P. *Bonhoeffer's Theological Formation: Berlin, Barth, and Protestant Theology.* Oxford: Oxford University Press, 2012.

Denecke, Axel. *Gotteswort als Menschenwort. Karl Barths Predigtpraxis.* Hannover: Lutherisches Verlagshaus, 1989.

Dix, Gregory. *The Shape of the Liturgy.* New ed. New York: Continuum, 2005.

Dorrien, Gary J. *The Barthian Revolt in Modern Theology: Theology without Weapons.* Louisville: Westminster John Knox, 2000.

Ebeling, Gerhard. *Word and Faith.* Philadelphia: Fortress, 1963.

Edwards, David M. *Worship Three Sixty-Five: The Power of a Worshiping Life.* Nashville: Broadman & Holman, 2006.

Eichorn, Christian David. "Ecclesial Preaching: The Homiletical Theology of Vatican II and Its Influence Upon Protestant Homiletics of the Twentieth Century." PhD diss., Drew University, 2001.

Eslinger, Richard L. *A New Hearing: Living Options in Homiletic Methods.* Nashville: Abingdon, 1987.

Fagerberg, David W. *Theologia Prima: What Is Liturgical Theology?* 2nd ed. Chicago: Liturgy Training Publications, 2003.

Farley, Edward. *Divine Empathy: A Theology of God.* Minneapolis: Fortress, 1996.

———. *Ecclesial Reflection: An Anatomy of Theological Method*. Philadelphia: Fortress, 1982.

———. *The Fragility of Knowledge: Theological Education in the Church and the University*. Philadelphia: Fortress, 1988.

———. *Practicing Gospel: Unconventional Thoughts on the Church's Ministry*. Louisville: Westminster John Knox, 2003.

———. "Preaching the Bible and Preaching the Gospel." *Theology Today* 51, no. 1 (1994) 90–104.

———. *Theologia: The Fragmentation and Unity of Theological Education*. Philadelphia: Fortress, 1983.

———. "Theology and Practice Outside the Clerical Paradigm." In *Practical Theology: The Emerging Field in Theology, Church, and World*, edited by Don S. Browning, 21–41. San Francisco: Harper & Row, 1988.

———. "Toward a New Paradigm for Preaching." In *Practicing Gospel: Unconventional Thoughts on the Church's Ministry*, 83–92. Louisville: Westminster John Knox, 2003.

Florence, Anna Carter. *Preaching as Testimony*. Louisville: Westminster John Knox, 2007.

Forbes, James. *The Holy Spirit and Preaching*. Nashville: Abingdon, 1989.

Frei, Hans W. *The Eclipse of Biblical Narrative: A Study in Eighteenth and Nineteenth Century Hermeneutics*. New Haven: Yale University Press, 1974.

Fulkerson, Mary McClintock. *Places of Redemption: Theology for a Worldly Church*. Oxford: Oxford University Press, 2007.

Furr, Gary, and Milburn Price. *The Dialogue of Worship: Creating Space for Revelation and Response*. Faithgrowth. Macon, GA: Smyth & Helwys, 1998.

Fynsk, Christopher. *Language and Relation: . . . That There Is Language*. Stanford, CA: Stanford University Press, 1996.

Gaarden, Marianne, and Marlene Ringgaard Lorensen. "Listeners as Authors in Preaching: Empirical and Theoretical Perspectives." *Homiletic* 38, no. 1 (2013) 28–45.

Gadamer, Hans-Georg. *Truth and Method*. 2nd ed. New York: Crossroad, 1989.

Garrod, Simon. "Referential Processing in Monologue and Dialogue with and without Access to Real-World Referents." In *The Processing and Acquisition of Reference*, edited by Edward Gibson and Neal J. Pearlmuter, 273–96. Boston: MIT Press, 2011.

Gerrish, B. A. *The Old Protestantism and the New: Essays on the Reformation Heritage*. Chicago: University of Chicago Press, 1982.

Green, Clifford. "Editor's Introduction." In *Sanctorum Communio*, by Dietrich Bonhoeffer, 1–20. Minneapolis: Fortress, 1998.

———. "Human Sociality and Christian Community." In *The Cambridge Companion to Bonhoeffer*, edited by John W. De Gruchy, 113–23. Cambridge: Cambridge University Press, 1999.

Greer, Rowan A. *Broken Lights and Mended Lives: Theology and Common Life in the Early Church*. University Park, PA: Pennsylvania State University Press, 1986.

Gregory, Brad S. *The Unintended Reformation: How a Religious Revolution Secularized Society*. Cambridge, MA: Belknap Press of Harvard University Press, 2012.

Gregory. *The Book of Pastoral Rule*. Popular Patristics. Crestwood, NY: St. Vladimir's Seminary Press, 2007.

Grice, H. P. "Logic and Conversation." In *Syntax and Semantics, vol. 3: Speech Acts*, edited by P. Cole and J. L. Morgan, 41–58. New York: Academic, 1975.

Griffiths, Paul J. *Lying: An Augustinian Theology of Duplicity*. Grand Rapids: Brazos, 2004.

Grossberg, Lawrence. *Cultural Studies in the Future Tense*. Durham, NC: Duke University Press, 2010.

Habermas, Jürgen. *Communication and the Evolution of Society*. Translated by Thomas McCarthy. Boston: Beacon, 1979.

Hall, Thor. *The Future Shape of Preaching*. Philadelphia: Fortress, 1971.

Hancock, Angela Dienhart. *Karl Barth's Emergency Homiletic, 1932–1933: A Summons to Prophetic Witness at the Dawn of the Third Reich*. Grand Rapids: Eerdmans, 2013.

Hedahl, Susan. "All the King's Men: Constructing Homiletical Meaning." In *Preaching as a Theological Task: World, Gospel, Scripture*, edited by Thomas G. Long and Edward Farley, 82–90. Louisville: Westminster John Knox, 1996.

Hodgson, Peter. *Winds of the Spirit: A Constructive Christian Theology*. Louisville: Westminster John Knox, 1994.

Holloway, Charles Stewart. "The Homiletical Theology of Jonathan Edwards, Gilbert Tennent, and Samuel Davies." PhD diss., Southwestern Baptist Theological Seminary, 2008.

Hopkins, Dwight N. *Introducing Black Theology of Liberation*. Maryknoll, NY: Orbis, 1999.

Howard, Thomas Albert. *Protestant Theology and the Making of the Modern German University*. Oxford: Oxford University Press, 2006.

Hughes, Graham. *Worship as Meaning: A Liturgical Theology for Late Modernity* Cambridge Studies in Christian Doctrine. Cambridge: Cambridge University Press, 2003.

Hughes, Robert G., and Robert Kysar. *Preaching Doctrine for the Twenty-First Century*. Fortress Resources for Preaching. Minneapolis: Fortress, 1997.

Hurston, Zora Neale. *The Sanctified Church*. Berkeley, CA: Turtle Island, 1983.

Hymes, Dell. "Competence and Performance in Linguistic Theory." In *Language Acquisition: Models and Method*, edited by R. Huxley and E. Ingram, 3–26. New York: Academic Press, 1971.

Jacobsen, David Schnasa. "Preaching as the Unfinished Task of Theology: Grief, Trauma, and Early Christian Texts in Homiletical Interpretation." *Theology Today* 70, no. 4 (2014) 407–16.

———. "The Unfinished Task of Homiletical Theology: A Practical-Constructive Vision." In *Homiletical Theology: Preaching as Doing Theology*, edited by David Schnasa Jacobsen, 23–38. Eugene, OR: Cascade, 2015.

———. "What Is Homiletical Theology?: An Invitation to Constructive Theological Dialogue in North American Homiletics." *The Papers of the Annual Meeting of the Academy of Homiletics*, 347–59. Academy of Homiletics. Louisville, 2013.

Jacobsen, David Schnasa, and Robert Allen Kelly. *Kairos Preaching: Speaking Gospel to the Situation*. Minneapolis: Fortress, 2009.

Jacobsen, David Schnasa, and Günter Wasserberg. *Preaching Luke-Acts*. Nashville: Abingdon, 2001.

Jenson, Robert W. "Luther's Contemporary Theological Significance." In *The Cambridge Companion to Martin Luther*, edited by Donald K. McKim, 272–88. Cambridge: Cambridge University Press, 2003.

Johns, Cheryl. "Preaching Pentecost to the 'Nones.'" *Journal for Preachers* 36, no. 4 (2013) 3–10.

Jones, Serene, Paul Lakeland, and Workgroup on Constructive Christian Theology. *Constructive Theology: A Contemporary Approach to Classical Themes with CD-ROM*. Minneapolis: Fortress, 2005.

Jordan, Mark D. *Rewritten Theology: Aquinas after His Readers'*. Challenges in Contemporary Theology. Malden, MA: Blackwell, 2006.

Kaufman, Gordon D. *An Essay on Theological Method: Reflection and Theory in the Study of Religion*. 3rd ed. Atlanta: Scholars Press, 1995.

Kearney, Richard. *The God Who May Be: A Hermeneutics of Religion*. Indiana Series in the Philosophy of Religion. Bloomington, IN: Indiana University Press, 2001.

Kinnaman, David, and Gabe Lyons. *Unchristian: What a New Generation Really Thinks About Christianity—and Why It Matters*. Grand Rapids: Baker, 2007.

Kinneavy, James L., and Catherine R. Eskin. "*Kairos* in Aristotle's Rhetoric. *Written Communication* 11:1 (January 1994), 131–42.

Kruschwitz, Robert B., and Robert Campbell Roberts. *The Virtues: Contemporary Essays on Moral Character*. Belmont, CA: Wadsworth, 1987.

Lathrop, Gordon. *Holy Things: A Liturgical Theology*. Minneapolis: Fortress, 1993.

Lazareth, William Henry. *Christians in Society: Luther, the Bible, and Social Ethics*. Minneapolis: Fortress, 2001.

Legaspi, Michael C. *The Death of Scripture and the Rise of Biblical Studies*. Oxford Studies in Historical Theology. Oxford: Oxford University Press, 2010.

Levison, John R. *Filled with the Spirit*. Grand Rapids: Eerdmans, 2009.

Lindbeck, George A. *The Nature of Doctrine: Religion and Theology in a Postliberal Age*. Philadelphia: Westminster, 1984.

Lischer, Richard. "Preface." In *Faith and Freedom: An Invitation to the Writings of Martin Luther*, edited by John F. and Susan B. Varenne Thornton, xiii–xxviii. New York: Vintage Books, 2002.

Long, Thomas G. *The Witness of Preaching*. 2nd ed. Louisville: Westminster John Knox, 2005.

Lowell, James Russell. "To Us All, to Every Nation." In *The Chalice Hymnal*, 634. St. Louis: Chalice, 1995.

Lund, Eric. *Documents from the History of Lutheranism, 1517–1750*. Minneapolis: Fortress, 2002.

Luther, Martin. "The Blessed Sacrament of the Holy and True Body and Blood of Christ, and the Brotherhoods." In *Martin Luther's Basic Theological Writings*, edited by Timothy F. Lull, 242–66. Minneapolis: Fortress, 1989.

———. "A Brief Instruction on What to Look for and Expect in the Gospels (1521)." In *Martin Luther's Basic Theological Writings*, edited by Timothy F. Lull, 104–11. Minneapolis: Fortress, 1989.

Maier, Harry O. "Heresy, Households, and the Disciplining of Diversity." In *A People's History of Christianity, Volume 2: Late Ancient Christianity*, edited by Virginia Burrus, 213-33. Minneapolis: Augsburg Fortress, 2005.

McClure, John S. *The Four Codes of Preaching: Rhetorical Strategies*. Minneapolis: Fortress, 1991.

———. *Other-Wise Preaching: A Postmodern Ethic for Homiletics*. St. Louis: Chalice, 2001.

———. "Preaching and the Pragmatics of Human/Divine Communication in the Liturgy of the Word in the Western Church: A Semiotic and Practical Theological Study." PhD diss., Princeton Theological Seminary, 1984.

———. "Preaching Theology." *Quarterly Review* 24, no. 3 (2004) 249–61.

———. *The Roundtable Pulpit: Where Leadership and Preaching Meet*. Nashville: Abingdon, 1995.

McKenzie, Alyce M. *Hear and Be Wise: Becoming a Preacher and Teacher of Wisdom*. Nashville: Abingdon, 2004.

———. *Preaching Biblical Wisdom in a Self-Help Society*. Nashville: Abingdon, 2002.

Meuser, Fred M. "Luther as Preacher of the Word of God." In *The Cambridge Companion to Martin Luther*, edited by Donald K. McKim, 136–48. Cambridge: Cambridge University Press, 2003.

Meyer, Michel. *Of Problematology: Philosophy, Science, and Language*. Chicago: University of Chicago Press, 1995.

Miller, Carolyn. "Kairos in the Rhetoric of Science." In *A Rhetoric of Doing: Essays on Written Discourse in Honor of James Kinneavy*, edited by Stephen, Neil Nakadate, and Roger Cherry Witte, 310–27. Carbondale, IL: Southern Illinois University Press, 1992.

Mitchell, Henry H. *Black Preaching: The Recovery of a Powerful Art*. Nashville: Abingdon, 1990.

Moses, John A. "Bonhoeffer's Germany: The Political Context." In *The Cambridge Companion to Dietrich Bonhoeffer*, edited by John W. De Gruchy, 3–21. Cambridge: Cambridge University Press, 1999.

Muller, Richard A. *Post-Reformation Reformed Dogmatics: The Rise and Development of Reformed Orthodoxy, Ca. 1520 to Ca. 1725*. 4 vols. 2nd ed. Grand Rapids: Baker Academic, 2003.

Nappi, Brandon A. "First, Empty Your Cup: Zen Gifts to Christian Preachers." DMin thesis, Aquinas Institute of Theology, 2010.

Niebuhr, Reinhold. *Does Civilization Need Religion? A Study in the Social Resources and Limitations of Religion in Modern Life*. New York: Macmillan, 1927.

O'Malley, John W., SJ. "Luther the Preacher." In *The Martin Luther Quincentennial*, edited by Gerhard Dunnhaupt, 3–16. Detroit: Wayne State University Press, 1985.

Oberman, Heiko Augustinus. *Luther: Man between God and the Devil*. New Haven, CT: Yale University Press, 2006.

———. "Preaching and the Word in the Reformation." *Theology Today* XVIII, no. 1 (1961) 16–29.

Old, Hughes Oliphant. *Themes and Variations for a Christian Doxology*. The Clinton Lectures, delivered Spring Semester, 1989, University of Dubuque Theological Seminary, Dubuque, Iowa. Grand Rapids: Eerdmans, 1992.

Pasquarello, Michael. *Christian Preaching: A Trinitarian Theology of Proclamation*. Grand Rapids: Baker Academic, 2006.

———. *God's Ploughman, Hugh Latimer: A "Preaching Life" 1485–1555*. Milton Keynes, UK: Paternoster, 2014.

———. *John Wesley: A Preaching Life*. Nashville: Abingdon, 2010.

———. *Sacred Rhetoric: Preaching as a Theological and Pastoral Practice of the Church*. Grand Rapids: Eerdmans, 2005.

———. *We Speak Because We Have First Been Spoken: A Grammar of the Preaching Life*. Grand Rapids: Eerdmans, 2009.

Pelikan, Jaroslav. *Luther the Expositor: Introduction to the Reformer's Exegetical Writings*. St. Louis: Concordia, 1959.

Perelman, Chaim. *The Realm of Rhetoric*. Notre Dame, IN: University of Notre Dame Press, 1982.

Plantinga, Cornelius, and Sue A. Rozeboom. *Discerning the Spirits: A Guide to Thinking About Christian Worship Today*. Calvin Institute of Christian Worship Liturgical Studies Series. Grand Rapids: Eerdmans, 2003.

Poling, James N. *Rethinking Faith: A Constructive Practical Theology*. Minneapolis: Fortress, 2011.

Powery, Luke A. *Dem Dry Bones: Preaching, Death, and Hope*. Minneapolis: Fortress, 2012.

———. *Spirit Speech: Lament and Celebration in Preaching*. Nashville: Abingdon, 2009.

Quicke, Michael J. *Preaching as Worship: An Integrative Approach to Formation in Your Church*. Grand Rapids: Baker, 2011.

Randolph, David James. *The Renewal of Preaching*. Philadelphia: Fortress, 1969.

Rashkover, Randi. "Introduction: The Future of the Word and the Liturgical Turn." In *Liturgy, Time, and the Politics of Redemption*, edited by Randi Rashkover and C. C. Pecknold, 1–28. Grand Rapids: Eerdmans, 2006.

Redmond, M. V. "The Relationship between Perceived Communication Competence and Perceived Empathy." *Communication Monographs* 52 (1985) 377–82.

Ricoeur, Paul. *Interpretation Theory: Discourse and the Surplus of Meaning*. Fort Worth, TX: Texas Christian University Press, 1976.

———. "Toward a Hermeneutic of the Idea of Revelation." *Harvard Theological Review* 70, no. 1–2 (1977) 1–37.

Rognlien, Bob. *Experiential Worship: Encoutering God with Heart, Soul, Mind, and Strength*. Colorado Springs: NavPress, 2005.

Rogers, Eugene F. *After the Spirit: A Constructive Pneumatology from Resources Outside the Modern West*. Radical Traditions. Grand Rapids: Eerdmans, 2005.

Rose, Lucy Atkinson. *Sharing the Word: Preaching in the Roundtable Church*. Louisville: Westminster John Knox, 1997.

Rumsscheidt, Martin. "The Formation of Bonhoeffer's Theology." In *The Cambridge Companion to Dietrich Bonhoeffer*, edited by John W. De Gruchy, 50–70. Cambridge: Cambridge University Press, 1999.

Russell, Bertrand. *Portraits from Memory, and Other Essays*. London: G. Allen & Unwin, 1956.

Russell, Helene Tallon. "Introduction to Feminist Theology." In *Creating Women's Theology: A Movement Engaging Process Thought*, edited by Helene Tallon Russell, Nancy R. Howell, and Monica A. Coleman, 3–11. Eugene, OR: Pickwick, 2011.

Saunders, Stanley P., and Charles L. Campbell. *The Word on the Street: Performing the Scriptures in the Urban Context*. Grand Rapids: Eerdmans, 2000.

Sauter, Gerhard. *Gateways to Dogmatics: Reasoning Theologically for the Life of the Church*. Grand Rapids: Eerdmans, 2003.

Schiffman, Lawrence. *From Text to Tradition: A History of Second Temple and Rabbinic Judaism*. Hoboken, NJ: Ktav, 1991.

Schlingenslepen, Ferdinand. *Dietrich Bonhoeffer, 106–1945: Martyr, Thinker, Man of Resistance*. London: T & T Clark, 2010.

Schreiter, Robert J. *Constructing Local Theologies*. Maryknoll, NY: Orbis, 1985.

Shivers, Mark McCheyene. "Finding Something to Say: Reconsidering the Rhetorical Practice of Invention in Homiletics." PhD diss., Vanderbilt University, 2011.

Sigmund, Paul E. *Liberation Theology at the Crossroads: Democracy or Revolution?* New York: Oxford University Press, 1990.

Simon, Marcel. "From Greek Hairesis to Christian Heresy." In *Early Christian Literature and the Classical Tradition: In Honorem R. M. Grant*, edited by W. R. Schoedel and R. L. Wilken, 101–16. Berkeley, CA: University of California Press, 1979.

Smith, Ted A. *The New Measures: A Theological History of Democratic Practice*. New York: Cambridge University Press, 2007.

Soosten, Joachim Von. "Editor's Afterword." In *Sanctorum Communio*, by Dietrich Bonhoeffer, 290–306. Minneapolis: Fortress, 1998.

Steinmetz, David C. "Luther and Formation in Faith." In *Educating People of Faith: Exploring the History of Jewish and Christian Communities*, edited by John Van Engen, 252–62. Grand Rapids: Eerdmans, 2004.

Stone, Howard W., and James O. Duke. *How to Think Theologically*. Minneapolis: Fortress, 1996.

Stone, Ronald H. *Professor Reinhold Niebuhr: A Mentor to the Twentieth Century*. Louisville: Westminster John Knox, 1992.

———. *Reinhold Niebuhr, Prophet to Politicians*. Nashville: Abingdon, 1971.

Stricklen Eisenlohr, Teresa. "Analgesic Jesus and the Power of God for Salvation: The Importance of Theological Method for Preaching." *Collected Papers of the 38th Annual Meeting of the Academy of Homiletics*, 2003, 232–42.

———. "Preaching and Theology in Light of Theological Education." PhD diss., Vanderbilt University, 2001.

Taylor, Charles. *Sources of the Self: The Making of the Modern Identity*. Cambridge, MA: Harvard University Press, 1989.

Teilhard de Chardin, Pierre. *The Future of Man*. 1st American ed. New York: Harper & Row, 1964.

Thompson, Bard. *Liturgies of the Western Church*. Philadelphia: Fortress, 1980.

Thurman, Howard. *Meditations of the Heart*. New York: Harper, 1953.

Tisdale, Leonora Tubbs. *Preaching as Local Theology and Folk Art*. Fortress Resources for Preaching. Minneapolis: Fortress, 1997.

Tracy, David. *The Achievement of Bernard Lonergan*. New York: Herder and Herder, 1970.

———. *The Analogical Imagination: Christian Theology and the Culture of Pluralism*. New York: Crossroad, 1981.

———. *Blessed Rage for Order, the New Pluralism in Theology*. New York: Seabury, 1975.

Trilling, Lionel. *Sincerity and Authenticity*. Cambridge, MA: Harvard University Press, 1972.

Tsai, Tzu-Lun. "Preaching as 'Testimony, Publication, Prophesying': A Study of Horace Bushnell's Christological Preaching and Homiletics in Light of his Religious Experience, 1833–1876." PhD diss., Drew University, 2008.

Wannenwetsch, Bernd. *Political Worship: Ethics for Christian Citizens*. Oxford: Oxford University Press, 2004.

Wasserberg, Günter. "Die Haltung der beiden grossen Kirchen in Deutschland nach 1945 zu Auschwitz." In *Abrahams Enkel: Juden, Christen, Muslime Und Die Schoa*, edited by N. Günter and S. Zanke, 53–70. Stuttgart: Franz Steiner Verlag, 2006.

Webb, Stephen H. *The Divine Voice: Christian Proclamation and the Theology of Sound*. Grand Rapids: Brazos, 2004.

Welker, Michael. *God the Spirit*. Minneapolis: Fortress, 1994.

Whitehead, Alfred North. *Modes of Thought*. New York: Macmillan, 1938.

Whitehead, Alfred North, David Ray Griffin, and Donald W. Sherburne. *Process and Reality: An Essay in Cosmology*. Corrected ed. Gifford Lectures. New York: Free Press, 1978.

Williams, Daniel Day. "Niebuhr and Liberalism." In *Reinhold Niebuhr: His Religious, Social and Political Thought*, edited by Charles W. Bretall and Robert W. Kegley, 193–214. New York: MacMillan, 1956.

Williams, James G. *Those Who Ponder Proverbs: Aphoristic Thinking and Biblical Literature*. Bible and Literature Series. Sheffield: Almond, 1981.

Williams, Rowan. *On Christian Theology*. Malden, MA: Blackwell, 2000.

Willimon, William H. *Acts: Interpretation, a Bible Commentary for Teaching and Preaching*. Atlanta: John Knox, 1988.

Wilson, Paul Scott. "Is Homiletics Academic?" *Homiletic* 13, (1988) 1–4.

———. "Is Homiletics Making a Theological Turn?" *Homiletic* XXIII, no. 1 (1998) 15.

———. *The Practice of Preaching*. Nashville: Abingdon, 1995.

Wood, Charles Monroe. *Vision and Discernment: An Orientation in Theological Study*. Scholars Press Studies in Religious and Theological Scholarship. Decatur, GA: Scholars Press, 1985.

Wuthnow, Robert. *After Heaven: Spirituality in America Since the 1950s*. Berkeley, CA: University of California Press, 1998.

Yang, Sung Gu. "Martin Luther King Jr.'s Homiletic Theology of Preaching on Violence and Reconciliation." PhD diss., Emory University, 2009.

Yarbrough, Stephen R. *Inventive Intercourse: From Rhetorical Conflict to the Ethical Creation of Novel Truth*. Carbondale, IL: Southern Illinois University Press, 2006.

Made in the USA
San Bernardino, CA
01 September 2015